Natural Language Processing for Online Applications

D0989005

Natural Language Processing

Volume 5

Natural Language Processing for Online Applications: Text Retrieval, Extraction and Categorization
by Peter Jackson and Isabelle Moulinier

Natural Language Processing for Online Applications

Text Retrieval, Extraction and Categorization

Peter Jackson
Isabelle Moulinier
Thomson Legal & Regulatory

John Benjamins Publishing Company
Amsterdam / Philadelphia

™ The paper used in this publication meets the minimum requirements of American National Standard for Information Sciences – Permanence of Paper for Printed Library Materials, ANSI z39.48-1984.

Library of Congress Cataloging-in-Publication Data

Jackson, Peter, 1948-
    Natural language processing for online applications : text retrieval, extraction, and categorization / Peter Jackson, Isabelle Moulinier.
        p.   cm. (Natural Language Processing, ISSN 1567–8202 ; v. 5)
    Includes bibliographical references and index.
        I. Jackson, Peter. II. Moulinier, Isabelle. III. Title. IV. Series.

QA76.9.N38 I33 2002
006.3'5--dc21   2002066539
ISBN 90 272 4988 1 (Eur.) / 1 58811 249 7 (US) (Hb; alk. paper)
ISBN 90 272 4989 X (Eur.) / 1 58811 250 0 (US) (Pb; alk. paper)

John Benjamins Publishing Co. · P.O. Box 36224 · 1020 ME Amsterdam · The Netherlands
John Benjamins North America · P.O. Box 27519 · Philadelphia PA 19118-0519 · USA

Table of contents

Preface

There is no single text on the market that covers the emerging technologies of document retrieval, information extraction, and text categorization in a coherent fashion. This book seeks to satisfy a genuine need on the part of technology practitioners in the Internet space, who are faced with having to make difficult decisions as to what research has been done, and what the best practices are. It is not intended as a vendor guide (such things are quickly out of date), or as a recipe for building applications (such recipes are very context-dependent). But it does identify the key technologies, the issues involved, and the strengths and weaknesses of the various approaches. There is also a strong emphasis on evaluation in every chapter, both in terms of methodology (how to evaluate) and what controlled experimentation and industrial experience have to tell us.

I was prompted to write this book after spending seven years running an R&D group in an Internet publishing and solutions business. During that time, we were able to put into production a number of systems that either generated revenue or enabled cost savings for the company, leveraging technologies from information retrieval, information extraction, and text categorization. This is not a chronicle of these exploits, but a primer for those who are already interested in natural language processing for online applications. Nevertheless, my treatment of the philosophy and practice of language processing is colored by the context in which I function, namely the arena of commercial exploitation. Thus, although there is a focus on technical detail and research results, I also address some of the issues that arise in applying such systems to data collections of realistic size and complexity.

The book is not intended exclusively as an academic text, although I suspect that it will be of interest to students who wish to use these technologies in an industrial setting. It is also aimed at software engineers, project managers, and technology executives who want or need to understand the technology at some level. I hope that such people find it useful, and that it provokes ideas, discussion, and action in the field of applied research and development. Each chapter begins with lighter material and then progresses to heavier stuff, with some of the later sections and sidebars being marked with an asterisk as optional. Every attempt has been made to cover more ground, and make the material more accessible, than one would expect from the typical textbook.

Thanks are due to Khalid Al-Kofahi, Chris Dozier, David Lewis, Jane Lund, Ruslan Mitkov, and two anonymous referees, for providing insightful comments on one or more chapters. I would also like to thank James Allen and David Israel for helping me get started in information extraction back in 1995, and Chris Wolff for backing that project at Thomson Legal Publishing. I thank my colleagues at Thomson Legal & Regulatory for bearing with me while I finished the book, and for providing a stimulating work environment. Finally, I thank my wife Sandy for putting up with me while I devoted long hours to this project.

Peter Jackson
St Paul, MN

Chapter 1

Natural language processing

A conversation with Eliza

Eliza:	how are you today?
PJ:	not so good
Eliza:	why do you say not so good?
PJ:	i suffer from allergies
Eliza:	that's interesting
PJ:	i come out in spots
Eliza:	i'm not sure i know what you're talking about
PJ:	spots on my face
Eliza:	your face
PJ:	that's right
Eliza:	is it really that right?
PJ:	you're a program, aren't you?
Eliza:	does it please you to believe i am a program, am not i?
PJ:	it sure does
Eliza:	i see
PJ:	yup
Eliza:	a while back you talked about your face
PJ:	what about your face?
Eliza:	what is it you really want to know?
PJ:	are you my kind of girl?
Eliza:	perhaps in your fantasies i am your kind of girl
PJ:	in my fantasies you are blonde
Eliza:	what makes you think i am blonde?
PJ:	i don't know
Eliza:	don't you really know?
PJ:	no
Eliza:	are you saying no just to be negative?
PJ:	no
Eliza:	you are being a bit negative
PJ:	no i'm not
Eliza:	how long have you been not?

The above dialogue took place recently between one of the authors and a computer program called Eliza,[1] downloaded from the World Wide Web. Eliza was an AI brainchild of the 1960s that employed rather primitive pattern-matching methods to respond to inputs and sustain a conversation of sorts. She now exists in many incarnations,[2] but it is fair to say that she has never grown up, in the sense of having learned any new linguistic tricks.

Many apocryphal tales exist of people having been fooled by Eliza into thinking that they were dealing with a sentient being, but as you can see from the above conversation, her replies can rather quickly deteriorate into nonsense.[3] The errors that she makes often reveal the simplistic strategies that the program uses to construct its responses, e.g., "How long have you been not?" Clearly there is a rule in there which matches an input of the form:

"... i am *blah* ... "

and constructs the response

"how long have you been *blah*?"

Nonetheless, one of the interesting things about Eliza is that sometimes her replies appear to be quite prescient, e.g., the sly "Perhaps in your fantasies I am your kind of girl." Just as human beings are prone to see human faces in the flames of a fire, so we seem to be programmed to extract meaning from phenomena, even if this task involves the total suspension of disbelief. We are capable of being emotionally affected by scenes in books and cinema that we know are not real, and we have a tendency to anthropomorphize animals and even artifacts, such as automobiles and computer programs, as the Eliza example shows. The program appears to be flirting, or perhaps sarcastic, but it clearly isn't. How could it be?

This book is not about the psychology or philosophy of human language, but about how we can program computers to process language for commercial ends. The emphasis will be upon particular tasks that we want computers to perform and the techniques that are currently available. The applications will be largely drawn from domains associated with electronic publishing, particularly on the World Wide Web.

1.1 What is NLP?

The term 'Natural language processing' (NLP) is normally used to describe the function of software or hardware components in a computer system which analyze or synthesize spoken or written language. The 'natural' epithet is meant to distinguish human speech and writing from more formal languages, such as mathematical or logical notations, or computer languages, such as Java, LISP, and C++. Strictly speaking, 'Natural Language Understanding' (NLU) is associated with the more ambitious goal of having a computer system actually comprehend natural language as a human being might.

It is obvious that machines can be programmed to 'comprehend' Java code, e.g., in the sense that an interpreter can be written which will cause an applet to execute correctly in a browser window. It is also possible to program a computer to solve many mathematical and logical puzzles,[4] as well as prove theorems,[5] and even come up with novel conjectures.[6] But the computer analysis of speech and text remains fraught with problems, albeit interesting ones (see Sidebar 1.1).

None of these problems would be of the slightest commercial interest, were it not for the fact that the need for information defines the fastest growing market on the planet. Business information is increasingly available online in a relatively free text format, both on the World Wide Web and on corporate Intranets, instead of being in a database format. The issue is no longer lack of information, but an embarrassment of riches, and a lack of tools for organizing information and offering it at the right price and the right time. The vast majority of this information is still expressed in language, rather than images, graphs, sound files, movies, or equations. Much of the information residing in relational databases has been extracted from electronic documents, such as memos, spreadsheets, and tables, often by hand or with a significant amount of editorial assistance.

We contend that language processing has an important role to play in both the production and packaging of online information, and our book is intended to demonstrate this fact.

Sidebar 1.1 Ambiguity in NLP

Linguistic ambiguity is sometimes a source of humor, but many common words and sentences have multiple interpretations that pass unnoticed. For example, the noun 'bank' has many meanings. It can refer to a financial institution, or a river margin, or to the attitude of betting or relying upon something. Humans rarely confuse these meanings, because of the different contexts in which tokens of this word occur, and because of real world knowledge. Everyone who reads the newspapers knows that 'the West Bank of Jordan' does not refer to a financial institution.

'Bank' is an instance of lexical ambiguity. But whole sentences can be ambiguous with respect to their structure and hence their meaning. Here are some popular examples:

'Visiting aunts can be a nuisance.'

which could mean either 'It is a nuisance having to visit one's aunt' or 'It is a nuisance having one's aunt to visit' depending upon the syntactic analysis.[7]

A common manifestation of syntactic ambiguity is prepositional phrase attachment. Consider the following example:

'John saw the man in the park with the telescope.'

To whom does the telescope belong? John? The park? The man in the park? Each would suggest a different interpretation, based on a different attachment of the prepositional phrase 'with the telescope.'

More subtly, sentences that no human would deem ambiguous can cause problems to computer programs, e.g.,

'She boarded the airplane with two suitcases.'

which appears superficially similar to

'She boarded the airplane with two engines.'

It's obvious to you and I that the suitcases belong to the woman, and the engines belong to the airplane, but how is a computer supposed to know this? The ability to understand the two sentences listed above would hardly be deemed evidence of superior intelligence, yet the desire to deal with this kind of ambiguity automatically fuels a number of Ph.D. theses every year.

Given this motivation, there are many ways in which one can approach the study of NLP/NLU. Most texts[8] begin with some background in linguistics, proceed directly to syntax (the analysis of grammatical structures), continue with a study of semantics (the analysis of meaning), and end with a treatment of pragmatics (the problem of context or language use). Such an organization of material is fine for academic study, but will not serve in a book focused upon applications and their associated techniques.

This chapter provides a brief overview of NLP that filters the legacy of modern linguistics, pattern recognition and artificial intelligence through a set of concerns that arise in many commercial applications. Some of these concerns may appear to be mundane, compared with the goals of artificial intelligence or linguistic philosophy, but there are also some fundamental issues that are unavoidable and need to be addressed. Thus questions like:

- 'how can a retrieval system satisfy a user's information need?' (see Chapter 2), or
- 'what makes a good summary of a document?' (see Chapter 5), are of both theoretical and practical interest.

Other issues focus upon rather specialized tasks. For example, a typical commercial problem involves finding names in free text, such as the names of people or companies. An online provider of news or business information may wish to link such names to public records or to a directory of companies.[9]

The syntax of names (e.g., the internal structure of compounds, such as first name/last name pairs) is a somewhat different problem from that of determining the structure of a typical English (or French or German) sentence. Similarly, the problem of determining the referent of a name is in many ways different from that of unraveling the meaning of a sentence. The role of context in name identification and disambiguation is also quite specialized when compared with general-purpose techniques for disambiguating sentences such as those listed in Sidebar 1.1.

These are nonetheless problems that need to be solved, if we wish to provide consumers of online information with superior search functionality, targeted news clips or banner ads, and customized browsing. The alternative to using some degree of automation for identifying, marking, and linking such text features is an editorial effort that few companies can afford. As information is increasingly commoditized, managing the cost structure of the information supply chain becomes a crucial factor in the success or failure of an information provider.

1.2 NLP and linguistics

Some brief definitions of traditional linguistic concepts are necessary, if only to provide an introduction to the literature on NLP. The following sections will serve to introduce some terminology and concepts that are the common currency of discussion in this field. Our coverage of these topics is meant to be superficial, but not simplistic.

1.2.1 Syntax and semantics

In a seminal book,[10] Noam Chomsky distinguished between sentences that are syntactically anomalous, such as

> 'Furiously sleep ideas green colorless.'

and sentences which are grammatically well-formed but semantically anomalous, such as

> 'Colorless green ideas sleep furiously.'

The fact that we can break the rules of language in these two quite different ways has often been adduced as evidence for the decomposability of syntax and semantics in language. An attendant assumption is that one can analyze the syntactic structure of a sentence first (without reference to meaning) and analyze its semantic structure afterwards, although the 'airplane' example in Sidebar 1.1 ought to be enough to refute this hypothesis for natural language applications.

The separation of form and meaning is typically a design feature of more formal notations, such as logical calculi and computer languages. In such (unnatural) languages, the meaning of a statement can be determined entirely from its form. In other words, the semantics of such a language can be defined over the valid structures of the language without regard to contextual or extralinguistic factors.[11] We are not in that happy position with regard to natural languages, where ambiguity and subjectivity make poetry, crossword puzzles, and international misunderstandings possible.

1.2.2 Pragmatics and context

Pragmatics is usually defined as the rules that govern language use. Thus if I say,

> 'You owe me five dollars'

this might be more a request for payment than an assertion of fact, regardless of how it is actually phrased. Hence the primacy often accorded to intention in the modern analysis of meaning.

For example, if I type the words

> 'natural language processing'

in the query box of a search engine, what am I really looking for? A definition? References to the literature? Experts in NLP? Courses in NLP? An 'intelligent' search engine might be able to figure this out, by looking at my previous queries. Each of the candidate preceding queries listed below might point the search engine in a different direction:

> 'what is natural language'
> 'ai textbook'
> 'rochester university.'

Use and context are inextricably intertwined. Some contexts radically affect the intention behind an utterance. Thus I may quote the words of Adolf Hitler without endorsing the sentiments expressed, or embed a sentence in a linguistic context that affects its interpretation, e.g., '*I doubt that* the Government will break up Microsoft.'

Although there have been attempts to construct grand theories of language use, it has also been argued that patterns of use are so specific to particular domains that a general theory is impossible. Documents as diverse as newspaper articles, court reports, public records, advertisements, and resumes are bound to exhibit very different patterns of language use in their different real world contexts. Having said that, it is possible to distinguish two broad approaches to NLP, which tackle these problems in different ways.

1.2.3 Two views of NLP

One approach to NLP is rooted in the kinds of linguistic analyses outlined in the previous section. It is sometimes characterized as 'symbolic', because it consists largely of rules for the manipulation of symbols, e.g., grammar rules that say whether or not a sentence is well formed. Given the heavy reliance of traditional artificial intelligence upon symbolic computation, it has also been characterized informally as 'Good Old-Fashioned AI.'

A second approach, which gained wider currency in the 1990s, is rooted in the statistical analysis of language. It is sometimes characterized as 'empirical', because it involves deriving language data from relatively large text corpora, such as news feeds and Web pages.[12] This nicely chosen term has the added bonus of imputing Rationalism to the opposing view, a designation that acquired some derogatory connotations in the arena of twentieth-century scholarship.

One way of looking at this distinction is purely methodological. Symbolic NLP tends to work top-down by imposing known grammatical patterns and meaning associations upon texts. Empirical NLP tends to work bottom-up from the texts themselves, looking for patterns and associations to model, some of which may not correspond to purely syntactic or semantic relationships.

Another way to think of this distinction is to see how the two schools handle the complexity of language processing, particularly the problem of uncertainty, exemplified by phenomena such as ambiguity. It is clear that a purely symbolic approach must resolve uncertainty by proposing additional rules, or contextual factors, which must then be formalized in some fashion. This is a 'knowledge based' methodology, because it relies upon human experts to identify and describe regularities in the domain. The empirical approach is more quantitative, in that it will tend to associate probabilities with alternate analyses of textual data, and decide among them using statistical methods. Various sophisticated tools are available for mixing and blending mathematical models in the service of this endeavor.

To misquote Oscar Wilde, NLP is rarely pure and never simple, so one can expect to find attempts to solve real problems combining these two approaches. Applications featured in the book will be chosen partly for pedagogical reasons, such as accessibility and ease of explanation, but they will mostly feature some innovative use of current NLP technology. There will also be a deliberate bias towards applications that can or could be scaled to drive applications on the World Wide Web.

1.2.4 Tasks and supertasks

The primary application of language processing on the Web is still *document retrieval*:[13] the finding of documents that are deemed to be relevant to a user's query.[14] One can perform document retrieval without doing significant NLP, and many search engines do, but the trend in the 1990s has been towards increasing sophistication in the indexing, identification and presentation of relevant texts (see Chapter 2). A related, but not identical, task is *document routing*, where items in a document feed are automatically forwarded to a user, e.g., one with a certain profile.[15]

Document routing is in turn related to the task of *document classification* (see Chapter 4). In this task, we are concerned with assigning documents to classes, usually based upon their content. In the most general case, a document could be assigned to more than one class, and the classes could be part of some larger structure, such as a subject hierarchy. It is possible to distinguish this activity from *document indexing*, where we would like a program to automatically assign selected keywords or phrases to a document, e.g., to build a 'back of the book' style index.

Sometimes the focus is not upon finding the right document, but upon finding specific information targets in a document or set of documents. For example, given a set of news articles about corporate takeovers, you might want to distil, from each article, who bought whom. This is usually called *information extraction*, and it provides a way of generating valuable metadata[16] that would otherwise remain buried inside a document collection (see Chapter 3). At least some forms of *document summarization* can be regarded as a special kind of information extraction, in which a program attempts to extract the salient information from a document and present it as a surrogate document.

These tasks can be combined in interesting ways to form 'supertasks', e.g., a program could select documents from a feed based on their content, sort them into categories, and then extract some pertinent pieces of information from each document of interest. Depending upon the level of accuracy required, some manual intervention may be necessary, but we shall see concrete examples which show that programmatic processing of text feeds can be an effective adjunct to human editorial systems. Such supertasks are now being considered under the rubric of 'text mining' (see Chapter 5) which, by analogy with the field of 'data mining', is meant to represent the myriad ways in which useful metadata can be derived from large online text repositories.

In the next section, we outline some NLP tools that we shall refer to from time to time throughout the text. Most of these tools are potentially useful in all of the tasks listed above, and some of them are essential to at least one task. Many of them are freely available for research purposes; others are available as commercial products.[17]

1.3 Linguistic tools

Linguistic analysis of text typically proceeds in a layered fashion. Documents are broken up into paragraphs, paragraphs into sentences, and sentences into individual words. Words in a sentence are then *tagged* by part of speech and other features, prior to the sentence being *parsed* (subjected to grammatical analysis). Thus parsers typically build upon sentence delimiters, tokenizers, stemmers, and part of speech (POS) taggers. But not all applications require a full suite of such tools. For example, all search engines perform a tokenization step, but not all perform part of speech tagging.

We now treat each of these layers in turn.

1.3.1 Sentence delimiters and tokenizers

In order to parse sentences from a document, we need to determine the scope of these sentences and identify their constituents.

Sentence delimiters

Detecting sentence boundaries accurately is not an easy task, since punctuation signs that mark the end of a sentence are often ambiguous. For instance, the period can denote a decimal point,[18] an abbreviation, the end of a sentence, or an abbreviation at the end of a sentence. Similarly, sentences begin with a capital letter, but not all capitalized words start a sentence, even if they follow a period.

As an example of such an exception, consider:

> Periods followed by whitespace and then an upper case letter, but preceding a title are not sentence boundaries.

Sample titles might include 'Mr.', 'Mrs.', 'Dr.', 'Pres.', V.P.', 'C.T.O.', 'H.M.S.', 'U.S.S.', and so on.

To disambiguate punctuation signs, sentence delimiters often rely on regular expressions[19] or exception rules.[20] Other sentence segmentation tools rely on empirical techniques, and are trained on a manually segmented corpus.[21] In addition to rules and exceptions, and to training corpora, segmenters may use additional information such as part-of-speech frequencies.[22]

Tokenizers

Sentence delimiters sometimes need help from tokenizers to disambiguate punctuation characters. Tokenizers (also known as lexical analyzers or word segmenters) segment a stream of characters into meaningful units called tokens. At first sight, tokenization appears rather straightforward: a token can be taken as any sequence of characters separated by white spaces.[23]

Such a simple approach may be appropriate for some applications, but it can lead to inaccuracies.

For instance, it does not take into account punctuation signs, such as periods, commas and hyphens. Is 'data-base' composed of one or two tokens? Clearly, the number '1,005.98' should be one token. What about '$1,005.98'? Should the '$' sign be part of the token, or identified as a token in its own right?

Until now, we have relied on white spaces to indicate word breaks. This is not always the case. The white spaces in 'pomme de terre' (French for potato) do not actually indicate a break between tokens. Moreover, some languages, in fact the major East-Asian languages, do not put white spaces between words.[24] Other languages, like German, Finnish or Korean, retain most of white spaces, but allow the dynamic creation of compound words, for instance 'Lebensversicherungsgesellschaft' (German for 'life insurance company'). These compounds can be considered as a single word, but in a document retrieval task, we may benefit from limited word segmentation identifying the parts. Tokenization tools usually rely on rules,[25] finite state machines,[26] statistical models (see Note 21), and lexicons to identify abbreviations or multi-token words.

1.3.2 Stemmers and taggers

Parsing cannot proceed in the absence of lexical analysis, and so it is necessary to first identify the root forms of word occurrences and determine their part of speech.

Stemmers

In linguistic parlance, stemmers are really morphological analyzers that associate variants of the same term with a root form. The root can be thought of as the form that would be normally be found as an entry in a dictionary. For instance, 'go', 'goes', 'going', 'gone' and 'went' will be associated with the root form 'go'.

There are two types of morphological analyzers: inflectional and derivational.

- *Inflectional morphology* expresses syntactic relations between words of the same part of speech (e.g., 'inflate' and 'inflates'), while derivational morphology expresses lexical relations between words that can be different parts of speech (e.g., 'inflate' and 'inflation'). More specifically, inflectional morphology studies the variation in word forms needed to express grammatical features, such as singular/plural or past/present tense.
- *Derivational morphology* expresses the creation of new words from old ones, and attempts to relate different words to a root form. Derivation usually involves a change in the grammatical category of a word, and may also involve a modification to its meaning. Thus 'unkind' is formed from 'kind', but has the opposite meaning. Derivational morphological analyzers are less widespread than inflectional morphological analyzers.

Morphological analyzers make extensive use of rules and lexicons. The lexicon typically relates all forms of a word to its root form. These rules and lexicons can be efficiently encoded using finite state machines[27] (see Chapter 3) and support limited word segmentation for compound terms.

For instance, 'Lebensversicherungsgesellschaft' will be stemmed as

'Leben#Versicherung#Gesellschaft',

which identifies the parts of the compounds. Because morphological analyzers do not use the context of a word, they do not resolve ambiguities, and may output more than one root for a given term. For instance 'being' corresponds to the verb 'to be' and the noun 'being', as in 'human being.'

Building lexicons to support morphological analyzers is time consuming and somewhat expensive. Many applications, such as document retrieval, often do not require morphological analyzers to be linguistically correct. In this case, we call the analyzer a 'heuristic' stemmer, because it uses 'rules of thumb' instead of linguistic rules.

A heuristic stemmer attempts to remove certain surface markings from words directly in order to discover their root form. In theory, this involves discarding both affixes ('un-', 'dis-', etc.) and suffixes ('-ing', 'ness', etc.), although most stemmers used by search engines only remove suffixes. Affix stripping is a quick way of performing both inflectional and derivation morphology that does not require access to a lexicon.

For instance, the Porter stemmer[28] has inflectional rules to remove the suffixes '-ed' and '-ing', but also derivational rules to remove '-ation' or '-ational'. Such stemming is rather a rough process, since the root form is not required to be a proper word. Thus the terms 'abominable', 'abominably' and 'abomination' all share the same root, 'abomin', which is not a valid word.

Part of speech taggers

Part of speech taggers build upon tokenizers and sentence delimiters,[29] as they label each word in a sentence with its appropriate tag. We decide whether a given word is a noun, verb, adjective, etc. Here are two possible tagged sentences associated with the ambiguous sentence about visiting aunts.

> 'Visiting/ADJ aunts/N-Pl can/AUX be/V-inf-be a/DET-Indef nuisance/ N-Sg.'

> 'Visiting/V-Prog aunts/N-Pl can/AUX be/V-inf-be a/DET-Indef nuisance/ N-Sg.'

In the first sentence, 'visiting' is an adjective that modifies the subject 'aunts'. In the second sentence, it is a gerund[30] that takes 'aunts' as an object.

If words were assigned a single POS tag, and there were no words unknown to the tagger, POS tagging would be a simple task. However, as the example above illustrates, words may be assigned multiple POS tags, and the role of the tagger is to choose the correct one. In the 'aunts' example, there is not enough information in the sentence to decide between the two tags. You need some kind of context, along the lines of:

> 'I ought to invite her, but visiting aunts can be a nuisance.'

or

> 'I ought to visit her, but visiting aunts can be a nuisance.'

Even then, the program would need to draw a few inferences to choose the right tag.

Following the two views of NLP, there are two main approaches to POS tagging:[31] *rule-based* and *stochastic.*

A rule-based tagger tries to apply some linguistic knowledge to rule out sequences of tags that are syntactically incorrect. This can be in the form of contextual rules such as:

> If an unknown term is preceded by a determiner and followed by a noun, then label it an adjective.

Some taggers also rely on morphological information to aid the disambiguation process. For instance,

> If an ambiguous/unknown word ends in '-ing' and is preceded by a verb, then label it a verb.

While some rule-based taggers[32] are entirely hand-coded, others leverage from training procedures on tagged corpora.

Stochastic taggers rely on training data, and encompass approaches that rely on frequency information or probabilities to disambiguate tag assignments. The simplest stochastic taggers disambiguate words based solely on the probability that a word occurs with a particular tag. This probability is typically computed from a training set, in which words and tags have already been matched by hand.

One drawback of this simple approach is that syntactically incorrect sequences can be generated, even though each individual tag assignment may be valid. Thus, in our 'visiting aunts' example above, 'visiting' might be tagged as a verb instead of an adjective, simply because it occurs more frequently as a verb than as an adjective in the training corpus. More complex taggers may use more advance stochastic models, such as Hidden Markov Models[33] (see Chapter 5) or maximum entropy.[34]

1.3.3 Noun phrase and name recognizers

We often need to go beyond part-of-speech tagging. For instance, let us assume that we want to build system that extracts interesting business news from a document feed, and need to identify people and company names and their relationships. It may be helpful to know that a given word is a proper noun (say 'George'), but POS tagging alone does not help us recognize first and last names in a sentence (say 'George Bush').

Noun phrase parsers can help us perform such a task. These are typically partial (or *shallow*) parsers,[35] rather than the complete (or *deep*) parsers that we encountered earlier in this section. Partial parsers address a simplified version of the parsing task, where the goal is to identify major constituents, such as noun phrases, or 'noun groups', which are partial noun phrases. However, they often disregard ambiguities,[36] such as prepositional phrase attachment, the treatment of which would be required by a complete parse.

Noun phrases extractors can be symbolic or statistical. Symbolic phrase finders usually define rules for what constitutes a phrase, and use relatively simple heuristics.[37] For example, many noun phrases start with a determiner ('the', 'a', 'this', etc.) and end just before a common verb ('is', 'are', 'has', 'have', etc.).

Thus 'visiting aunts' could be identified as a noun phrase of the form AD-JECTIVE + NOUN, while 'a nuisance' is of the form DET + NOUN. Noun phrases can be embedded in other noun phrases; thus the phrase 'two engines' is embedded in the phrase 'the airplane with two engines'. Many noun phrase extractors concentrate on identifying *base* noun phrases, which consist of a *head* noun, i.e., the main noun in the phrase, and its *left modifiers*, i.e., determiners and adjectives occurring just to the left of it.

Name finders, also called 'named entity' recognizers, identify proper names in documents, and may also classify these proper names as to whether they designate people, places, companies, organizations, and the like. In the sentence:

> 'Italy's business world was rocked by the announcement last Thursday that Mr. Verdi would leave his job as vice-president of Music Masters of Milan, Inc to become operations director of Arthur Andersen.'

'Italy' would be identified as a place, 'last Thursday' as a date, 'Verdi' as a person, 'Music Masters of Milan, Inc' and 'Arthur Andersen' as companies. Breaking out 'Milan' as a place, and identifying 'Arthur Andersen' as a person would be an error in this context.

Unlike noun phrase extractors, name finders choose to disregard part of speech information and work directly with raw tokens and their properties (e.g., capitalization). As with taggers, some name finders rely on hand crafted rules, while others learn rules from training data,[38] or build statistical models such as Hidden Markov Models.[39] However, most of the name finders currently available as commercial tools are rule based.

1.3.4 Parsers and grammars

Parsing is done with respect to a *grammar*, basically a set of rules that say which combinations of which parts of speech generate well-formed phrase and sentence structures. Thus:

'Colorless green ideas sleep furiously.'

might be judged syntactically well-formed, since

ADJECTIVE + ADJECTIVE + NOUN

is a valid noun phrase pattern,

VERB + ADVERB

is a valid verb phrase pattern, and

NOUN PHRASE + VERB PHRASE

forms a valid sentence. By contrast,

'Furiously sleep ideas green colorless.'

would be judged ungrammatical, since none of the grammatical patterns

ADVERB + VERB + NOUN + ADJECTIVE + ADJECTIVE

ADVERB + VERB + NOUN + NOUN + ADJECTIVE

ADVERB + NOUN + NOUN + ADJECTIVE + ADJECTIVE

ADVERB + NOUN + NOUN + NOUN + ADJECTIVE

is sanctioned by the rules of English.[40]

Semantic analysis involves identifying different types of words or phrases, e.g., recognizing a word or phrase as a proper name, and also identifying the role that they play in the sentence, e.g., whether subject or object. Different semantic types have different features, e.g., a word or noun phrase may refer to something animate or inanimate, to a company, an organization, a place, a date, or a sum of money. Semantic roles may differ from syntactic roles, e.g., in the two sentences,

'The Federal Court chastised Microsoft.'

and

'Microsoft was chastised by the Federal Court.'

the grammatical subject is different in each case, but the basic meaning is the same, and the semantic roles associated with the two participants is also the same. The Federal Court is the 'agent' and Microsoft is the 'recipient' in the event.[41]

Identifying noun phrases is an important and non-trivial task. Such phrases may have complicated internal structures, e.g.,

"A small screw holding the cylinder assembly in the frame of the revolver"

or

"The cat that ate the mouse that ate the cheese."

Many programs settle for identifying simple or 'base' noun phrases, such as

"the cat"
"a small screw".

Linguistic engineering by writing grammar rules is very labor-intensive. Although large general-purpose grammars of English have been written, none has 100% coverage of all the constructs one might encounter in random texts, such as news articles. Similarly, although machine-readable lexicons exist for many languages, none has excellent coverage. Thus, any program that sets out to analyze unseen text will have to cope with unrecognized words and unanticipated phrase structures.

But even unknown words can be marshaled into patterns. Thus the legal term 'res judicata' can be recognized as a two-word pattern (called a *bigram*) if it occurs often enough in a corpus of documents, such as a collection of court cases, in spite of the fact that these words may not be in the program's lexicon. Many software tools[42] neglect parsing altogether in favor of this kind of analysis, in which occurrences of words and word patterns are counted and tabulated.

There are also corpus-based resources that the researcher and developer can draw upon. For example, the Penn Treebank Project at the University of Pennsylvania annotates documents in extant text collections for linguistic structure. This project inserts part of speech tags into documents and produces 'skeletal parses' that show the rough syntactic structure of a sentence to generate a 'bank' of linguistic trees.[43]

Syntactic structure is most often annotated using brackets to produce *embedded lists*, e.g.,

(S: (NP: Green ideas) (VP: sleep furiously))

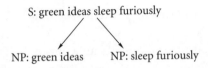

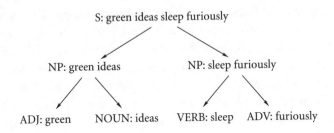

Figure 1.1 Phrase structure represented as a tree

Figure 1.2 More complex phrase structure

denotes the concatenation of a noun phrase and a verb phrase to form a sentence,[44] and this structure can also be represented as a *parse tree* (see Figure 1.1).

Trees and embedded lists are isomorphic recursive structures, and can therefore be embedded to arbitrary depth in order to tease out structural details, e.g.,

(S: (NP: (ADJ: Green) (NOUN: ideas))
   (VP: (VERB: sleep) (ADV: furiously)))

shows a more complex bracketing with a corresponding tree (see Figure 1.2).

Thus manually tagged corpora and statistical analysis tools provide a number of resources that can be brought to bear upon the problem of building a natural language system for an application.

1.4 Plan of the book

The purpose of this introductory chapter was to show the reader that there are both theoretical and practical resources available to aid in the construction of natural language processing systems. In much shorter supply are guidelines on how to utilize such resources for commercial ends, discussion of the various options available to the system builder, and warnings concerning possible pitfalls, complications, and the like. This book attempts to address some of these issues, in order to facilitate the understanding and deployment of this technology.

Given our focus on applications, it is different kinds of language processing task that will give the book its basic structure, rather than theoretical constructs such as syntax and semantics, or tools such as parsers and taggers. Linguistic concepts and tools will not be neglected, but we shall examine their import in the context of specific tasks, rather than attempting a review of the underlying theory or techniques. Such reviews can be found elsewhere, and a number of well-respected works are listed in the bibliography at the end of this chapter.

Chapter 2 looks at document retrieval and outlines the basic logic behind Boolean and ranked retrieval. The simple mathematics behind these systems is applicable to other application areas, and will therefore receive a thorough treatment. Techniques for query processing and index construction are explained in detail. Methods for evaluating retrieval systems are also examined in depth, since this topic turns out to be more complex than one might think. We review the Text Retrieval Conferences and some recent research advances that have found their way into commercial systems.

Chapter 3 addresses the information extraction task, surveying programs for identifying events described in free text. We review the Message Understanding Conferences and look at parsing techniques, such as finite automata and context-free parsers. The workings of such programs are exemplified by applications in the domains of general news and legal information, and some key evaluation studies are summarized.

Chapter 4 turns to document classification algorithms, and attempts to categorize such tasks in order to understand the space of applications that they might support. Then we survey the many methods that have been applied to problems of this kind, including 'Naïve Bayes', *tf-idf*, nearest neighbor, decision lists and trees, and so forth. Again, there is a strong emphasis on how such systems should be evaluated, both in the laboratory and in production.

Chapter 5 covers some major research areas that are beginning to generate commercial applications. We focus particularly upon named entity extraction, summarization, and topic detection, both within single documents and across sets of documents. We end with a summary of the state of the art, and some predictions[45] about what the future will hold.

Pointers

Eliza-like programs are now called 'chatbots', or 'chatterbots', but they seem to be no more advanced.[46]

For an accessible overview of linguistics, we recommend Finegan.[47] If you are serious about learning the foundations of syntactic theory, then Chomsky[48] is one place to start. For semantics, we would suggest Leech.[49]

For a computational view of language, Allen[50] is excellent, although it is short on applications and leans heavily towards 'Good Old Fashioned AI,' as opposed to more modern corpus-based approaches. For the latter, consult Charniak[51] or Manning and Schütze.[52]

For an overview of the Penn Treebank Project at the University of Pennsylvania, see Marcus et al.[53] All data produced by the Treebank is released through the Linguistic Data Consortium.[54]

Notes

1. Weizenbaum, J. (1966). ELIZA – A computer program for the study of natural language communication between man and machine. *Communications of the ACM, 9*, 36–45.

2. See e.g., http://www.neuromedia.com, where (as of October 2001) an ELIZA-style program poses as a sales representative.

3. The human in the dialogue isn't behaving very intelligently either, but that's a different problem.

4. See e.g., Korf, R. E. (1997). Finding Optimal Solutions to Rubik's Cube Using Pattern Databases. *Fourteenth National Conference on Artificial Intelligence* (AAAI-97), pp. 700–705.

5. Kalman, J. A. (2001). *Automated Reasoning with Otter*. Princeton, NJ: Rinton Press.

6. Lenat, D. B. & Brown, J. S. (1984). Why AM and EURISKO Appear to Work. *Artificial Intelligence, 23*, 269–294.

7. In fact, they're both a nuisance.

8. E.g., Allen, J. (1995). *Natural Language Understanding* (2nd edition). Redwood City, CA: Benjamin/Cummings.

9. Or the information provider may wish to categorize news stories with respect to the industries that they would be of interest to. Such a categorization may need to be done in close to real time, to retain the currentness of the feed.

10. Chomsky, N. (1957). *Syntactic Structures*. The Hague: Mouton & Co. Reprinted 1978, Peter Lang Publishing.

11. Some attempts have been made to argue that natural languages are really a kind of (highly complex) formal language, but we will not consider these here. See, e.g.,

Montague, R. (1974). English as a formal language. In Thomason, R. (Ed.), *Formal Philosophy*. New Haven: Yale University Press.

12. 'Empirical' suggests experience and experimentation, not summary statistics. One might prefer another term, such as 'predictive', since the normal purpose of these data analyses is to predict linguistic patterns in unseen texts.

13. We shall reserve the more general term 'information retrieval' for when we wish to include the retrieval of images, audio, and documents containing notations other than text (e.g., musical notation, tabular data, equations, and so on).

14. It is common to talk about a user's 'information need' in this context, but we shall see in Chapter 2 that deducing this need from a user's query is a non-trivial process that begs many questions.

15. This profile is typically nothing more than a standing query.

16. We shall use the term 'metadata' to mean machine-readable data about data. A simple inverted file index contains metadata, i.e., data about the original text data.

17. We give pointers to a number of these offerings, without endorsing them in any way. Also, although URLs are a useful mechanism for such pointers, they are obviously not archival. In the event of a dead link, we suggest using an effective search engine, such as Google (http://www.google.com), to track down the reference.

18. The interpretation of punctuation signs is language dependent. In French, for instance, it's the comma that denotes the decimal point, while the period may mark a thousand as in 1.000,00 (equivalent to the American 1,000.00).

19. We cover regular expressions, a fundamental pattern matching technique, in Chapter 3.

20. See for instance the *mtsegsent* tool of in the Multext project (http://www.lpl.univ-aix.fr/projects/multext/MUL7.html), or the *inxight::document_analysis* class in the LinguistX toolkit commercialized by *Inxight* (http://www.inxight.com).

21. One example is the use of maximum entropy to derive sentence and word segmenters. Maximum entropy is a powerful technique for building statistical model of natural language. A sample Java class can be found at http://www.cis.upenn.edu/~adwait/statnlp.html, or at http://grok.sourceforge.net/.

22. See http://elib.cs.berkeley.edu/src/satz/ for instance.

23. The *java.util.StringTokenizer* class in Java is an example of a simple tokenizer, where you can define the set of characters that mark the boundaries of tokens. Another Java class, *java.text.BreakIterator*, is language dependent and identify word or sentence boundaries, but does not handle ambiguities.

24. Resource for tokenizing Chinese can be found at http://www.chinesecomputing.com/. ALTJAWS (http://www.kecl.ntt.co.jp/icl/mtg/resources/altjaws.html) and *Chasen* (http://chasen.aist-nara.jp.com) include tokenization for Japanese text.

25. See the *Intex* (http://ladl.univ-mlv.fr/INTEX/) tool, for instance.

26. Most NLP toolkits include lexical analyzers for English. The Xelda toolkit (http://www.xrce.xerox.com/ats/xelda/overview.html) includes tokenizers for various languages. Other

links can be found at http://registry.dfki.de/sections.php3?f_mainsection=
2&f_section=11.

27. The LinguistX platform, the XELDA toolkit or the product line commercialized by
Teragram all rely on similar 'finite state' technology.

28. Source code for the Porter stemmer can be found on-line at http://www.tartarus.org/
~martin/PorterStemmer/.

29. POS taggers and morphological analyzers may be used in conjunction or independent
of one another.

30. A gerund is a noun-like use of a verb, e.g., "Gun control is *hitting* your target."

31. A list of POS taggers can be found at: http://registry.dfki.de/sections.php3?f_mainsection
=2&f_section=20

32. A well-known rule-based tagger has been developed by Brill. There are several, more or
less efficient, implementations available. See http://www.markwatson.com/opensource/
opensource.htm or http://www.inalf.cnrs.fr/cgi-bin/mep.exe?HTML=mep_winbrill.txt?
CRITERE=ENGLISH.

33. An example of an HMM-based tagger is the *TATOO – ISSCO tagger*. Another can be
found at http://www.coli.uni-sb.de/~thorsten/tnt/.

34. See Adwait Ratnaparkhi's *MXPOST* tagger.

35. The *Natural Language Software Registry* contains two different entries for partial and
shallow parsing. However all systems classifying under shallow parsing are also classified
under partial parsing.

36. The *Link Grammar* parser attempts to produce the complete analysis of a sentence, but
is able to skip over portions it can not understand.

37. The *FASTR system* includes a noun phrase extractor component. Most NLP vendors,
such as Inxight, Teragram and Xerox, provide noun phrase extractors.

38. The *Alembic* tool allows for both writing hand-coded rules and automatically generating
rules using a tagged corpus as training data. *NetOwl extractor* is another example of rule-
based named entity recognizer.

39. The *Identifinder* system is based on Hidden Markov Models (see Chapter 5).

40. We need to consider four patterns, because 'sleep' can be a noun or a verb, and 'green'
can be a noun or an adjective.

41. There isn't as much standardization of terminology in semantics as there is in syntax,
where the grammatical notions of 'subject', 'verb', and 'object' are well established. So you
may also see 'actor' and 'patient' as terminology for semantic roles corresponding to the
notions of subject and object in meaning relations. But the basic idea is always the same:
one party is doing something, and the other party is having that something done to them.

42. See, e.g., http://nlp.stanford.edu/links/statnlp.html

43. The Treebank project is located in the LINC Laboratory (http://www.cis.upenn.edu/
~linc/home.html) of the Computer and Information Science Department at the University
of Pennsylvania.

44. We will use some common abbreviations, such as 'S' for sentence, 'NP' for noun phrase, etc., explaining as we go.

45. Predictions of this kind nearly always turn out to be wrong, but everyone makes them, so we will too.

46. See e.g., http://www.alicebot.org

47. Finegan, E. (2001). *Language: Its Structure and Use* (3rd edition). Fort Worth: Harcourt Brace.

48. Chomsky, N. (1965). *Aspects of a Theory of Syntax*. Cambridge, MA: MIT Press.

49. Leech, G. N. (1974). *Semantics*. Baltimore: Penguin. 2nd edition published in 1981.

50. Allen, J. (1995). *Natural Language Understanding* (2nd edition). Redwood City, CA: Benjamin/Cummings.

51. Charniak, E. (1993). *Statistical Language Learning*. Cambridge, Massachusetts: MIT Press.

52. Manning, C. & Schütze, H. (1999). *Foundations of Statistical Natural Language Processing*. Cambridge, Massachusetts: MIT Press.

53. Marcus, M., Santorini, B., & Marcinkiewicz, M. (1993). Building a Large Annotated Corpus of English: The Penn Treebank. *Computational Linguistics, 19* (2), 313–330.

54. http://www.ldc.upenn.edu

CHAPTER 2

Document retrieval

The case of the missing guitar

In 1993, the guitar manufacturer C. F. Martin made a special version of the legendary Martin D18 guitar played by, among others, Elvis Presley. They called it the D93, and made very few of them. If you wanted to find one on the World Wide Web, you might be tempted to go your favorite search engine and type:

'martin d93 guitar.'

An optimist might expect to find a Web page describing this guitar, maybe even offering one for sale. A less optimistic person would at least expect to bring up the Web page for C. F. Martin & Co. A pessimist might expect to find only pages about other, less rare, Martin guitars. A real curmudgeon might expect to find only pages about guitars made by other companies. All we can say to these people is: "Dream on."

Here are AltaVista's top-ranked sites.

Perikles Vänner, funktionärer 95/96
Styrelse samt övriga funktionärer i. Ølföreningen Perikles Vänner 95/96. Ordförande. Thomas Jonsson V91. Vice ordförande. Lisa Bodén A93. ...
URL: http://www.tlth.lth.se/~perikles/arkiv9798/styrelse95.htm

Home of **d93**-alo
Welcome user! If you're from out of town, you're probably looking for this: C64 page. or this: XPilot. This rest is my personal linklist and nothing... URL: http://www.student.nada.kth.se/~d93-alo/ ● Translate
More pages from www.student.nada.kth.se

E$33) 9(/'D92J2 **'D93**'A 'D*,'1J)
Enghlish. #*5D (F' 1H'(7 'D,/J/ D/JF' EF*,'*F' 'D9FH'F H'DA1H9 'DEB/E) F(0) *#33* E$33) **'D93**'A DD*,'1) H 'D%3*J1'/ AJ 'D9'E 1355G@ AJ E/JF) -'&D AJ... URL: http://www.alassaf.net/Aindex.htm

[COM3-**D93**] Deutsche Telekom AG (Q6/3): D.atm - Informationflow between Network
English Español. Copie Imprimable. Bureau du Secrétaire Général. Radio-communication (ITU-R)Normalisation (ITU-T)Développement (ITU-D)Expositions et. URL: http://www.itu.int/itudoc/itu-t/com3/dco...v98/093-fr.html ● Translate More pages from www.itu.int

D93-00013 MICROSOFT - BACKOFFICE: APPLICATION CENTER 1PROC .
APPLICATION CENTER 1PROC .
URL: http://saleonall.com/cat/software/suites...
oneproduct.html • Translate
More pages from saleonall.com
Index of /~ **d93**-msr
Index of /~**d93**-msr. Name Last modified Size Description. Parent Directory 06-Apr-2001 00:14 - 2000/ 15-Dec-1999 16:56 - foton/ 04-Aug-2000 17:14 -...
URL: http://jota.sm.luth.se/~d93-msr/ • Translate More pages from jota.sm.luth.se
Microsoft **D93**-00013 D9300013 Application Center 1proc .
Microsoft **D93**-00013 d9300013 application center 1proc .. 30 day return policy. Free ground shipping.
URL: http://www.ichq.com/partnum/msoft_d9300013a.html • Translate More pages from www.ichq.com

See anything about guitars, Martin or otherwise? None of these documents seems to address either of the query terms 'martin' and 'guitar.' Well, maybe Altavista's having a bad day. Let's try another search engine, Google. Here are the top-ranked results.

Echoes Playlist Week of 2.1.99
... Quartet Gongan LAGQ LA **Guitar** Quartet Fiesta LAGQ Rudiger ... Ancient Key Richie Buckley **Martin**, Frances The General & ... The Water Garden $16.98 **D93** Delgado, Luis El ... www.echoes.org/playlists/wk06-99.html - 20k - Cached - Similar pages
C64 - game music
... PSID files: ... For the greatest SID collection, check out The High ... from the same game (30k); He slimed me from Ghostbusters (10k); **Guitar** from Wizball (46k). ... www.d.kth.se/~d93-alo/c64/sid/ - 2k - Cached - Similar pages
other
... vg/vg+ 10.00. Ivan Csudai / **Martin** Burlas 9 Easy Pieces ... vg+ 5.00. Sonny Sharrock **Guitar** (ENEMY EMY102 GB86) LP ... BACK RECORDS MMLP 66006 **D93**) LP vg+/vg+ 7.00. ... www.abyss.pwp.blueyonder.co.uk/other.html - 101k - Cached - Similar pages
Records Added to the Library Catalog : July 30 - August 5 ...
... Music Library Audio CD7585 **Guitar** paradise of East Africa ... **Martin**. Pinter : the playwright / **Martin** Esslin. Hodges Library ... book QA76.575.**D93** 2001 DVD Studio ... www.lib.utk.edu/research/utkcats/about/recentadds/010730.html - 80k - Cached - Similar pages
Result of searching for "va-".
... master,wlp 47527 VA-**Guitar** Album: Historic Town Hall ... Positive Noise, Richard Strange, **Martin** Hannett 14680 VA-Capitol ... songs 30696 VA-**D93**: Basement Tapes II ... vinylrevival.com/cgi-bin/srch?va- - 101k - Cached - Similar pages

---

GuitareTAB: Presidents Of The Usa - Kitty
... questions, comments or whatever!!! - **Martin** Aaserud – - Bente Moe From ...
DST) Message-ID: <31D2FBA9.**D93**@aft.sn.no> Date ... Version: 1.0 To: GUI-
TAR@NEVADA.EDU Subject ... www.guitaretab.com/gtab/t/15001 - 14k - Cached -
Similar pages
Guestview
... 02/08/01 - **Martin** Sinclair - eMail: sinclairmartin@hotmail ... you learn to play **guitar**
like that!!! Absolutely breath ... Denny Daniels - eMail: Double **D93**@aol.com. Hi ...
www.kraigkenning.com/guestview.htm - 71k - Cached - Similar pages
[**PDF**] www.cg26.fr/gb/tourisme/GUIDE_GB.pdf
File Format: PDF/Adobe Acrobat - View as Text
... 04.75.76.01.72 INTERNATIONAL **GUITAR** FESTIVAL. Theatre, concerts, folklore ...
D122 D132 ST **MARTIN**-DES ROSIERS BEAUSEMBLANT ... Glass blower - CREST
D93 ETOILE (C8) Old ... Similar pages

At least Google figured out that the query had something to do with guitars,
but Martin's home page is nowhere to be seen, and *not one* of these pages is
about guitars made by C. F. Martin. To find out why this search is such an
unmitigated disaster, you will have to read the rest of the chapter!

Electronic document retrieval used to be a task most commonly associated
with librarians, or specialized business and legal analysts, working with proprietary online information services, such as Dialog, Westlaw and Lexis-Nexis.
The advent of the World Wide Web has transformed everyone into a document
retriever of sorts, and it has also commoditized retrieval technology.[1] People of
all ages and walks of life are now becoming familiar with search engines and
their limitations.

In the context of this chapter, we shall concentrate on document retrieval
by *full-text search*, rather than alternative methods. For example, many library
systems[2] and proprietary online systems[3] associate a set of keywords with each
document, and retrieval is via those keywords, rather than via any process that
matches a query against the actual text of a document.[4] Such keywords are often chosen from a controlled vocabulary, compiled by subject matter experts or
library scientists, and may be used in conjunction with thesauri. These vocabularies may be quite large, and may or may not be well known to the information
seeker. Keywords, ISBN numbers, and other devices, can be considered as *surrogates* for the documents themselves.[5] Clearly, their effectiveness as retrieval
agents depends upon the appropriateness of the keywords, the convenience of
the numbering scheme, and so forth. The advantages and disadvantages of var-

ious indexing schemes and their associated mechanisms are well known and are discussed elsewhere.[6]

This chapter begins by explaining the basic indexing and retrieval model upon which all full-text retrieval is based. It outlines the logic behind traditional Boolean search engines, and explains the concepts of term frequency and inverse document frequency, which form the basis of modern ranked retrieval in the *tf-idf* model. We then cover attempts to improve search results by using a variety of linguistic and statistical techniques, such as thesauri, query expansion, and relevance feedback. This is followed by a survey of experimental designs and statistical measures for assessing retrieval performance.

Then we go on to examine Web search engines in some detail, with respect to both their implementation and performance. Large claims have been made for commercial search engines, but we shall see that coverage, freshness, and retrieval performance vary greatly from one to another. The chapter ends with an up-to-date examination of new techniques that promise to improve Web search.

2.1 Information retrieval

Information Retrieval (IR) can be defined as the application of computer technology to the acquisition, organization, storage, retrieval, and distribution of information. The associated research discipline is concerned with both the theoretical underpinnings and the practical improvement of search engine technology, including the construction and maintenance of large information repositories. In recent years, researchers have expanded their concerns from the bibliographic and full-text search of document repositories to Web search, with its associated hypertext and multimedia databases.

Information retrieval is an activity, and like most activities it has a purpose. A user of a search engine begins with an *information need*, which he or she realizes as a *query* in order to find relevant documents. This query may not be the best articulation of that need, or the best bait to use in a particular document pool. It may contain misspelled, misused, or poorly selected words. It may contain too many words or not enough. Nevertheless, it is usually the only clue that the search engine has concerning the user's goal.[7]

We often speak of documents in the result set as being more or less relevant to the query, but, strictly speaking, this is inaccurate. The user will judge relevance with respect to the information need, not the query. If irrelevant documents are returned, the user may or may not realize why this is the case, and may or may not find ways to improve the query. The relationship between the query and the documents is explained entirely by the logic of the search engine. There is no need to invoke the concept of relevance at this point.

To emphasize this distinction, one can conceive of two different users who enter identical queries but have different information needs. The query

'British beef imports'

could be looking for information about the importation of British beef (by other countries), or the importation of beef (from other countries) by the British. There is no way of knowing which the user meant without asking him or her.

Another distinction that needs to be made is that between relevance considered as topicality and relevance considered as utility. A document can be on the topic associated with a user's information need without actually being useful. Utility can only be assessed in the context of a larger task that the user is trying to perform, such as writing an article or representing a client in court.

The whole concept of relevance is a difficult one that entertained linguists and philosophers for much of the 20th century, and will no doubt continue to do so in the 21st and beyond. Our concern here is less with theoretical conundrums than with the practical difficulty of obtaining relevance judgments for the purposes of evaluating and improving search systems. We shall return to this topic in Section 2.4.

2.2 Indexing technology

It is easy to forget that document retrieval starts not with a query but with the indexing of documents. Everyone is familiar with a 'back of the book' index, in which selected words and phrases from a text are associated with the numbers of the pages where the relevant contents appear. It is also well known that such indexes leave quite a lot to be desired, although any index is better than none at all.

An index for the full-text search of electronic documents is generally more exhaustive than the index of any book. One would like to be able to query a collection of documents by matching terms in the query with terms actually occurring in the text of those documents. This ability requires that a document be indexed with all of the words[8] that occur in it, instead of being indexed only by keywords or subject headings provided by an editor or a librarian.

INVERTED DICTIONARY

Token	DocCnt	FreqCnt	Head
ABANDON	28	51	•
ABIL	32	37	•
ABSENC	135	185	...
ABSTRACT	7	10	...

POSTING

DocNo	Freq	Word Position
67	2	279 283
424	1	24
1376	7	137 189 481...
206	1	170
4819	2	4 26 32

Figure 2.1 Part of an inverted file index, showing the basic structure

An index consisting of a list of all the words occurring in all the documents in the collection is called an *inverted file*, or dictionary (see Figure 2.1). Words are typically *stemmed* before being stored, as described in Chapter 1, Section 1.3.2. Thus, we attempt to conflate all the variants of a word, reducing words like 'anticipate', 'anticipating', 'anticipated', and 'anticipation' to a common root, 'anticipat', for indexing purposes.

For each token,[9] we store the following information:

- *Document Count.* How many documents the token occurs in. This allows us to compute a useful statistic, called 'inverse document frequency' (IDF), for ranking purposes. We discuss the uses of IDF in Section 2.3.2.
- *Total Frequency Count.* How many times the token occurs across all the documents. This is a basic 'popularity' measure that tells you how common the token is.

In addition, for each token, we store the following indexing information on a *per document* basis:

- *Frequency.* How often the token occurs in that document. This number is a very rough indicator of whether or not the document is really 'about' the concept encoded in the token, or whether it simply mentions the concept in passing.

– *Position*. The offsets[10] at which these occurrences are found in the document. Offsets can be retained for different reasons. Some search engines allow users to search for a query term within n words, say 3, of another term. Other search engines, like Google, use offsets to generate word-in-context snippets for display, which can be quite effective abstracts for retrieved documents, because they are query dependent. Finally, offsets are sometimes used to highlight query terms in retrieved documents.[11]

These records are usually linked in a structure similar to the one shown in Figure 2.1. We now proceed to examine how such indexes are used at retrieval time.

2.3 Query processing

The first full-text document retrieval systems were 'Boolean' or 'terms and connectors' search engines. Such a designation characterizes properties of the query submitted to the system, rather than the mode of indexing employed.

2.3.1 Boolean search

A Boolean search is one in which the user searches a database with a query that connects words with operators, such as AND, OR, and NOT. Such a search is often called a 'terms and connectors' search, since there is a clear distinction made in the query between content-bearing terms and content-free operators based on logical connectives. The operators derive their meaning from the truth tables of Boolean logic (see Sidebar 2.1), hence 'Boolean search.'

Sidebar 2.1 Boolean logic and truth tables

The truth tables for AND, OR, and NOT are shown in Table 2.1. Thus, the entry 'true' in the cell with column 'true' and row 'true' in the AND table shows that 'true' AND 'true' begets 'true'. Any other combination of truth values ANDed together results in 'false.'

Table 2.1 Boolean truth tables

and	true	false	or	true	false	not	
true	true	false	true	true	true	true	false
false	false	false	false	true	false	false	true

A Boolean engine returns the set of documents in the database that satisfy the logic of the user's query. For example, the query 'computer AND virus' would return all documents containing both terms, by intersecting the postings for 'computer' and 'virus' in the inverted file, thus

$$POSTING_{computer} \cap POSTING_{virus}$$

The query 'computer OR virus' would return all documents containing either term, by forming the union of the postings for 'computer' and 'virus':

$$POSTING_{computer} \cup POSTING_{virus}$$

The NOT operator allows users to exclude terms and conditions from their search result terms. Thus 'Jordan NOT Michael' would return all documents containing the term 'Jordan' but not the term 'Michael', namely

$$POSTING_{Jordan} - POSTING_{Michael}$$

where '−' denotes set difference.

There is normally a precedence established between operators, in order to avoid ambiguity. Thus

'Jordan NOT Michael AND Nike'

would be interpreted as

$$(POSTING_{Jordan} - POSTING_{Michael}) \cap POSTING_{Nike}$$

rather than

$$POSTING_{Jordan} - (POSTING_{Michael} \cap POSTING_{Nike})$$

where NOT has broader scope.

Most Boolean systems also allow non-Boolean operators, such as those governing term proximity. Thus the query 'computer /5 virus' would return all documents where the terms 'computer' and 'virus' occur within five words of each other – assuming that the inverted file also contains information about word positions, as shown in Figure 2.1. This can be useful for name searching, e.g., 'President /3 Kennedy' will find documents containing the phrase 'President John Kennedy' and 'President John F. Kennedy' as well as 'President Kennedy', but not necessarily retrieve a document that mentions President Johnson and Robert Kennedy.

There are also stemming operators that allow a user to enter the root form of a word to retrieve documents containing its morphological variants. This is useful for older Boolean systems in which words were not stemmed at index compilation time. Thus the term 'assassin!', where '!' is the stem operator, will find occurrences of 'assassin', 'assassinated', 'assassination', etc. There are various ways of supporting such an operator, e.g., by identifying roots at indexing time, allowing partial matching against index entries, or expanding queries by adding morphological variants as disjoined terms.

Some query languages also allow grammatical connectors that permit the user to search for terms that occur within the same paragraph or sentence. Clearly sentence and paragraph boundaries must have been determined at index time. This is not very common, because identifying sentence, or even paragraph, boundaries is not trivial.

However, documents are often broken into fields by mark up, and then users are allowed to search within a field. The contents of such fields receive additional indexing, to enable searches across just those fields of a document. For example, in the legal online information service Westlaw, one can search for 'eminent domain' in just the synopses of a collection of court reports by entering a query in the following syntax:

SY(eminent domain).

Even more common is phrase searching. Phrases in queries can be specified by including multiple terms within quotation marks. This stipulates that the user is looking for the enclosed terms occurring adjacent to each other and in a certain order.

Such features are now familiar to all from online search engines. Thus Altavista allows AND, OR and NOT in its 'advanced search' facility, as well as the connective NEAR, which means 'within 10 words.' Despite the introduction of other search methods, particularly on the Web, Boolean search remains popular in many commercial and library applications.[12]

Its power can be enhanced by the use of thesauri in query processing, and by special purpose indexing techniques. Thesauri are used to add synonyms[13] to a query in order to gain coverage. This kind of 'query expansion' is discussed below in Section 2.5.

In spite of such enhancements, the problems with Boolean search are well known.[14]

Large result set. The result set contains all documents that satisfy the query. This may be an extremely large set. Boolean search tends to be highly iterative, involving more than one round of query refinement. The user adds terms and connectives until a result of manageable size is returned. There is no way to know ahead of time how many documents a query will find, so this is something of a trial and error process.[15]

Complex query logic. Effective Boolean queries can therefore be quite compli-cated. The simple queries that untrained searchers devise often bring back too few or too many documents. For example, a query that does not contain dis-joined synonyms may fail to find documents about automobiles because it only uses the term 'car.'

Unordered result set. The result set is not ordered by relevance. Typically, docu-ments are ordered by some other criterion, such as recency of publication. This may work well for some tasks, such as obtaining news updates, but less well for others, such as finding out when a certain story broke.

Dichotomous retrieval. The result set does not admit degrees of relevance. A Boolean query effectively partitions the collection into two subsets: documents that satisfy the query and documents that do not. There is no notion of partial satisfaction, which would be useful in those cases where an overly restrictive search returns nothing at all.

Equal term weights. All query terms are accorded equal importance by the basic Boolean model. Yet, in many contexts, some terms are more probable than others. For example, a document about the assassination of President John F. Kennedy ought to contain the term 'Kennedy', and may contain the term 'Dallas', but may or may not contain more obscure terms like 'Dealey' or 'Zapruder.'[16]

These problems are properties of the logic underlying Boolean search, and are therefore hard to fix without changing the whole formalism. Professional searchers are capable of adapting to this logic and can become extremely skilled in formulating productive queries. Some prefer Boolean search to other meth-ods because of the degree of control the experienced user can exercise over the documents that are returned. The crisp logic of Boolean queries also helps the user decide when to stop searching; this is particularly important in applica-tions where completeness is at a premium, e.g., in legal research. But occa-sional searchers, or seasoned searchers inexperienced in searching a particular domain, may get disappointing results.

2.3.2 Ranked retrieval

As noted above, a Boolean search typically returns sets of documents that are either unordered, or ordered by criteria unrelated to relevance, such as recency. Most Web search engines are based on a different technology that ranks search results based upon the frequency distribution of query terms in the document collection. Roughly speaking, if a document contains many occurrences of a query term (e.g., 'aardvark') which is rather rare in the collection as a whole (e.g., all Web documents), this suggests that the document might be highly relevant to a query like

'where do aardvarks live'.

By contrast, many more documents will contain the word 'live', so this query term should not contribute as much to the ranking.

As the example suggests, ranked retrieval is usually employed in search interfaces where users are allowed to enter unrestricted 'natural language' queries, without Boolean or other operators. Such a query is then processed by removing stop words,[17] like 'where' and 'do', and performing various manipulations on the remaining words, the most common being stemming.[18] In modern search engines, words are stemmed at index time, and stemming algorithms attempt to identify the root forms of query terms automatically, so that the user does not have to resort to wild cards.

The question then arises as to how a query without operators could be processed so as to return good results most of the time. The naïve approach of translating natural language queries into Boolean ones is unlikely to work well. Disjoining the content words in such a query will typically produce too many hits, while conjoining them may produce too few.

The Boolean interpretation of the retrieval task was found to be simply inadequate for the processing of natural language queries, and so an alternative model had to be developed. Instead of regarding documents as sets of terms, and queries as operations on sets of documents, researchers began to think of documents as being arranged in a multi-dimensional vector space defined by the terms themselves.[19] If each term defines a dimension, and the frequency of that term defines a linear scale along that dimension, then queries and documents can be represented by vectors in the resulting space.[20]

For example, a (not very realistic) document, such as,

'A dog is an animal. A dog is a man's best friend. A man is an owner of a dog.'

might be represented as in Table 2.2.

Table 2.2 A simple vector representation of a document

a	an	animal	best	dog	friend	is	of	man	owner
5	2	1	1	3	1	3	1	2	1

Given that we can establish an implicit, e.g., alphabetical, ordering on terms, we can simply represent this document as a vector in a 10-dimensional space:

(5, 2, 1, 1, 3, 1, 3, 1, 2, 1).

Similarity between a query and a document (or between two documents) is now defined in terms of *distance*, rather than set inclusion or exclusion.[21] Given two vectors, e.g.,

(3, 2, 1, 1, 3, 1, 3, 1, 2, 1)

and

(2, 2, 0, 1, 2, 1, 5, 0, 2, 2),

there are various ways in which we can decide how close they are to each other in the 10-dimensional space. The idea of representing documents by vectors of term weights has turned out to be very fruitful for indexing, retrieval, and classification tasks.

It is convenient to assume that the terms are uncorrelated, in which case the dimensions are orthogonal. This simplifies the task of computing the similarity between two vectors to that of measuring the angle between them, based on the cosine[22] (see Sidebar 2.2). Of course, most content-bearing terms occurring in a collection will be highly correlated with other terms, but the assumption of linear independence among variables is a commonplace in many real-world applications of statistics.

A major technical issue is what function to use in computing term weights. As we stated earlier, a query term is a good discriminator for ranking purposes to the extent that it tends to occur in relevant documents but tends not to occur in nonrelevant ones. Unlike the Boolean paradigm, ranked retrieval does not limit itself to noting the presence or absence of features, but rather considers their frequency and distribution, both within individual documents and across the collection as a whole.

These intuitions suggest that any such function should have two components. One, the *term frequency* (*tf*) component, should depend upon the frequency with which a query term occurs in a given document that we are trying to rank. The other, the *document frequency* component, should depend upon how frequently the term occurs in all documents. In fact, we are really interested in *inverse document frequency* (*idf*), which measures the relative rarity of a term. It is usually given by

$$idf_t = \log\left(\frac{N}{n_t}\right),$$

where N is the number of documents in the collection, and n_t is the number of documents in which term t appears. We take the logarithm to compress the range.

Notice that the *idf* term is inversely proportional to the document frequency. For instance, a term appearing in all documents in the collection would have an *idf* value of zero. This makes sense, because such a term does not contain any information for retrieval purposes.

The weight of a term, t, in a document vector, d, is then given by

$$w_{t,d} = tf_{t,d} \times idf_{t,d}$$

where $tf_{t,d}$ is a simple count of how many times t occurs in the document.

Document retrieval is now accomplished by computing the similarity between a query vector, q, and a document vector, d, using the formula[23]

$$sim(q,d) = \frac{\sum_t w_{t,d} \cdot w_{t,q}}{\sqrt{\sum_t w_{t,d}^2} \cdot \sqrt{\sum_t w_{t,q}^2}}$$

and then ranking the found documents in decreasing order with respect to this measure.[24]

Sidebar 2.2 A simple vector space model

Let us consider a simple three-dimensional case with a collection of three documents. The dimensions are: 'yes', 'no', and 'maybe,' and the documents are

D_1: 'yes yes yes'
D_2: 'no no no'
D_3: 'yes maybe yes'.

The dimensions of the space can be viewed as *features* that distinguish documents from each other. The components of the document vectors can be viewed as *weights* that code the importance of the corresponding feature for that document.

We can represent each document in our collection with a three-dimensional vector. Assuming that the components of the vector are raw frequencies associated with the dimensions and appearing in the order 'yes', 'maybe', 'no', then the following vectors:

$d_1 = (3, 0, 0)$
$d_2 = (0, 0, 3)$
$d_3 = (2, 1, 0)$

can be used to represent the documents D_1, D_2, and D_3 respectively.

It can be seen by inspection that d_1 is closer to d_3 than d_2 in the vector space defined by the terms. Vectors d_1 and d_2 are at right angles in the vector space, whereas d_1 and d_3 meet at an acute angle. This is in accordance with our intuition that the document D_1 is more similar to the document D_3 than it is to D_2.

Similarity between documents can be measured by the inner product of their corresponding vectors. Recall that the cosine measure is the inner product of the vectors, normalized by their length. Here, we omit the normalization. Thus

$$Sim(D_1, D_2) = d_1 \cdot d_2 = (3, 0, 0) \cdot (0, 0, 3) = 0$$

while

$$Sim(D_1, D_3) = d_1 \cdot d_3 = (3, 0, 0) \cdot (2, 1, 0) = 6$$

The documents D_1 and D_2 have no words in common, and are therefore totally dissimilar. This is reflected by the geometric fact that their vectors are orthogonal, and the algebraic fact that their inner product is zero. D_1 and D_3 share the first dimension ('yes') so their vectors are correlated and their inner product is non-zero.

More generally, given any two documents D_1 and D_2, with vectors

$$d_1 = (d_{1,1}, \ldots, d_{1,t})$$

and

$$d_2 = (d_{2,1}, \ldots, d_{2,t})$$

the similarity between the two documents can be computed by

$$sim(D_1, D_2) = \sum_{i=1}^{i=t} d_{1,i} \cdot d_{2,i}$$

A more realistic example would have higher dimensionality, normalize by the length of each vector and compute a more sophisticated weight function than raw term frequency, but the essentials are the same.[25]

2.3.3 Probabilistic retrieval*[26]

Probabilistic retrieval technology derives from work done at Cambridge University in the late 1970s.[27] This school of thought takes the usual term and document frequency statistics and feeds them as parameters to a Bayesian model that estimates how relevant a document is to a given query. The approach gave rise to the Muscat[28] and Autonomy[29] search engines in the UK, as well as IN-QUERY and WIN in the US, which both have their roots in the University of Massachusetts' Center for Intelligence Information Retrieval.[30] The primary research engine is Okapi,[31] which has gone through many incarnations as a testbed, primarily in a research context.

Probabilistic ranking

Probabilistic IR is an attempt to formalize the ideas behind ranked retrieval in terms of probability theory. Although basic ranked retrieval algorithms employ frequency counts, the underlying mathematics is fairly *ad hoc*, and the scores assigned to documents in a result set are not probabilities, but 'weights' that attempt to estimate how much evidence there is in favor of a document. Consequently they are not subject to the axioms of probability theory, nor can they be combined using the standard formulas.

Probabilistic IR is based on a theory that incorporates a number of underlying assumptions. The most common form of the theory frames the document retrieval problem as one of *computing the probability that a document is relevant to a query*, given that it possesses certain attributes or features.[32] These features are typically words or phrases occurring in the document, as in the ranked retrieval model.

Some key assumptions behind the probabilistic model of retrieval are the binary nature of relevance judgments and the belief that documents can be rated for relevance independently of each other. In other words, we assume:

- that each document is either relevant or irrelevant to a given query, and
- that judging one document to be relevant or irrelevant tells us nothing about the relevance of another document.

Thus the theory does not admit degrees of relevance, nor does it allow for the fact that finding one document may then render another irrelevant. These two points show how far this theoretical notion of relevance is from any practical notion of utility, which would attempt to quantify how useful a document is to a searcher. Clearly utility admits of degrees, and finding one document may render another document redundant to a user's information need.

The probabilities of relevance associated with documents do have a practical aspect, however. They are used to determine the order in which hits are presented to the user. The Probability Ranking Principle[33] states that ranking documents by decreasing probability of relevance to a query will yield 'optimal performance,' i.e., the best ordering, based on the available data. Transformations of the probabilities are allowed, as long as they are order-preserving.

Probability of relevance

We can express the probability of relevance of a document D given a query Q as

$$P(R_Q = X|D).$$

We assume that $X \in \{0, 1\}$, in accordance with the binary nature of relevance. Our 'similarity measure', or matching score, between the query and the document will be the *odds* in favor of relevance. This can be expressed as the ratio between the probability of relevance and the probability of nonrelevance:

$$\frac{P(R_Q = 1|D)}{P(R_Q = 0|D)}.$$

By "odds likelihood" form of Bayes' rule, we can compute this ratio as follows,

$$\frac{P(R_Q = 1|D)}{P(R_Q = 0|D)} = \frac{P(R_Q = 1)P(D|R_Q = 1)}{P(R_Q = 0)P(D|R_Q = 0)}$$

so long as we can estimate the quantities on the right-hand side of the equation.

$P(R_Q = 1)$ is the probability that a document chosen at random from the collection is relevant to the query, i.e., the document is chosen without knowledge of its contents. Since this quantity is the same for all documents, we can ignore it without affecting the final ranking of results. A similar argument applies to $P(R_Q = 0)$.

Thus we are left with the equation

$$\frac{P(R_Q = 1|D)}{P(R_Q = 0|D)} \propto \frac{P(D|R_Q = 1)}{P(D|R_Q = 0)},$$

with just the likelihood ratio on the right hand side. It is also common to see this formula expressed as log-odds:

$$\log \frac{P(R_Q = 1|D)}{P(R_Q = 0|D)} \propto \log \frac{P(D|R_Q = 1)}{P(D|R_Q = 0)}.$$

$P(D|R_Q = 1)$ is the probability of selecting the document from the relevant set, and is not so easily dismissed. Neither is $P(D|R_Q = 0)$, the probability of selecting the document from the non-relevant set. One way to estimate these quantities is to look at the query terms in

$$Q = \{t_1, \ldots, t_m\}$$

and see how they are distributed, both within the document and within the collection as a whole. Moreover, independence assumptions (and the use of logarithms) lead to the decomposition of the ratio into additive components such as individual terms weights, rather as we did in the vector space model.

As before, we would like to be able to compute a weight, $w_{t,d}$, for each term t in the context of a given vector d, representing the document D.

Term weights
Let N be the size of the collection and n_t be the number of documents containing a given query term, t. (We will subsequently omit subscripts where there is no ambiguity.) One component of the weight is usually given by

$$IDF_t = \log \left(\frac{N - n_t + 0.5}{n_t + 0.5} \right).$$

This is recognizable as a smoothed version of inverse document frequency[34] (IDF[35]). Smoothing prevents division by zero in the case where a term does not occur in the document collection at all.

If within-document frequency counts were not available, a simple matching score that respects the Probability Ranking Principle could be derived by summing these components, by computing

$$\sum_t \log \left(\frac{N - n_t + 0.5}{n_t + 0.5} \right),$$

where the summation is over all the terms in the query.

However, there is usually another component of the term weight, one that is a function of the frequency, f, with which t occurs in a document. We say a function of f, rather than f itself, because we may need to take document length into account. Long documents will tend to have multiple occurrences of terms. They deserve some credit for this in the final ranking. A Web page that contains the single sentence:

'Gravity sucks.'

should not be deemed as relevant to a query containing 'gravity' as a longer article that contains 50 occurrences of the word 'gravity'. On the other hand, we should not assume that the longer page is 50 times more relevant. The longer page may simply be a wordier statement of the contents of the shorter page.

Many engines attempt to control for document length by normalizing, so that the average length of a document in the collection is set to unity. A common term frequency (TF) expression is then:

$$TF = \frac{f(K + 1)}{f + KL},$$

where L is the *normalized* length of document D. If the document is of average length, then $L = 1.0$. K is a constant, usually set between 1.0 and 2.0.

The TF component is designed to increase in value quite modestly as f increases. If f, K and L are 1, then $TF = 1.0$. If f were 9, then $TF = 1.8$. L modulates this effect, giving more credit to shorter documents.[36]

The term weight would then be given by:

$$w_{t,d} = \frac{f(K+1)}{f+KL} \log \left(\frac{N-n+0.5}{n+0.5} \right).$$

Clearly, if the term does not occur in the document, its weight will be zero. Another variation, used by the INQUERY search engine mentioned earlier, is given by:

$$w_{t,d} = \alpha + (1-\alpha)\frac{f}{f+0.5+KL} \left(\frac{\log \frac{N+0.5}{n}}{\log N + 1} \right).$$

α is a constant which states that, even if the term does not occur in the document, its probability of occurrence isn't zero, while $(1-\alpha)$ weights the contribution of *TF.IDF*.

$\alpha = 0.4$ is chosen to fix a minimum value for $w_{t,d}$. This value was derived from experiments in which the range for $P(R_Q = 1|D)$ was varied systematically by manipulating α. There was judged to be a performance improvement in the rankings as α increased to 0.3, with a 'sweet spot' in the region of [0.3, 0.4], beyond which performance dropped again, mostly due to ties.

K is typically set to 1.5. Other variants of *TF.IDF* use even more constants, and choosing their values is something of a black art.[37] The *IDF* term is based on the ratio between the *IDF* of the term t (the numerator) and an estimate of the *IDF* of the term that occurs in the most documents (the denominator).

The WIN[38] search engine employs a somewhat modified formula that differs mostly in the *TF* term.

$$w_{t,d} = 0.4 + 0.6 \left(\frac{0.5 \times \log f}{\log f^*} + 0.5 \right) \left(\frac{\log \frac{N}{n}}{\log N} \right).$$

Instead of normalizing *TF* with respect to document length directly, by standardizing actual document lengths, the denominator of *TF* ratio features a quantity, f^*, which is the frequency of the most frequent term in the document. This will clearly tend to increase with document length, but it is a much cheaper statistic to compute.[39]

For a multi-term 'natural language' query, the probability of a document being relevant is often computed by summing[40] the query term weights in the context of that document

$$P(D|R_Q = 1) = \sum_{t \in Q} w_{t,d},$$

thereby giving us the numerator of our ratio, while the denominator can be computed by

$$P(D|R_Q = 0) = 1 - P(D|R_Q = 1),$$

giving us the measure we need to rank the document. This weighting scheme can also be applied to Boolean queries (see Sidebar 2.3).

We have seen that the basic formulation of probabilistic IR relies heavily upon Bayes' Rule in order to compute the probability of that a given document is relevant to a query. The rule enables us to perform two essential tasks.

– We can compute the probability that a document is relevant from an estimate of the probability of that document being selected, given that it is relevant.
– We can combine the evidence of relevance provided by occurrences of individual query terms into a relevance estimate based on all the query terms.

The question then arises as to how to implement these tasks efficiently. Both INQUERY and WIN use inference networks to represent both documents and queries. *Inference networks* are directed acyclic graphs that enable the implementation of a direct and intuitive method for both the first estimation task and the second task of evidence combination.[41] They are based on Bayesian networks of the kind formalized by Pearl.[42] These structures offer a convenient mechanism for updating the probability, or degree of belief, in a hypothesis.

Sidebar 2.3 Term weights for boolean queries

Given a query containing Boolean operators, the weight of query term 'NOT t' with respect to document vector d is simply

$$1 - w_{t,d}$$

the weight of 's AND t' is computed by the product

$$w_{s,d} \cdot w_{t,d}$$

and the weight of a disjunctive term 's OR t' is given by

$$1 - [(1 - w_{s,d}) \cdot (1 - w_{t,d})]$$

since 's OR t' is equivalent to 'NOT (NOT s AND NOT t)'.

Summary of probabilistic IR

The Probability Ranking Principle suggests ranking a document according to its odds of being in the class of relevant documents, rather than the class of non-relevant documents.

The formulation of probabilistic IR given in this section is called the *Binary Independence Retrieval (BIR) model*.[43] Its usage of term frequency and inverse document frequency is not very different in practice from that of vector space models, and performance is typically no better. However, the approach lays claim to a more theoretically-motivated basis, in that it ranks documents with respect to probability of relevance to a user's need, rather than similarity to a query.[44]

The BIR model makes a number of assumptions. Its name implies that individual terms are distributed independently from each other throughout the documents in a collection. Thus we allow ourselves to combine term weights by multiplication (or summing logarithms). But it turns out that the key assumption is weaker than this. Given

$$\frac{P(R_Q = 1|D)}{P(R_Q = 0|D)} \approx \prod_{t \in Q} \frac{P(t|R_Q = 1)}{P(t|R_Q = 0)},$$

we are really assuming an equality among probability ratios, i.e., that such dependencies as exist between terms are the same across both relevant and non-relevant documents.[45]

Another assumption is that documents can be judged for relevance independently of each other, as noted earlier. In practice, finding one document can obviously make another document less useful, e.g., if one document subsumes another with respect to its information content.

2.3.4 Language modeling*

Probabilistic modeling of relevance is not the only application of probability theory to information retrieval. Since 1998, a new approach, called 'language modeling', has sparked some interest, deriving from work done at the University of Massachusetts.[46] Language modeling is a framework that, until recently, had been more commonly associated with speech recognition and generation.

The primary difference between what is now being called 'classical' probabilistic IR and language modeling is that the latter seeks to model the query generation process, rather than the pool of relevant documents. Query generation is viewed as a process of sampling randomly from a document, or rather from a document model consisting of terms and their frequencies of occurrence in the document. In other words, we consider the probability that a given document model could have produced the query, and rank the corresponding document accordingly. Documents with a relatively high probability of generating the query are ranked high in the results list.

This is rather different from the classic approach, where we seek to construct a model of the relevant documents, and then estimate the probability that a word occurs in such documents. Language modeling models each document individually, rather than assuming that documents are members of a predefined class. A language model is in fact a probability distribution that captures the statistical regularities that govern query generation viewed as a random process.

More formally, given a query, Q, and a document model, M_d, for document d, we would like to estimate

$$P(Q|M_d).$$

The maximum likelihood estimate (MLE) of this quantity for a query consisting of a single term, t, is

$$P_{MLE}(t, d) = \frac{tf_{t,d}}{d_{len}}$$

where $tf_{t,d}$ is the frequency of the term t in document d, as usual, and d_{len} is the sum of the frequencies of all the tokens in d.

If we then seek to estimate the probability of a multi-term query, we might assume independence among query terms, and compute

$$P(Q|M_d) = \prod_{t \in Q} P_{MLE}(t, d).$$

However, there are two main problems with this estimator. Firstly, it needs to be smoothed, else

$$P_{MLE}(t, d) = 0$$

for any query term, t, will lead to

$$P(Q|M_d) = 0.$$

Thus a term, t, not occurring in d is assigned a non-zero MLE, according to its probability of occurrence in the collection as a whole.

Secondly, even if t occurs in d, a document-sized sample may be too small for our estimate, so we fortify the probability of observing t in d with the probability of observing t in those documents where it in fact occurs.[47]

Then the probability of the query given the document can be estimated by:

$$P(Q|M_d) = \prod_{t \in Q} P(t|M_d) \times \prod_{t \notin Q} 1 - P(t|M_d).$$

Ponte and Croft found that ranking documents by this method produced better results than the usual *TF.IDF* weighting. Subsequent work[48] has investigated more sophisticated forms of smoothing, such as 'semantic smoothing', which takes synonyms and word senses into account. Finally, language models have recently used to estimate relevance models of the kind computed by 'classic' probabilistic IR.[49]

2.4 Evaluating search engines

Prior to any discussion of evaluation methods and metrics, it makes sense to ask what an evaluation of a search engine is really setting out to achieve.

2.4.1 Evaluation studies

During the course of its working life, a full-text search engine will typically be used to retrieve documents that were not indexed or even written at the time it was created by means of queries that the designers and programmers could not be expected to anticipate. Consequently, there is no sense in which a search engine can be tested on a representative sample from a target population of queries or documents. A search engine that works well on today's Web may not work well on tomorrow's, just because there is no guarantee that the content and structure of today's Web pages or queries are a representative sample of to-morrow's. Consider the growth in commercial uses of the Web that took place between 1995 and 2000, which radically changed the content mix of material available through the Internet.

Ideally, search engine evaluations ought to be concerned with estimating an interval that predicts, at a certain level of confidence, how well a particular engine will perform on the next several randomly selected queries over a grow-ing document collection. Thus we are not sampling a population, but rather a process extending into the future, only part of which is in existence and avail-able for sampling.[50] In addition to identifying a target population (e.g., general Web queries), and a sampled population (e.g., all AltaVista queries submit-ted on January 1st, 2001), we need to consider the differences between the two and what the consequences of those differences are in predicting future performance.

Such evaluations are hard to perform, but significant progress has been made in the area of evaluation methodology, thanks largely to an initiative started by the US Government in 1992.

The purpose of the Text REtrieval Conference[51] (TREC) was to support research within the information retrieval community by providing the infrastructure necessary for large-scale evaluation of text retrieval methodologies. It consists of a series of workshops with the following goals:[52]

- To encourage IR research based on large test collections.
- To increase communication among industry, academia, and government.
- To speed the transfer of technology from research laboratories into commercial products.
- To increase the availability of appropriate evaluation techniques for use by industry and academia.

TREC is probably the greatest single source of information about IR evaluation methods and metrics. It has certainly made an effort to encourage experimentation with test collections of realistic size. Another shift that has taken place within the IR community in recent years is an increased focus upon the quality of the user's experience, and his or her level of satisfaction.

2.4.2 Evaluation metrics

Two performance metrics gained currency in the 1960s, when researchers began performing comparative studies of different indexing systems.[53] These are *recall* and *precision*, and they can be defined as follows.

Let us assume a collection of N documents. Suppose that in this collection there are $n < N$ documents that are relevant to the specific information need represented by a query. The search on the query retrieves m items, a of which are actually relevant. Then the recall, R, of the search engine on that query is given by

$$R = a/n$$

and the precision, P, is given by

$$P = a/m.$$

Table 2.3 A contingency table analysis of precision and recall

	Relevant	Non-relevant	
Retrieved	a	b	$a + b = m$
Not retrieved	c	d	$c + d = N - m$
	$a + c = n$	$b + d = N - n$	$a + b + c + d = N$

Thus recall can be thought of as the 'hit ratio', the proportion of target documents returned. Precision can be thought of as the 'signal to noise' ratio, the proportion of returned documents that are actually targets.

One way of looking at recall and precision is in terms of a 2×2 contingency table (see Table 2.3).

Recall and precision are usually expressed as percentages based on the following ratios:

$$R = 100a/(a + c)$$

$$P = 100a/(a + b).$$

Clearly, there is a trade-off between recall and precision, and so it is customary to present precision results at different levels of recall in an easy to read graph. Researchers sometimes report 'average precision', derived by averaging precision scores over some number of evenly spaced recall points, such as 10%, 20%, ..., 100%.

The above measures are all well and good, but they do not take relevance ranking into account. In addition to finding relevant documents, we would like a ranked retrieval engine to also assign relevant documents higher ranks than irrelevant documents. Two common and easy to compute measures that fit the bill are *rank recall* and *log precision*.[54]

Suppose that the *i*th *relevant* document has a rank r_i associated with it, where ranks are assigned in decreasing order of relevance to the query. (Thus the most relevant document gets a rank of one.) Then the measures can be defined as follows.

$$Ranked\ Recall = \frac{\sum_{i=1}^{n} i}{\sum_{i=1}^{n} r_i}$$

and

$$Log\ Precision = \frac{\sum\limits_{i=1}^{n} \log i}{\sum\limits_{i=1}^{n} \log r_i}.$$

Measuring effectiveness based on a pair of numbers, which co-vary in a loosely specified way, has been sometimes seen as dissatisfactory.[55] This has led various composite measures, which make use of the entries in the contingency table, but combine them into a single measure. One of these measures is the E_α measure defined as follow:

$$E_\alpha = 1 - \frac{1}{\alpha\dfrac{1}{P} + (1-\alpha)\dfrac{1}{R}}.$$

α is a weight for calibrating the relative importance of recall versus precision. Thus if α is set to 1, $E_\alpha = 1 - P$, while if α is set to 0, $E_\alpha = 1 - R$. Intermediate values of α introduce a deliberate bias for one over the other.

In Chapters 3 and 4, we will see how variants of a related measure, the F–measure, where

$$F_\alpha = 1 - E_\alpha,$$

are used to evaluate both information extraction and text classification systems.

2.4.3 Relevance judgments

Over 30 years later, precision and recall are still the most widely used metrics in IR. However, before they can be computed, it is necessary to obtain *relevance judgments*. In a perfect world, one would know, for each query, which documents in the collection are relevant to the corresponding information need, and which are not. For example, the experiments done at the Royal Air Force College of Aeronautics in Cranfield, England in the 1960s relied upon the ability to rate the relevance of retrieved bibliographic references on a scale of 1 to 4.

For modern document collections of commercial value, obtaining complete relevance judgments on all queries of interest is clearly impossible. Thus the normal problems involved in performing an analytic, predictive study of IR systems are compounded by the inherent difficulty of obtaining the necessary ground data. TREC has certainly made a contribution by providing relevance judgments for selected queries[56] with respect to nontrivial test collections.[57]

TREC adopted the following working definition of relevance:

> 'If you were writing a report on the subject of the topic and would use the information contained in the document in the report, then the document is relevant.'[58]

A document is judged to be either relevant or irrelevant, so there are no degrees of relevance in TREC. A document is deemed to be relevant if any piece of it is relevant.

TREC adopted the following method, called *pooling*, for identifying documents in a collection that are relevant to a given information need or topic.[59] A sample of possibly relevant documents is created by running each of the participating search system and taking the top 100 documents returned by each system for a given topic. These documents are then merged into a pool for review by judges, who determine whether or not each document really is relevant. For the sake of consistency, a single judge assessed the documents for each topic; tests had suggested that inter-judge agreement was only about 80% on such a task.

TREC was fortunate in having access to multiple search engines. The STAIRS project at IBM[60] generated another method, involving only a single search engine. Given a conjunctive query of the form:

$$Q_1 \& Q_2 \& \ldots \& Q_n$$

generate the set of queries

$$\cancel{Q_1} \& Q_2 \& \ldots \& Q_n$$
$$Q_1 \& \cancel{Q_2} \& \ldots \& Q_n$$
$$\ldots$$
$$Q_1 \& Q_2 \& \ldots \& \cancel{Q_n}$$

formed by leaving out each of the query terms in turn, and then form the union of the documents. The set difference between this union and those documents returned by the original query form a useful pool in which to look for relevant documents not returned by the original query.

2.4.4 Total system evaluation

Precision and recall do not, in themselves, tell us whether a particular search engine is pleasant to use, or provides a cost-effective service.

We shall not concern ourselves with user interface issues in this book, but screen design and general ergonomics are obviously important factors in user acceptance. Also important is the recall-precision trade-off inherent in providing editorial features that help focus search. Having editors (or programs) create metadata that organizes documents into a taxonomy can significantly enhance the user experience.

For instance, industry evaluations of portals like Open Directory and Yahoo![61] stress the convenience that comes with having hundreds of thousands of sites categorized into thousands of categories. This allows the merging of search and browsing behaviors, and guarantees a high level of precision. But, if recall is a user's main concern, he or she is more likely to subscribe to an archival online service, such as Dialog or Lexis-Nexis, or use a high coverage search engine, such as Google (see Section 2.6).

Cost-effectiveness is another large issue, and one that any commercial provider must address. The issue is not merely 'What can I charge for this service?' Cost also enters into any consideration of whether or not to improve the speed or accuracy of an existing system. Many things can be done to improve system performance,[62] but will users notice, and will they pay the premium?

Studies suggest that user satisfaction with search experiences is more a function of expectations than expertise,[63] and that users have 'erroneous mental models' of search engine operation.[64] If this research is accurate, then commercial providers of search facilities should be as least as concerned with expectation management and transparency as they are with performance. Many successful Web sites[65] provide only rudimentary search capabilities, but provide tools for browsing documents and do a good job of managing their customers' perceptions.

We return to the topic of evaluation when we focus upon Web search engines in Section 2.6 below.

2.5 Attempts to enhance search performance

As mentioned earlier, various devices have been employed in an attempt to improve the basic performance of search engines, whether based on the Boolean or the ranked retrieval model. This section reviews the better-understood methods, such as query expansion, relevance feedback, and local content analysis, which have been both well researched and adequately documented in the literature.

2.5.1 Query expansion and thesauri

The most obvious problem with free text searching is that there is often a mismatch between the terms used in a query and the terms that appear in a relevant document. Thus the query

> who sells complete email solutions for cell phones

will fail to find a document containing only the following relevant fragment

> Gizmotron is a leading vendor of electronic messaging services for cellular devices.

An equally obvious solution is to try and 'expand' the query by adding terms that stand in some useful meaning relation to original query terms. A thesaurus is a traditional source of relations among words and phrases, and so it is natural to think of looking up terms in an online database that encodes such information.

Does this help? Not always, and not as much as you might think. Here are some reasons why.

- Synonymy is not the only relationship we are interested in. Thus a phone is a device, but 'device' is a *hyponym*[66] of 'phone,' not a synonym. Not all thesauri will enable you to make this kind of connection. Neither is the relationship between 'sells' and 'vendor' one that can easily be looked up in a thesaurus. Grammatical and morphological issues intervene.
- *Polysemy*[67] gets in the way. Thus the term 'cell' can refer to a locked room in a prison or a unit in some structure, depending upon the context. A thesaurus won't help much unless it encodes all and only the meaning relations that are relevant to the domain of interest. Query expansion using a general thesaurus will typically add noise that degrades retrieval performance.
- Regional variants can also cause problems, as noted earlier. Thus American English prefers 'automobile' to describe personal vehicles, while British English prefers 'car'. Slang or abbreviated terms, such as 'mobiles' for 'mobile phones', are often highly regional in usage.

Electronic thesauri such as Wordnet[68] can be fairly sophisticated. Wordnet is a hand-built thesaurus that organizes words into synonym sets (called 'synsets'), each of which represent a single sense of a word. These sense are organized into taxonomies by meaning inclusion, e.g., the synset for containing 'vehicle' is superior to the synset containing 'car' in the hierarchy. Such an organization captures hyponymic relations and also attempts to distinguish the different senses of polysemous words. Nevertheless, early attempts to harness Wordnet to improve retrieval were disappointing.[69]

Hand crafting isn't the only way to build a thesaurus. Another approach is to associate words on statistical grounds, e.g., because they tend to occur together in some corpus of documents, or because they occur in similar sentential contexts. The criteria for association will obviously determine what such word groups look like. For example, if co-occurrence is the criterion, then one can imagine a grouping such as

{bird, nest, feather, egg, swallow, robin},

where the meaning relations among group members are something of a mixed bag. If occurrence in similar contexts is the criterion, then

{swallows, warblers, finches, USAir, New Yorkers}

might be grouped because they all fly down to Florida in the winter. Swallows and New Yorkers don't share many other characteristics,[70] but if the focus of interest is Florida, then such a grouping might still make sense.

Co-occurrence thesauri have sometimes been shown to improve retrieval performance on small collections.[71] However, there is a convincing argument[72] that queries so expanded will tend to contain high frequency terms that are not good discriminators. More linguistically motivated thesauri based on contextual cues, such as head-modifier[73] relations, have found modest, albeit uneven, improvements that depend upon the methods and collections used.[74] Such lukewarm results have led many people to conclude that natural language processing has not achieved much in the service of document retrieval.

Yet a recent prototype by Woods[75] employs natural language processing and knowledge representation techniques to achieve more impressive improvements on a typical retrieval task than previous literature would lead one to expect. His approach, called 'conceptual indexing' integrates morphological variation and semantic relationships into a single taxonomy to support query expansion and passage retrieval. The idea is to exploit both linguistic and real-world knowledge to get better results while pinpointing relevant passages in found documents. This ability is termed 'Precision Content Retrieval.'

The query expansion capability is provided by a lexicon that contains subsumption information for about 15,000 words, i.e., it delineates specificity/generality relationships such as

a *car* is a kind of *vehicle*,
walking is a kind of *moving*.

The lexicon also records morphological information, so that the query processor can recognize different word roots without resorting to ad hoc stemming rules. When you combine these two knowledge sources, you are able to recognize that the phrase *turns red* is a more specific instance of the phrase *color change*, since *red* is a kind of *color*, and *turns* is an inflected form of the root form *turn*, which is a kind of *change*.

Woods found that using these knowledge sources added 20% to the success rate[76] of a state-of-the-art search engine, albeit over a small document collection of 1800 files. The contribution of passage retrieval is harder to evaluate, but anecdotal evidence suggests that the identification of relevant passages in found documents greatly enhances the productivity of knowledge workers as they sift through search results.

In summary, it seems that straightforward approaches to query expansion based on general-purpose thesauri are very unlikely to enhance search engine performance. Methods based on statistically generated thesauri also tend to be ineffectual, because they only succeed in adding common terms, which are poor discriminators. Methods involving linguistic engineering still hold promise, but require a serious hand crafting and knowledge engineering effort, and have yet to prove themselves on large collections.

2.5.2 Query expansion from relevance information*

An alternative to thesauri for query expansion relies upon having some kind of relevance information. One can use information about whether some documents in the collection are relevant or not in a number of different ways. For example, one can

- add significant terms from known relevant documents to the query, or
- modify the weights of terms in the query to optimize performance, or both.

Relevance information for a given query is typically obtained through feedback from the user, who can be asked to mark the top ranked documents in a result set as relevant or not. However, the user can implicitly provide such feedback by clicking on a "More Like This" button next to a document. Alternatively, the system can simply assume that the top ranked documents are relevant, and expand the query automatically by selecting significant terms from those documents.

Query expansion using relevance feedback was originally designed in the context of the vector space model,[77] while the probabilistic model included the idea of re-evaluating term weights using relevance information.[78]

Vector space models of query expansion
In the vector space model, queries and documents are represented as vectors
of term weights. Query expansion using relevance feedback can then be seen
as adjusting weights in the query vector. Adding a new term to the query corresponds to giving that term a non-zero weight. Emphasizing or reducing the
importance of a query term corresponds to increasing or decreasing its weight.

Similarity between a document vector, D, and a query vector, Q, is computed as the inner product between these vectors, a specialization of the earlier
formula, where weights in the query vector, $w_{t,q}$, were set to 1:

$$sim(Q, D) = \sum_{t \in Q} w_{t,d} \cdot w_{t,q}.$$

Given a query represented by the vector

$$Q = (w_{1,q}, w_{2,q}, \cdots, w_{t,q}),$$

the relevance feedback process generates a new vector

$$Q' = (w'_{1,q}, w'_{2,q}, \cdots, w'_{t,q}, w'_{t+1,q}, \cdots, w'_{t+k,q}),$$

where old weights, w, have been updated and replaced by new weights, w', and
k new terms have been added.

Rocchio[79] has shown that, given all relevance information about a query,
the query formulation leading to the retrieval of many relevant documents
from a collection is of the form:

$$Q_{opt} = \frac{1}{n} \sum_{\substack{relevant \\ documents}} \frac{D_i}{|D_i|} - \frac{1}{N - n} \sum_{\substack{non-relevant \\ documents}} \frac{D_i}{|D_i|},$$

where D_i represent document vectors, and $|D_i|$ is the Euclidean vector length. N
is assumed to be the collection size, and n is the number of relevant documents
in the collection.

This information cannot be used in practice to formulate the query, since
finding which documents are relevant is the purpose of search, and not a given.
However, the formula can help in generating a feedback query from relevance
assessments for documents retrieved from an initial search. If we substitute "all
relevant" by "known relevant" documents, and "all non-relevant" documents
by "known non-relevant" documents, the original query can be expanded in
the following manner:

$$Q_1 = Q_0 + \frac{1}{n_1} \sum_{\substack{known \\ relevant}} \frac{D_i}{|D_i|} - \frac{1}{n_2} \sum_{\substack{known \\ non-relevant}} \frac{D_i}{|D_i|},$$

where Q_0 is the initial query and Q_1 the reformulated query after the first round of relevance feedback. n_1 is the number of known relevant documents, and n_2 is the number of known non-relevant documents.

More generally, query reformulation via relevance feedback can be expressed as an iterative process,

$$Q_{i+1} = \alpha Q_i + \beta \sum_{\substack{known \\ relevant}} \frac{D_j}{|D_j|} - \gamma \sum_{\substack{known \\ non-relevant}} \frac{D_j}{|D_j|},$$

where α, β, and γ are set experimentally, and term weights are normalized and their range restricted from 0 to 1. Usually, parameters α, β, and γ are set arbitrarily,[80] and have no relations with the number of known relevant and non-relevant documents in the original formulation.

Probabilistic models of query expansion

Probabilistic retrieval models also integrate to various degrees the use of relevant information for query expansion. In the vector space model, selecting terms for expansion and computing the weights for the new query are done at the same time. In a probabilistic framework, selecting terms and computing relevance weights are treated as two different problems.

Computing relevance weights seeks to answer the question: "How much evidence does the presence of this term provide for the relevance of this document?" Probability estimates can be rendered more accurate when more information (e.g., from relevance feedback) is available. Selecting new terms to add to a query should answer a different question, namely: "How much will adding this term to the request benefit the overall performance of the search formulation?"[81]

In the probabilistic model developed by Robertson and Sparck-Jones, relevance information is used to compute more accurate weight estimates. Consider the term incidence contingency table in Table 2.4, where R is the number of relevant documents for this query, and r is the number of these documents containing the term. The term weight from the equation

$$w_{t,d} = \frac{f(K+1)}{f+KL} \log \left(\frac{N-n+0.5}{n+0.5} \right),$$

which we encountered earlier, would then be re-expressed as

$$w'_{t,d} = \frac{f(K+1)}{f+KL} \log \frac{(r+0.5)(N-n-R+r+0.5)}{(R-r+0.5)(n-r+0.5)}$$

to take account of the relevance information.

Table 2.4 Term incidence contingency table

	Relevant	Non-relevant	Total
Containing the term	r	$n - r$	n
Not containing the term	$R - r$	$(N - n) - (R - r)$	$N - n$
Total	R	$N - R$	N

Let us now address how terms are selected for query expansion. For each expansion candidate, the model discussed by Robertson[82] considers the distribution of scores for relevant and non-relevant documents, with the candidate term present or absent. The model leads to an 'offer weight', which is used to rank candidate terms (the larger the offer weight, the better the candidate):

$$OW_t = r_t \log \frac{(r_t + 0.5)(N - n_t - R + r_t + 0.5)}{(R - r_t + 0.5)(n_t - r_t + 0.5)}.$$

The model proposed by Robertson tightly integrates query expansion using relevance information and probabilistic retrieval.

By contrast, relevance feedback using the inference network model (see Section 2.3.3) is more akin to relevance feedback in the vector space model.[83] In the inference network framework, relevance information is not used to re-estimate individual term contributions as above. Rather, adding new terms to the query causes the re-estimation of the probability that a document satisfies the information need, by changing the structure of the network.

Relevance feedback from the user is not always available. Not all users are willing to participate in such an exercise, which may be viewed as an imposition or a distraction. Nevertheless, it is still possible to perform query expansion, in the following way.

In recent years, systems participating in TREC (see Section 2.4) have included query expansion using *blind relevance feedback*. In this approach, also called *pseudo relevance feedback*, the search engine retrieves a ranked list of documents with the original query formulation. The top n (typically between 5 and 30) documents retrieved by the system are labeled (blindly) as 'known to be relevant.' The methods introduced earlier in the section can then be applied to using those top ranked documents in place of documents judged by a user. (In this case, there are no known non-relevant documents.)

Experiments at TREC have shown that pseudo relevance feedback can significantly improve performance. However, experiments have also shown that the technique may not be very robust. Indeed, it can harm performance when there are few relevant documents in the top ranked documents retrieved, since the words added to the query will be selected from non-relevant documents. Moreover, this is still a relatively expensive process.

First, we need to run a search using the original query in order to get relevance information (either by interacting with the user, or by selecting the top n documents) Next, we need to select terms and modify their weights. To do so, we need to access the terms of a given document. In a typical system that relies on inverted index files, this information (which terms appear in a given document) is not stored and needs to be computed on the fly.

In summary, query expansion using relevance information looks more promising than query expansion based on thesauri. In past years, there has been experimental evidence that such a process may be effective but not always reliable. By the same token, users of Web search engines know from experience that devices purporting to deliver 'similar documents' are sometimes wide of the mark.

Sidebar 2.4 Improving relevance feedback

A couple of new approaches have been proposed to improve the robustness of pseudo relevance feedback: *local context analysis* and *query expansion using summaries*. The latter is a very recent technique[84] where summaries are used in place of full text documents to perform blind relevance feedback. The results look very promising compared to blind relevance feedback based on full documents.

Local context analysis (LCA) is a blind relevance feedback technique based on co-occurrence analysis between candidate expansion features and query terms. The underlying hypothesis is that a good expansion term tends to co-occur with all query terms in the top-ranked set. This hypothesis leads to a novel selection function for candidate expansion terms.

Experiments using local context analysis typically use nouns and noun phrases as expansion features. They also rely on top-ranked paragraphs rather than top-ranked documents, mostly for efficiency purposes. In those experiments, local context analysis has been shown more effective than earlier approaches to blind relevance feedback, and it also appears to be more robust.[85]

2.6 The future of Web searching

Traditional search engines were never intended to deal with a vast, distributed, heterogeneous collection of documents such as the WWW. The almost complete absence of editorial control over Web documents poses special problems, such as coverage, currentness, spamming, dead links, and the manipulation of rankings for commercial advantage. In this section, we examine new techniques that seek to address such problems and explore a number of avenues for improving Web search.

2.6.1 Indexing the Web

The Web is indexed by 'crawling' it. A *Web crawler* is a program that visits remote sites over the Internet and automatically downloads their pages for indexing. Today this is typically done in a distributed fashion, using more than one program.

In the 1990s, many commercial search engines claimed to index the entire Web, and to be able to find 'anything on the Internet'.[86] However, systematic studies showed that there was significant room for improvement in search engines' ability to produce comprehensive, up-to-date indices.[87] For example, Lawrence and Giles[88] of NEC Research Institute estimated the coverage of a number of popular search engines in 1997, and also counted the number of invalid links returned. The results are shown in Table 2.5.

At the time of the study, the authors estimated a lower bound on the publicly indexable Web to be 320 million pages. This estimate was derived by examining the overlap between the result sets of pairs of search engines. Their method used one engine as a yardstick to estimate the coverage of the other, based on the assumption that the two engines sample the Web independently.

The fraction of the Web covered by engine a, written W_a, was approximated by

$$W_a = N_{ab}/N_b,$$

where N_{ab} is the number of documents returned by both engine a and engine b, and N_b is the number of documents returned by engine b.

The authors used the two largest engines studied in order to derive this approximation. The estimate was deemed to be a lower bound, because the independence assumption may not be entirely valid, given that search engines tend to index more 'popular' pages. Using this method, it was estimated that no

Table 2.5 Estimated coverage of popular Web search engines and percentage of invalid links returned. Data collected in December 1997. Results based on 575 typical queries submitted by scientists

Search Engine	Hotbot	AltaVista	Northern Light	Excite	Infoseek	Lycos
Coverage wrt est. size of Web	34%	28%	20%	14%	10%	3%
Dead links returned	5.3%	2.5%	5.0%	2.0%	2.6%	1.6%

search engine indexed much more than one-third of the Web, and that search engine coverage could vary by an order of magnitude.

Search engine indexes have grown significantly since 1997. By the end of 2001, Google was indexing an estimated 1.5 billion pages,[89] with runners-up Fast, Altavista, and Inktomi indexing half a billion or more.[90] Indexing the Web is a non-trivial business. A crawler may connect to half a million servers and download millions of pages. Downloaded documents need to be compressed and stored, parsed to extract index terms, and then sorted to generate an inverted index of the kind described in Section 2.2.

The crawler serving Google also parses out the links on each page, and stores this information in an 'anchors' file. A program called the URLresolver converts relative URLs into absolute URLs,[91] and puts the anchor text into the index associated with the document that the anchor points to. Every page has a unique name associated with it, called a 'docID', and a database of links is generated, consisting of docID pairs. This information is later used to rank retrieved documents, according to the principle that pages that are well-linked deserve higher rankings than pages that are not. The PageRank algorithm, and the thinking behind it, is described in Section 2.6.3.

Sidebar 2.5 Finding highly relevant documents

In 1999, the Text Retrieval Conference (TREC) set out to evaluate web searching for the first time, and initiated a 'web track.' Its first task was to assemble several web-based collection of documents, based on a spidering of the Web called the Internet Archive.[92] Queries were taken from query log of the Excite search engine and massaged to fit the TREC notion of a 'topic.'[93] Search engine evaluation was conducted by having assessors rate retrieved documents as 'non-relevant', 'relevant', or 'highly relevant', instead of the usual binary judgments. Assessors were also asked to indicate the 'best document' for each topic.

The results, reported at the 2001 SIGIR Conference,[94] showed that:

– Correlations between system rankings were lower than anticipated, indicating that distinguishing highly relevant documents does produce somewhat different results than evaluation by the usual 'relevant' versus 'non-relevant' split.
– Using only highly relevant documents resulted in unstable measures,[95] and it was necessary to tune the balance between the contributions of the highly relevant and the merely relevant to overcome this.
– The 'best document' standard turned out to be useless for judging systems, since assessors disagreed over which were the best documents, and when they selected the same document did so for different reasons.

Another interested finding was that finding highly relevant documents did not correlate strongly with 'high early precision', i.e., having a system which trades off recall in order to get many relevant documents in the early ranks.

Thus there would appear to be some justice to the contention by search engine vendors that the task of finding highly relevant documents on the Web is somewhat different from the traditional TREC task of finding relevant documents in other collections. The very heterogeneity, redundancy, and lack of quality control on the Web emphasizes the importance of not just finding documents about a topic, but finding highly relevant, authoritative documents. New techniques for satisfying this need form the subject matter of the next section.

2.6.2 Searching the Web

The Web has been well described by Kleinberg[96] as a form of 'populist hypermedia' in which millions of parties act independently to create hundreds of millions of pages. As we stated earlier, this creates obvious problems for searching, since there is no overall scheme that organizes this content, beyond the addresses provided by URLs. A global structure is nonetheless formed by the hundreds of millions of uncoordinated local actions that individuals take in linking pages together.

It is a commonplace to observe that searchers often have difficulty in locating the information they desire on the Web, even when it is present. But different information needs result in different queries that pose different problems. For example, the problems faced by very specific queries are not the same as those faced by very general queries. Very precise queries (such as "is there a parrot indigenous to North America") face the problem of scarcity, in that there are not many pages that address this issue, and the query must be worded just right to find them.[97] Very general queries (such as "Bill Clinton") face the problem of overabundance, in that there are very many pages that contain the search terms, but many of them are probably irrelevant to the user's need.

Very precise queries typically require multiple searches, involving many different wordings, to find relevant documents. Query expansion techniques may help, but the user may ultimately have to resort to finding pages that are 'close' and then following links in the hope of tracking down the desired information. Very general queries can also be improved by adding terms, but the user may once again be forced to resort to browsing (i.e., following links) in order to find pages relevant to their interests.

Some pages are much more useful than others in facilitating browsing, namely pages that provide a well-organized set of outgoing links to other pages on a particular topic. Kleinberg calls such pages 'hubs'. Conversely, pages that have incoming links from many other pages are called 'authorities', since linking to a page is a way of conferring authority or credibility upon that page. Thus, even if your initial Web query does not turn up a highly relevant page, i.e., an authority on the topic of interest, it may nonetheless find a hub that will take you to such a page.

What can we say about this process of mixing search and browsing? To better understand the prospects and problems of this behavior, we must first gain some insights into the structure of the Web. Fortunately, there is a branch of mathematics (graph theory), which is specifically designed for describing and reasoning about linked structures.

The pattern of hyperlinks among WWW pages can be represented as a directed graph,

$$G = (V, E),$$

in which vertices, $v \in V$, represent pages and directed edges, $(v_1, v_2) \in E$, represent links. One way of looking for pages on a broad topic is to find a subgraph of the Web likely to contain authorities, and then analyze the structure of this subgraph to identify which pages are rich in incoming links. Kleinberg and his coworkers explored this idea in the context of a search engine called CLEVER.[98] Their basic approach is as follows.

Collect the highest-ranked 200 or so pages that satisfy a query using a text-based search engine, such as AltaVista. This collection of pages, called the 'root set,' is small enough to perform non-trivial computations upon and is a good source of relevant pages. Now all that is required is to identify the authorities that such pages point to. These pages may or may not be in the root set. In fact, the pages in the root set are not guaranteed to point to each other at all.

The algorithm for homing in on the authorities is formally described in Sidebar 2.6. But the basic idea is to build a 'base set' of possible authorities on top of the root set R by adding both pages that are pointed to by pages in R and pages that point to pages in R. There is one restriction: we only allow so many pages that point to a page in R to be included. Some Web pages are pointed to by thousands of pages, but we want to keep the base set small and easy to search. The algorithm typically builds a base set of 1,000–5,000 pages.

Sidebar 2.6 Authority finding algorithm

Let B be the 'base set' of authorities we seek for a given query, and let R be the 'root set' derived by taking the top-ranked pages for that query on some search engine. Let d be a constant (typically 50).

1. set B to be R.
2. *for* each page p in R,

    2.1. let $O(p)$ denote the set of all pages p points to via outgoing links,
    2.2. let $I(p)$ denote the set of all pages that point to p via incoming links,

2.3. add all pages in $O(p)$ to B,
2.4. *if* $|I(p)| \leq d$, *then* add all pages in $I(p)$ to B
    else add an arbitrary subset of d pages from $I(p)$ to B
    end if

3.   *end for*
4.   *return B*.

Clearly, the result of the base set algorithm is a (not necessarily connected) subgraph of the Web that contains many relevant pages and very likely some good authorities. It now remains to identify the hubs and authorities for the user to browse.

There are many ways in which one could go about this, but some obvious approaches do not appear to work very well. Considering nodes in the subgraph with high in-degree to be authorities can result in low precision, especially on short queries, due to the ambiguity of single words. For example, Java is an island as well as a programming language, and it is also as term associated with coffee.

What we really want is a set of pages on a consistent theme that addresses the users information need. One way of achieving this focus, without analyzing the text of the pages, is to require that there be some overlap among the sets of pages that point to potential authorities. Pages on different topics will tend to have disjoint sets of pages pointing to them, e.g., pages on culture or tourism versus pages on computers or programming in the Java example given above.

As we noted earlier, pages that cite many other pages are called 'hubs'. Good hubs point to many good authorities, while good authorities are pointed to by many hubs. This circular definition suggests an iterative means of identifying hubs and authorities.

For each page, $p \in B$, derived by the algorithm above, we compute an authority weight, p_A, and a hub weight, p_H. We can think of these page weights as being awarded increments in an iterative process. Hubs should be rewarded for pointing to pages with high A-values, while authorities should be rewarded for pointing to by pages with high H-values.

Authority weights are updated by the following operation:

$$p_A \leftarrow \sum_{q:(q,p) \in E'} q_H$$

while hub weights are updated by a similar process:

$$p_H \leftarrow \sum_{q:(p,q) \in E'} q_A$$

where E' is the set of edges in the directed subgraph structure representing hypertext links among pages.

We constrain these weights so that their squares sum to one, i.e.,

$$\sum_{p\in B} (p_A)^2 = \sum_{p\in B} (p_H)^2 = 1.$$

To find final values for these weights, we apply these operations alternately, normalizing after each pair of operations, and look for a fixed point.

The authors report that convergence is typically quite rapid (about 20 iterations), and that reporting the most highly weighted pages with respect to p_A and p_H yields authorities and hubs, respectively. They recommend collecting the 5–10 best-scoring pages of each kind.

2.6.3 Ranking and reranking documents

In Section 2.3.2, we studied ranked retrieval and walked through a simple example of how an engine might rank the documents returned by a query. However, modern search engines for the World Wide Web employ a number of variations upon the basic term frequency approach. 'Hit lists' of documents that match a given query are typically computed and manipulated in ways that extent the traditional model.

For example, Google's ranking algorithm for search results relies on the fact that their crawlers capture a fair amount of information about Web pages in addition to the usual inverted term index. Font and capitalization information are recorded along with position, and a distinction is drawn between 'plain' and 'fancy' hits.

- Fancy hits involve a match between a query term and part of a URL, page title, anchor text, or meta tag.
- Plain hits involve all other matches against the text of a document.

Google tries to address the question of how important a Web page is. Importance is estimated by analyzing the number of links between a given page and the rest of the Web. To this end, they introduce the notion of a *page rank*, who is computed as follows.

Suppose that p is a Web page. As in Section 2.6.2, let $O(p)$ denote the set of all pages that p points to through outgoing links, so that $|O(p)|$ denotes the number of such pages, and let $I(p) = \{i_1, i_2, \ldots, i_n\}$ denote the set of all pages that point to p through incoming links. The PageRank of any page p, $\pi(p)$, is then given by

$$\pi(p) = (1 - d) + d(\pi(i_1)/|O(i_1)| + \cdots + d(\pi(i_n)/|O(i_n)|)$$

where d is a damping factor between 0 and 1, usually set to 0.85 or 0.90. In other words, we calculate the importance of a page as a function of the importance of the pages that point to it. As with the page weights used by CLEVER, this can be accomplished through a straightforward iterative algorithm. PageRanks form a probability distribution over the set of all Web pages, and so the sum of all these ranks over the entire Web will be unity. The PageRanks for 26 million Web pages can apparently be computed in a few hours on a medium size workstation.[99]

So why does Google perform badly on the Martin guitar example we encountered at the start of the chapter? And why does it nonetheless perform better than Altavista? The answer is that PageRank helps to some extent with the reranking of pages that are well-ranked, but it is not going to fix a poorly ranked result set derived mostly from plain hits ranked by *tf-idf*.[100] Also, Google may have been deceived by fancy hits, such as

D93@aft.sn.no,
GUITAR@NEVADA.EDU,
D93@aol.com,

on the query terms 'd93' and 'guitar'.

On the other hand, a recent study[101] showed that link-based ranking, such as that used by Google's fancy hits, can be very effective at finding the main entry points to Web sites. A fair number of Web queries appear to be looking for specific sites, rather than documents about a particular topic, e.g.,

"Where is the CNN home page?"

For such inquiries, link-based methods have been shown to perform about twice as well as more conventional, content-based methods.

2.6.4 The state of online search

Commercial search engines were once custom-built, often proprietary, pieces of software that served specific data collections for some business or public purpose. Professional users were expected to undergo some kind of training in their use, e.g., to master the niceties of Boolean syntax, proximity operators, and field searching. The advent of the Internet made searching everyone's business, and created a demand for search engines as entry points to the vast, undisciplined document store that is the World Wide Web. Ranked retrieval 'natural language' engines filled this gap, often with Boolean features added in an 'advanced search' mode. At the time of writing, it seems that such engines have reached a plateau, both as a viable business proposition and as a useful tool for finding information on the Web.

Many of the features that have been added to search engines in the last few years, such as relevance feedback and query expansion, are based on research that is over a decade old. There do not appear to be many fundamental advances in the pipeline to provide new features for tomorrow.[102]

One exception is the work described in Section 2.6 on viewing the Web as a directed graph and capitalizing on its structure as an aid to determining the relevance and quality of pages. This appears to be a fruitful avenue that will bear further investigation. The analysis of link structure is also being used as a starting point for number of efforts to gain a better understanding of the Web and its contents, e.g.,

- Compilation of authoritative sites to populate a Yahoo!-like taxonomy of resources. This is often combined with *selective crawling*[103] of such sites, e.g., on a daily basis, to identify collections of high quality pages that are focused on particular topics.
- Identifying virtual communities on the Web with special business, scientific, or recreational interests.[104] This can be done by starting with a seed page and then using link analysis to find related pages.

Thus, as well as posing new problems for IR, the Web has also provided a freely available data set, rich in connections which suggest new approaches to ranked retrieval.

2.7 Summary of information retrieval

In its simplest terms, we can characterize information retrieval from a collection by the following 'equation':

RETRIEVAL = INDEXING + SEARCH.

Indexing is a tabulation of the contents of documents in the collection, while search consists of matching a query against these tables. Search can be thought of as follows:

SEARCH = QUERY PROCESSING + MATCHING (+ SCORING),

where scoring only takes place in the case of ranked retrieval. In the probabilistic version of ranked retrieval, the score assigned to a given document purports to be the probability that the document is relevant to the query.

Additional machinery can be added to the basic Boolean and ranked retrieval models, in the hope of improving search performance, but the addition of synonyms and other linguistic devices often do not help as much as one might suppose. The onus is still upon users to (i) formulate queries that capture their information needs, (ii) learn by trial and error how to exploit the features of the search engine, and (iii) mix search behavior with the browsing of result sets for possible links to other interesting documents.

The WWW has provided researchers with a new laboratory for conducting large-scale experiments in information retrieval. However, the Web does not obviate the need for relevance judgments in system tuning and testing. Neither has it provided us so far with any radical new means or measures for evaluating search engine performance.

Pointers

The ACM Special Interest Group on Information Retrieval[105] (SIGIR) defines its interests as lying at 'the interface between humans and unstructured or semi-structured information stored in computers.' They hold an international conference every year. This is a more academic meeting than the annual 'Search Engines' conference,[106] which tends to be dominated by vendors. The International World Wide Web Conference[107] provides as excellent mix of the two.

To explain some of the thinking behind probabilistic IR, we drew on an unpublished report,[108] which contains a fuller account than can be found in most published papers.

Various journals carry papers on information retrieval, some with a computer science bent, and some with more of a library science view of the world:

– Journal of the American Society for Information Science and Technology. New York, NY: Wiley, 1950-.
– Journal of Documentation. London: Aslib, 1955-.
– Information Processing & Management. Oxford: Elsevier, 1963-.

- Journal of Information Science. East Grinstead, England: Bowker-Saur, 1975-.
- Information Retrieval. Boston, MA: Kluwer, 1999-.

For a recent text on Web searching, we recommend Belew.[109]

Notes

1. It was estimated that the US Informational Retrieval market was worth about $30 billion in revenues at the beginning of 2000, and is likely to double about every 5 years.

2. See the Library of Congress, http://lcweb.loc.gov/rr/tools.html

3. E.g., the original DIALOG service, which was among the first commercial online information systems. The Dialog Corporation's databases have been estimated at about 9 terabytes, or 6 billion pages. This is still somewhat larger than the World Wide Web, which is currently (January 2001) estimated to be about 4 billion pages, and growing at 7 million pages a day.

4. Of course, for non-text materials, such as videos, audio recordings, etc., keyword searching is still the main location device.

5. Titles, abstracts and other summary material can also be used as document surrogates, and these can be full-text searched, with or without assistance in the form of keywords or thesauri.

6. Witten, I. H., Moffat, A., & Bell, T. C. (1999). *Managing Gigabytes*. San Francisco, CA: Morgan Kauffman.

7. In interfaces that combine browse and search capabilities, the domain of documents may already have been restricted by browsing. For example, when a user searches the auction site eBay (http://www.ebay.com) from a particular point in its classification hierarchy, the search engine knows to look only at certain categories of goods.

8. It is not always deemed necessary to index *all* the words. Some indexes omit so-called 'stop words.' These are typically what linguists would call function words, consisting mostly of a relatively small class of articles ('the', 'a', 'an', 'this', 'that' etc.), prepositions ('at', 'by', 'for', 'from', 'of', etc.), pronouns ('he', 'she', 'it', 'them', etc.), and verb particles ('am', 'is', 'be', 'was', etc.).
But many large online collections simply index every word. Otherwise you have to make awkward decisions, e.g., is this occurrence of 'will' a verb particle, or does it refer to a legal document? Similarly, short function words may coincide with acronyms, e.g., 'it' for 'information technology'. Many indexes do not store information about upper and lower case, and are therefore not able to distinguish acronyms from other words.

9. 'Token' is a more neutral term than 'word', since the indexed item may not be a word. It could be a stemmed word, like 'anticipat', or a number like '256', or even a symbol, such as '$'.

10. 'Offsets' are simply distances into the document, e.g., at offset of 95 might indicate that the word starts 95 characters into the document. Characters typically include whitespace, punctuation, and so forth.

11. Web search engines typically do not use word positions for highlighting purposes. Highlighting query terms in the snippets is performed using regular expressions.

12. For example, Boolean searching is still more popular than natural language searching on Westlaw (http://www.westlaw.com), while Gale Group (http://www.galegroup.com) still provides Boolean searching for periodicals on CD-ROM, which are sold into libraries.

13. Two words are synonyms if they have the same meaning. Not many terms are truly identical in meaning, but many pairs are sufficiently close to be treated as such for practical purposes, e.g., 'astronaut' and 'cosmonaut', 'student' and 'pupil', 'test' and 'exam', etc. Regional variations, such as British versus American English, are also sources of lexical variation, e.g., 'car' versus 'automobile.'

14. See e.g., Sparck Jones, K., & Willet, P. (Eds.). (1997). Readings in Information Retrieval. San Francisco, CA: Morgan Kaufmann, p. 258, for a brief summary.

15. Swanson, D. R. (1977). Information retrieval as a trial and error process. *Library Quarterly, 47* (2), 128–148.

16. Dealey Plaza is the part of Dallas in which the shooting occurred, and Zapruder was the bystander who shot the film of the motorcade that was later analyzed by the FBI.

17. Thanks to stop word removal, some search engines (e.g., Altavista) used to return no documents on a query such as 'to be or not to be.'

18. See Chapter 1, Section 1.3.2 for a discussion of stemming.

19. Consider tuples of the general form, $v = (x_1, \ldots, x_n)$, with quantities x_i lying in a field F. Each such n-tuple is called a *vector* with n components or coordinates. The totality of all such vectors, $V_n(F)$, is called the *n-dimensional vector space* over F. In IR, F is the field of term frequencies, or some function thereof.

20. There are a number of variations on this theme, such as projecting the vectors onto a sphere surrounding the origin, with each document being a point on this envelope.

21. It is possible to define distance over sets, using symmetric set differences, but this is a rather weak metric.

22. The cosine measure is the simple sum of products of the corresponding terms weights normalized by the length of each vector. However, the cosine is not the only similarity measure available, simply the most common. See van Rijsbergen, K. (1979). Information Retrieval, Butterworths. London (also at http://www.dcs.gla.ac.uk/Keith/Preface.html) for alternatives.

23. In this formula, sums range over all unique terms in the collection. In practice, however, when a simple tf-idf weight is used, sums only range over the terms appearing in query q and document vector d.

24. You now know enough to solve 'The case of the missing guitar.' Give it some thought, but don't fret. We'll string you along a little longer, but if you don't pick up on it, we'll divulge the solution shortly.

25. If we restrict ourselves to encoding presence or absence of terms with binary vectors, the computation still serves to define a degree of overlap in the range $[0, t]$ where t is the number of dimensions. But this may result in too many ties for ranking purposes.

26. Starred sections may be skipped on a first reading, as they represent more advanced material.

27. See Robertson, S. E., & Sparck Jones, K. (1976). Relevance weighting of search terms. *Journal of the American Society for Information Science, 27*, 129–146. The basic approach was first presented in Maron, M. E., & Kuhns, J. L. (1960). On relevance, probabilistic indexing and information retrieval. *Journal of the Association for Computing Machinery, 7*, 216–244.

28. http://www.muscat.com.

29. http://www.autonomy.com.

30. http://ciir.cs.umass.edu.

31. See Okapi (1997). Papers on Okapi. Special Issue of the *Journal of Documentation, 33*, 3–87.

32. Robertson, S. E., Maron, M. E., & Cooper, W. S. (1982). Probability of relevance: A unification of two competing models for document retrieval. *Information Technology: Research and Development, 1*, 1–21.

33. Robertson, S. E. (1977). The probability ranking principle in IR. *Journal of Documentation, 33*, 126–148.

34. Croft and Harper demonstrated how probabilistic retrieval without relevance information yields probability estimates that are very similar to the term weights, such as *idf*, used in ranked retrieval. See Croft, W., & Harper, D. (1979). Using propabilistic models without relevance information. *Journal of Documentation, 35*, 285–295. Also reprinted in K. Sparck Jones, & P. Willett (Eds.), *Readings in Information Retrieval*.

35. We will use capitals to distinguish '*TF*' and '*IDF*', as used in probabilistic retrieval, from the vector space notions '*tf*' and '*idf*' introduced earlier.

36. Normalizing document length may not be worthwhile, if documents are close to a standard length. Where documents differ greatly in length, one can expect some improvement in the final ranking as a result of the normalization. It turns out that any reasonable method of computing length, e.g., counting words or characters, gives sensible results. See Robertson, S. E., & Walker, S. (1994). Some simple effective approximations to the 2-Poisson Model. In *Proceedings of the 17th Annual International ACM-SIGIR Conference on Research and Development in Information Retrieval* (pp. 232–241).

37. Although logistic regression can help optimize them.

38. See Turtle, H. R. (1991). Inference Networks for Document Retrieval. Ph.D thesis, University of Massachusetts, Department of Computer and Information Science, p. 125 *et seq.*

39. WIN employs a number of patented optimizations that enable it to search large data collections in a reasonable time.

40. Summing is performed instead of multiplication, since we are dealing with logarithms of probabilities. Application of the multiplication rule is only permitted because of the independence assumptions we noted earlier.

41. See Turtle, H., & Croft, W. B. (1990). Inference networks for document retrieval. In *Proceedings of the 13th International Conference on Research and Development in Information Retrieval* (pp. 1–24).

42. Pearl, J. (1988). *Probabilistic Reasoning in Intelligent Systems: Networks of Plausible Inference*. San Mateo, CA: Morgan Kaufmann.

43. There is a more complex formulation called the '2-Poisson Model', which models term frequencies in documents as a mixture of two Poisson distributions. See Robertson, S., & Walker, S. (1994). Some simple effective approximations to the 2-Poisson Model. In *Proceedings of the 17th Annual International ACM-SIGIR Conference on Research and Development in Information Retrieval* (pp. 232–241).

44. Crestani, F., Lalmas, M., Van Rijsbergen, C. C., & Campbell, I. (1998). "Is this document relevant? … Probably": A survey of probabilistic models in information retrieval. *ACM Computing Surveys, 30* (4).

45. See Cooper, W. S. (1995). Some inconsistencies and misidentified modeling assumptions in probabilistic information retrieval. *ACM Transactions on Information Systems, 13* (1), 100–111.

46. Ponte, J. M. (1998). A Language Modeling Approach to Information Retrieval. Ph.D. Thesis, Department of Computer Science, University of Massachusetts, Amherst.

47. For the details of how this is done, we refer the interested reader to Ponte, J. M., & Croft, W. B. (1998). A Language Modeling Approach to Information Retrieval. In *Proceedings of SIGIR-98* (pp. 275–281).

48. Berger, A., & Lafferty, J. (1999). Information retrieval as statistical translation. In *Proceedings of SIGIR-99* (pp. 222–229).

49. Lavrenko, V., & Croft, W. B. (2001). Relevance-based language models. In *Proceedings of SIGIR-2001* (pp. 120–127). ACM Press.

50. Such studies have been called 'analytic.' See Deming, W. E. (1975). On probability as a basis for action. *The American Statistician, 29*, 146–152. By contrast, sampling an existing, well-defined population is called an 'enumerative' study.

51. TREC is co-sponsored by the National Institute of Standards and Technology (NIST) and the Defense Advanced Research Projects Agency (DARPA).

52. Adapted from http://trec.nist.gov.

53. See Cleverdon, C. W. (1967). The Cranfield tests on index language devices. *ASLIB Proceedings, 19*, 173–192. Also in Sparck Jones & Willet, Eds.

54. See Salton, G., & Lesk, M. E. (1968). Computer evaluation of indexing and text processing. *JACM, 15*, 8–36. Also in Sparck Jones & Willet, Eds.

55. Van Rijsbergen, K. (1979). Information Retrieval (2nd edition, Chapter 7). An electronic version of this book can be found on line at http://www.dcs.gla.ac.uk/Keith/Preface.html.

56. For each TREC, NIST provides a test set of documents and questions. Participants run their own retrieval systems on the data, and return to NIST a list of the top-ranked retrieved documents. NIST pools the individual results, judges the retrieved documents for correctness, and evaluates the results. The cycle then ends with a workshop that is a forum for participants to share their experiences.

57. Typical test collections include: the Los Angeles Times (1989, 1990), the Congressional Record of the 103rd Congress (1993), and U.S. Patents (1983–1991).

58. See http://trec.nist.gov/data/reljudge_eng.html

59. As described in Harman, D. K. (1995). The TREC conferences. In Kuhlen & Rittberger (Eds.) (see the 'Pointers' section at the end of this chapter).

60. Blair, D. C., & Maron, M. E. (1985). An evaluation of retrieval effectiveness for a full-text document retrieval system. *CACM, 20*, 1238–1242. See also Blair, D. C. (1996). STAIRS Redux: Thoughts on the STAIRS evaluation, ten years after. *JASIS, 47* (1), 4–22.

61. See e.g., Lidsky, D., & Sirapyan, N. (1998). Find it on the Web. *PC Magazine,* December 1st issue.

62. For example, speed can be improved dramatically by having enough RAM to hold indexes, while precision can be improved by various reranking techniques (see Section 2.6.3 below).

63. See e.g., Bruce, H. (1998). User satisfaction with information seeking on the Internet. *JASIS, 49* (6), 541–556. This study showed that the satisfaction of a sample of Australian academics with Internet searches was predicted by their expectations, but was not enhanced by Internet training.

64. Muramatsu, J., & Pratt, W. (2001). Transparent queries: Investigating users' mental models of search engines. In *Proceedings of SIGIR-2001* (pp. 217–224). ACM Press.

65. eBay (http://www.ebay.com) is a good example of this.

66. A word *v* is a hyponym of another word *w* if *v* is a more general or more abstract term than *w*. Thus the term 'vehicle' is more general than the term 'car', and may be said to *subsume* it. Looked at another way, the concept of CARHOOD contains the concept of VEHICLEHOOD, since a car is a vehicle, but not vice versa.

67. Polysemy occurs when a word has two or more meanings, e.g., 'bank' as a financial institution versus 'bank' as the margin of a river. Such words are said to be *polysemous*.

68. Miller, G. A. (1990). Wordnet: An on-line lexical database. Special Issue of the *International Journal of Lexicography, 3* (4).

69. Voorhees, E. M. (1994). Query expansion using lexical-semantic relations. In *Proceedings of SIGIR-94* (pp. 61–69).

70. Although they both move pretty fast.

71. Qui, Y., & Frei, H.-P. (1993). Concept based query expansion. In *Proceedings of SIGIR-93* (pp. 160–169). Measuring average precision over three recall points (0.25, 0.50, and 0.75), the authors found improvements of between 18 and 30% on three document collections (MED, CACM, and NPL). The largest collection contained about 11,500 documents.

72. Peat, H. J., & Willett, P. (1991). The limitations of term co-occurrence data for query expansion in document retrieval systems. *JASIS, 42* (5), 378–383.

73. Head-modifier is essentially the relation between a **noun** as subject and its associated *modifiers*, some of which may be adjectival uses of other parts of speech, e.g., '*ground attack* **plane**', '*aircraft communication* **device**', etc.

74. Grefenstette, G. (1992). Use of syntactic context to produce term association lists for text retrieval. In *Proceedings of SIGIR-92* (pp. 89–97).

75. Woods, W. A., Bookman, L. A., Houston, A., Kuhn, R. J., Martin, P., & Green, G. (2000). Linguistic knowledge can improve information retrieval. *6th ANLP*, 262–267.

76. Success rate was defined in terms of the system's ability to return a relevant document among the top ten hits.

77. Rocchio, J. J. Jr. (1971). Relevance feedback in information retrieval. In *The SMART system – Experiments in Automatic Document Processing* (pp. 313–323). Englewood Cliffs, NJ: Prentice Hall.

78. Robertson, S., & Spark-Jones, K. (1976). Relevance weighting for search terms. *Journal of the American Society for Information Science, 27*, 129–146.

79. Rocchio, J. J. Jr. (1966). Document retrieval systems – Optimization and evaluation. Doctoral Dissertation, Harvard University, Cambridge, MA.

80. E.g., the SMART system at TREC8 set all three parameters to the same value, i.e. the original query, a relevant document, and a non-relevant document contribute the same amount of information to select terms and update their weights. This assumes that the number of relevant and non-relevant documents are comparable.

81. The quotes are taken from page 30 of Sparck-Jones, K., Walker, S., & Robertson, S. E. (1998). A probabilistic model of information retrieval: Development and status. University of Cambridge Computer Laboratory Technical Report no. 446.

82. Robertson, S. E. (1990). On term selection for query expansion. *Journal of Documentation, 46*, 359–365.

83. Haines, D., & Croft, W. B. (1993). Relevance feedback and inference networks. In *Proceedings of SIGIR-93* (pp. 2–11). Pittsburgh, PA: ACM Press. See also Allan, J. (1996). Incremental relevance feedback for information filtering. In *Proceedings of SIGIR-96* (pp. 270–278). Zürich, Switzerland: ACM Press.

84. See Lam-Adesina, A., & Jones, G. (2001). Applying Summarization Techniques for Term Selection in Relevance Feedback. In *Proceedings of SIGIR 2001* (pp. 1–9), and also Sakai, T., & Sparck Jones, K. (2001). Generic Summaries for Indexing in Information Retrieval. In *Proceedings of SIGIR 2001* (pp. 190–198).

85. See Xu, J., & Croft, W. B. (2000). Improving the Effectiveness of Information Retrieval with Local Context Analysis. *ACM Transactions on Information Systems, 18* (1), 79–112.

86. See e.g., Seltzer, R., Ray, E., & Ray, D. (1997). *The Altavista Search Revolution: How to Find Anything on the Internet.* New York: McGraw-Hill.

87. Some search engine vendors have often retorted that the traditional recall and precision measures are less than fair, given the enormity and heterogeneous nature of the Web. Web

engines often seem to be tuned to find highly relevant documents and rank them highly, rather than going for overall recall and precision by finding all relevant documents. A recent study seems to bear out the intuition that different techniques are required for these two tasks (see Sidebar 2.5).

88. Lawrence, S., & Giles, C. L. (1999). Searching the Web: General and Scientific Information Access. *IEEE Communications, 37* (1), 116–122.

89. As we shall see, Google uses link data to index, and can therefore return listings for pages that its crawler has not visited, bringing its coverage up to an estimated 2 billion pages.

90. See Danny Sullivan's *Search Engine Report* of December 18, 2001, on-line at http://www.searchenginewatch.com.

91. A URL is a *Uniform Resource Locator,* an address specifies the location of a resource residing on the Internet. A complete URL consists of a scheme (such as ftp, http, etc.), followed by a server name, and the full path of a resource (such as a document, graphic, or other file).

92. http://www.archive.org.

93. TREC calls a natural language statement of an information need a 'topic' to distinguish it from a 'query', which is the data structure actually presented to the retrieval system. (This definition is taken verbatim from http://trec.nist.gov/data/testq_eng.html).

94. Voorhees, E. M. (2001). Evaluation by highly relevant documents. In *Proceedings of SIGIR-2001* (pp. 74–82). New Orleans, LA: ACM Press.

95. Such instability is mostly due to the small number of highly relevant documents, which allows small changes in document ranking to cause large differences in a system's evaluation score.

96. Kleinberg, J. (1998). Authoritative Sources in a Hyperlinked Environment. *Proceedings of the ACM-SIAM Symposium on Discrete Algorithms* (pp. 668–677).

97. There is no such parrot. There was one, but it was hunted to extinction. 'Negative' queries such as this can be especially problematical.

98. Chakrabati, S., Dom, B., Kumar, S. R., Raghavan, P., Rajagopalan, S., Tomkins, A., Gibson, D., & Kleinberg, J. (1999). Mining the Web's Link Structure. *Computer, 32* (8), 60–67.

99. Brin, S., & Page, L. (1998). The Anatomy of a Large-Scale Hypertextual Web Search Engine. *Computer Networks (Proceedings of WWW7), 30,* 107–117.

100. Both search engines perform poorly on the Martin guitar example thanks to their reliance on inverse document frequency (IDF). Given the query 'martin d93 guitar', the high weight derived from the IDF of the rare term 'd93' swamps the effect of the other two, much more common, terms. Thus we tend to get high-scoring documents that contain 'd93', regardless of whether or not they are about guitars, or have any association with the name Martin. If you omit the term 'd93' from the query, both search engines place C. F. Martin's home page at the top of the result set.

101. Craswell, N., Hawking, D., & Robertson, S. (2001). Effective site finding using link anchor information. In *Proceedings of SIGIR-2001* (pp. 250–257). ACM Press.

102. Although the increasing combination of document retrieval with information extraction and text categorization techniques represents an interesting new departure, see e.g., tools by ClearForest (http://www.clearforest.com/) and Vivissimo (http://www.vivissimo.com/). Question answering is another refinement of the document retrieval paradigm, see e.g., offerings by AskJeeves (http://www.askjeeves.com) and Primus (http://www.primus.com).

103. See Chakrabarti, S., M. Van den Berg, & B. Dom (1999). Focused crawling: A new approach to topic specific resource discovery. *Computer Networks (Proceedings of WWW8)*, *31*, 1623–1640.

104. See e.g., Gibson, D., J. Kleinberg, & P. Raghavan (1998). Inferring Web Communities from Link Topologies. Proceedings of *the Ninth ACM Conference on Hypertext and Hypermedia*. Also S. R. Kumar, P. Raghavan, S. Rajagopalan, & A. Tomkins (1999). Trawling the Web for emerging cyber-communities. *Eighth World Wide Web Conference*. Toronto, Canada.

105. http://www.acm.org/sigir

106. http://www.infonortics.com/searchengines/index.html

107. http://www.iw3c2.org

108. Sparck Jones, K., Walker, S., & Robertson, S. E. (1998). A probabilistic model of information retrieval: Development and status. TR-446, Cambridge University Computer Laboratory, September 1998.

109. Belew, R. K. (2000). *Finding out about: Search engine technology from a cognitive perspective*. Cambridge, England: Cambridge University Press.

CHAPTER 3

Information extraction

The plethora of material on the WWW is one of the factors that has sustained interest in automatic methods for extracting information from text. Information extraction differs from information retrieval, in that the focus is not upon finding documents but upon finding useful information inside documents. Typically, texts in an electronic document feed are examined to see if they contain certain target terms, and therefore merit further analysis.

Intelligence agencies have been using computers to screen electronic news feeds and communications traffic since the 1970s. In the past, programs would look for key terms, such as 'terrorist' and 'bomb,' and analysts would read the documents found. But modern extraction programs go further in attempting to identify, extract and present interesting content to speed the process.

Unlike more ambitious forms of NLP, information extraction programs analyze only a small subset of any given text, e.g., those parts that contain certain 'trigger' words, and then attempt to fill out a fairly simple form that represents the objects or events of interest. Thus, if our focus were corporate takeovers, we might be interested in who acquired whom, and for what price. Similarly, if we cared about personnel changes among senior executives in large corporations, we might want to know who vacated what position and who was hired to replace them.

Thus information extraction can be regarded as a subfield of NLP that focuses upon finding rather specific facts in relatively unstructured documents. No practitioner of this art would claim that his or her program 'understands' the text, or is artificially intelligent in the traditional sense. For the most part, such a program is simply recognizing linguistic patterns and collating them. It has been argued that shallow parsing followed by template filling is adequate for most of these tasks, and that nothing approaching natural language understanding is really needed. We present and examine this view, evaluating it in the light of recent applications.

This chapter summarizes relevant research and applications since 1990, and explains the basic techniques. For expository and evaluation purposes, we focus upon two problems: identifying incidents in news articles and finding the mandate[1] in an appellate court opinion. We chose these tasks because they have been studied in some depth and the results have been reported in the literature.

There are many other potential applications for such technology, e.g., generating meta data for Internet publishing, clustering search results with respect to key concepts occurring in found documents, and summarizing multiple documents with respect to a single theme. At the time of writing, these tasks have not been studied in depth, but preliminary research indicates that they pose interesting problems for future research. We defer discussion of such applications and their associated techniques until Chapter 5, where we discuss the topic of 'text mining.'

3.1 The Message Understanding Conferences

In the 1990s, the Defense Advanced Research Projects Agency (DARPA) initiated a series of seven annual workshops called the Message Understanding Conferences (MUCs, for short). The idea behind these meetings was to assemble teams of researchers that would focus upon the problem extracting information from free (i.e., unstructured) text. To participate, the team had to design and implement a system that would perform the chosen task and be capable of having its performance evaluated with respect to its competitors.

This initiative was extremely fruitful for a number of reasons.

- The emphasis on having a practical running system avoided the normal tendency of researchers to focus their eyes on the far horizon.
- The provision of a uniform set of training and testing materials encouraged rigorous evaluation using an agreed set of metrics (which we shall discuss below).
- The introduction of a competitive element involving direct feedback made the exercise more interesting than the normal technical conference.

Participants included both industrial sites (such as General Electric and Bolt Beranek & Newman), and universities (such as Edinburgh and Kyoto Universities and the University of Massachusetts). See Sidebar 3.1 for a brief overview of the main tasks addressed at these conferences.

Sidebar 3.1 A brief history of the Message Understanding Conferences

The first two conferences were held in 1987 and 1989, and analyzed naval operations messages.[2] MUC-3 (1991) and MUC-4 (1992) concentrated on event extraction, in particular finding details of terrorist attacks in newswires. MUC-5 (1993) introduced more business-oriented tasks, such as finding announcements of joint ventures.

In 1995, MUC-6 introduced Named Entity extraction as a component task, i.e., the finding of proper names of people, companies, places, etc. in free text, but also continued event extraction of management changes in the news. In 1996, the Multilingual Entity Task was initiated in a related conference (MET-1) to evaluate information extraction on non-English language texts. The first round focused on general extraction from Spanish, Chinese, and Japanese, while the following year MET-2 addressed Named Entity extraction from Chinese and Japanese.

In 1998, MUC-7 showed that Named Entity extraction from English language newswire articles was more or less a solved problem. The best MUC-7 programs scored about $F = 93\%$, compared to an estimated human performance of about $F = 97\%$. The F-measure is a combination[3] of precision and recall as defined in Chapter 2, Section 4.

The TIPSTER program of which MUC was a part was wound up after MUC-7.

For illustrative purposes, we focus on the MUC-3 event extraction task, in which a program had to extract information on terrorist incidents from plain text news articles.[4] A corpus of such materials was taken from an electronic database via a keyword query, with 1300 texts being specified as training data and a further 100 texts being held out for a blind test using a semi-automated scoring procedure. The details of the task and corpus construction are described elsewhere;[5] we shall only summarize them here along with the scoring mechanisms and performance measures used.

A typical text from this corpus begins as follows:

> Last night's terrorist target was the Antioquia Liqueur Plant. Four powerful rockets were going to explode very close to the tanks where 300,000 gallons of the so-called Castille crude, used to operate the boilers, is stored.[6]

The task facing each program was to extract and record specific features of the incident. Typical features included such things as date, location, target, instrument (e.g., bomb, rocket), and overall type (e.g., murder, arson). Blank 'answer' templates were provided to hold this information. Programs were expected to 'merge' filled templates providing full or partial descriptions of the same event. In other words, they were supposed to delivery a single template for each event, not multiple templates representing different descriptions found in the text.

A simplified template is shown in Table 3.1. About half the fields are omitted for brevity. An empty filler for a field means that the story did not specify the requisite information.

Table 3.1 MUC answer template for the 'terrorism' task (simplified)

Field	Filler
MESSAGE ID	TST-MUC3-0001
DATE OF INCIDENT	04 FEB 90
TYPE OF INCIDENT	ARSON
PERPETRATOR	"GUERRILAS"
PHYSICAL TARGET	"TANK TRUCK"
HUMAN TARGET	
INSTRUMENT	
LOCATION OF INCIDENT	GUATEMALA: PETEN: FLORES

Leaving the intricacies of scoring such templates to one side (based on partial credits for partial matches), we focus here upon results using the familiar metrics of precision and recall (see Chapter 2, Section 4).

The best MUC-3 systems reported results in the ballpark of 50% recall and 60% precision for event extraction. Roughly speaking, the programs could find about half of what they were looking for, with a false positive rate of less than 50%. By MUC-6, the best systems were scoring as high as 75% recall and 75% precision, where performance seems to have reached a plateau.

These are encouraging results for many applications. If you are an intelligence worker sifting the news for stories about terrorism, you might be quite satisfied to turn up 75% of all news reports on this topic, and have the key information extracted from them by automatic means, even if you had to discard 25% of the proposals as irrelevant or erroneous. On the other hand, if you were a lawyer looking for rulings that were on point to your current case, such a success rate might be less satisfactory.

We now move on to a description of the main NLP techniques used at the MUC conferences and beyond. These include pattern matching, finite state automata, context-free parsing, and statistical modeling. We treat them in the order listed above, since this will take us from the simplest to the most complex.

3.2 Regular expressions

Regular expressions (regexs) provide a means for specifying or defining regular languages. Many software engineers are familiar with these expressions from pattern-matching utilities such as UNIX 'grep', programming languages such as Perl, and lexical analysis tools for programming language compilers, such as 'lex'.[7] However, regexs are a general-purpose formalism for describing and matching patterns; this formalism is not specific to any particular programming language or tool.

In its simplest terms, a regex represents a *regular set* of strings in terms of three simple operations: adjacency, repetition, and alternation. A regex therefore provides a finite characterization of an infinite set.

A regex like

a(b|c)*a

represents the infinite language (set of strings)

L = {**aa, aba, aca, abba, abca, acba, acca,** . . .}

since (**b|c**) signifies 'choose **b** or **c**', '*' (the Kleene star) means 'zero or more times,' and adjacency of two symbols has its usual meaning.

As an example of a nonregular language, try representing the infinite set

{**ab, aabb, aaabbb, aaaabbbb,** . . .}

using only the three allowable operations.[8] (See Sidebar 3.2 for a more formal specification of these operations and a formal definition of regular expressions.)

Sidebar 3.2 Regular languages

Regular expressions can be defined formally as sequences over any finite alphabet $A = \{a_1, a_2, \ldots, a_n\}$ as follows.

1. If $a_i \in A$, for $1 \le i \le n$, then a_i is a regex.
2. If R and S are regexs, then so is (RS), where (RS) represents any sequence from the regular set R concatenated with any sequence from the regular set S.
3. If $R, S, \ldots, T$ are regexs, then so is $(R|S|\ldots|T)$, where $(R|S|\ldots|T)$ represents the union of the regular sets $R, S, \ldots, T$.
4. If R is a regex, then so is R^*, where R^* represents any stringing together of sequences represented by R.
5. Only expressions formed from applications of rules 1–4 are regexs.

For convenience, the empty string is defined as a regex, and denoted by Λ.

Thus a regular expression specifying a class of proper names might look like:

{Mr.|Mrs.|Ms.|Dr.} {A|B|C| . . . | Z}. **LASTNAME**

where **LASTNAME** stands for any selection from a list of last names, such as all last names occurring in an online Yellow Pages, or some other directory that a program can draw upon. All the other elements of the regular expression are *literals*, i.e., 'Mr.' and 'A' and '.' stand for themselves.

Figure 3.1 Typical cascade of modules in an information extraction system

A common approach to parsing free text using regular expressions is to separate different levels of linguistic processing into modules that are then pipelined together, as in Figure 3.1.

Earlier stages of processing recognize more local linguistic entities, such as words and sentence boundaries, and work in a more or less domain-independent fashion.

For example, a tokenizer[9] for breaking a sentence into words and punctuation can use purely linguistic knowledge to recognize word boundaries, requiring little or no modification as the system is moved to a new domain.[10] Part of speech tagging is a little more domain-dependent, being sensitive to different corpuses, particularly with respect to proper names. Later stages recognize more domain-specific patterns, necessitating knowledge of objects and events that will differ between applications. Thus the patterns to be recognized will differ across domains, as will the templates that need to be filled. Similarly, the knowledge required to merge filled templates successfully will be very domain-dependent.

Many Regex matchers have been written in the Perl programming language.[11] Perl stands for 'Practical Extraction and Report Language', which is a pretty good summary of what programs in the language are meant to achieve. Perl's economical syntax and powerful text-handling functions make it useful tool for shallow text analysis.

For example, it is relatively easy to write a stemmer in Perl, or a program that will guess a word's syntactic class based on morphological features, such as affixes and suffixes. Any non-capitalized English word ending in '-ful' can be recognized as an adjective, while one can stem a word like 'powerful' to 'power' in a single line of code. For example, the Perl match operator '=~' can be used to compare a string variable with a pattern of the form /.../ and return true or false, depending upon whether the match succeeds. Thus

$word =~/ful$/

looks to see if the value of the string variable '$word' ends in 'ful'. ('$' indicates 'end of word.') However, even short Perl patterns to perform simple tasks can look quite daunting, and be difficult to maintain. For example,

$$/\backslash([\hat{}(\backslash)]*(19|20)\backslash d\backslash d\backslash)/$$

matches citations such as

(Jackson & Moulinier 2002)

by finding a left parenthesis, followed by any number of chars that don't contain a left or a right parenthesis, followed by a year (within the last hundred years) and a closing right parenthesis.

In the next section, we look at a particular implementation of regular expression matching in a system that participated in MUC throughout the life of the conferences.

3.3 Finite automata in FASTUS

The FASTUS system[12] was in some ways a typical MUC entry. 'FASTUS' is a failed acronym[13] for 'Finite State Automata-Based Text Understanding System', and is so called because its basic parsing mechanism is a cascade of *finite automata*, sometimes called *finite state machines* (FSMs). It scored well in the MUC-4 tests on news about Latin American terrorism, with 44% recall and 55% precision on a blind test of 100 texts. On the MUC-6 template filling task, it scored 74% recall and 76% precision. It also performed well on the named entity recognition[14] task, with 92% recall and 96% precision.

3.3.1 Finite State Machines and regular languages

FSMs are idealized machines that move instantaneously from one internal state to another in a series of discrete 'steps'. Thus, they are nothing like real physical machines, which may move continuously with respect to time, be subject to friction, and so on. We assume that an FSM's current state can be completely described, and that it changes only as a function of its history of previous states and inputs from its environment. These inputs are characterized as symbols, fed to the machine on a tape. Such machines are called 'finite' because they have a finite number of internal states with which to remember their histories.

FSMs can be seen as both generators and recognizers of certain kinds of formal language.[15] But they cannot process all formal languages, as we shall see. It turns out that they can only recognize or generate *regular languages*, i.e., languages containing regular expressions of the kind we described in the last section. Regular languages are languages in which a symbol's position in

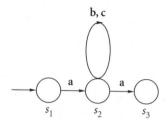

Figure 3.2 A Finite State Machine diagram for a(b|c)*a

a string can depend only upon a bounded number of previous positions. This linguistic restriction corresponds to the restriction concerning the finiteness of FSMs, noted earlier.

To illustrate this, let us return to our regex,

a(b|c)*a.

An FSM for recognizing a finite string as a member of this set would have the states and transitions as represented in Figure 3.2. The nodes of the graph represent states of the machine. s_1 is the *start state* and s_3 is the *end state*.

The arcs or arrows connecting states represent transitions. Note that symbols annotate transitions, not states. States are an FSM's (limited) memory of where it is in the computation. For example, the machine in Figure 3.2 does not keep track of how many times it has been round the loop emanating from state s_2. Consequently, it can only distinguish between a finite number of its infinitely many possible histories.

As we noted earlier, FSMs can be used to both recognize and generate strings.

– In *recognition mode*, the machine, in its start state, begins scanning the string provided, one character at a time (from a tape, say, using a read head). A single character of the string is consumed when the machine makes the corresponding transition to the next state. In our example of Figure 3.2, the machine consumes *a* when it moves to s_2. Reading the next character takes the machine to the next state, and so on, until the whole string is consumed. If this process of reading a character and finding a corresponding transition fails at any point, the machine halts, and the string is unrecognized. Similarly, if the string ends before the machine reaches an end state. Otherwise, the string is deemed to be recognized when the last character is consumed with a transition to an end state.

– In *generation mode*, the machine simply takes a random or guided walk through its states, following transitions until it chooses to halt in its end state. At each transition, it can select (randomly or in a guided manner) a symbol from the one or more annotating that arc. If we provide the FSM with a second tape (and a write head), we can make it emit each such symbol as it encounters it, in order of visitation.

An FSM with this kind of write capability is called a *finite state transducer* (FST). Note that the FST can't read the tape it is writing to, or move back and forth along the tape it is reading. Its input and output modes are strictly segregated and sequential, in that sense.

Sidebar 3.3 Finite State Machine tables

As well as drawing a machine diagram, we can represent an FSM by a table (see Table 3.2). Rows represent states of the machine and columns represent symbols. Thus s_3 in Row a, column s_2 means 'Move to s_3 if you read an a in state s_2.'

Table 3.2 A Finite State Machine table for a(b|c)*a

	a	b	c
s_1	s_2		
s_2	s_3	s_2	s_2
s_3			

3.3.2 Finite State Machines as parsers

The mathematical logician Kleene[16] showed that FSMs can recognize all and only regular sets of symbol sequences defined over a finite alphabet. As we noted in the previous section, 'recognition' means that the machine can read successive symbols in a sequence and tell you whether or not that sequence is 'regular.' It is therefore possible to specify an FSM that will function as a parser for a given regular language, by analyzing strings of words or symbols to see if they conform to the rules of the language.

The linguist Chomsky[17] showed that natural languages are not regular languages, since they contain embedded and crossed structures[18] that cannot be recognized by FSMs. More recently, Church[19] argued that FSMs might be nonetheless useful in modeling language, since the well-documented short-term memory limitations of humans make the full generality of more complex parsing schemes implausible as psychological models of language processing.

FSMs have been found to be a useful tool for extraction purposes in many applications where complex grammatical structures can sometimes be ignored. For example, if you are interested only in finding company names in news text, you might ignore the complexities of subordinate clauses and prepositional phrases and still meet with some success. Even event extraction can be accomplished from news in this fashion, if you are prepared to tolerate recall and precision in or around the 70% range, as the FASTUS experience shows.

The FASTUS approach to parsing follows the general sequence of operations shown earlier in Figure 3.1. This arrangement is sometimes called a 'cascade', so the FASTUS architecture is often described as one of 'cascaded finite automata.'

In the *Regular Expression Matching* phase, FSMs target specific noun and verb groups, and then match them up heuristically.[20] The *Template Filling* phase takes the patterns found in the previous two steps and puts them into some canonical form, storing them in a data structure. Thus the different sentences,

> 'Terrorists attacked the mayor's home in Bogota.'
> 'The mayor's Bogota home was attacked by terrorists.'
> 'The home of the mayor of Bogota suffered a terrorist attack.'

should, in theory, all result in the same information being extracted, and the same structure being generated, along the lines of Table 3.3.

Finally, similar structures deemed to represent the same event need to be merged, to avoid redundancy in the extracted data. Thus, given sentences like

> 'The mayor's home was attacked by terrorists.'
> 'Terrorists attacked the mayor's home in Bogota.'
> 'The home of the mayor of Bogota suffered a grenade attack.'

Table 3.3 FASTUS extraction template for the terrorist domain

Field	Filler
MESSAGE ID	TST-MUC3-0002
DATE OF INCIDENT	04 FEB 90
TYPE OF INCIDENT	ATTACK
PERPETRATOR	TERRORISTS
PHYSICAL TARGET	HOME
HUMAN TARGET	MAYOR
INSTRUMENT	
LOCATION OF INCIDENT	BOGOTA

Table 3.4 Merged extraction template for the terrorist domain

Field	Filler
MESSAGE ID	TST-MUC3-0003
DATE OF INCIDENT	04 FEB 90
TYPE OF INCIDENT	ATTACK
PERPETRATOR	TERRORISTS
PHYSICAL TARGET	HOME
HUMAN TARGET	MAYOR
INSTRUMENT	GRENADE
LOCATION OF INCIDENT	BOGOTA

the final *Template Merging* stage should merge the corresponding consistent but non-identical data structures to generate the structure in Table 3.4.

To promote generality in the specification of rules, a lexicon is required, so that patterns for breaking up sentences can be defined over parts of speech and other grammatical classes, instead of just over individual words.

For example, a noun group, **NG**, might be defined along the lines of:

> **NG = DET MOD NOUN**
> **DET** = the
> **MOD** = local
> **NOUN** = mayor

where bold uppercase items stand for categories of words or phrases, and lower case items denote actual words, kept in a dictionary or *lexicon*. Thus **DET** stands for the word class of determiners, such as 'the', 'a', and 'an', **MOD** stands for modifiers, mostly adjectives and adjectival uses of nouns, e.g., the use of 'house' in 'house call', and **NOUN** is the class of nouns.

Then a sentence such as

> 'The local mayor, who was kidnapped yesterday, was found dead today.'

could be matched against a regular expression containing pattern variables,[21] such as

> **NG RELPRO VG***

in FASTUS, where **NG** (Noun Group) and **VG** (Verb Group) match against phrases with the right constituents, and the pattern element **RELPRO** only matches against relative pronouns, such as 'who' and 'which'.

However, FASTUS also uses more specific patterns for extracting the details of an event. Thus the pattern

> PERP attacked HUMANTARGET's PHYSICALTARGET in LOCATION on DATE with DEVICE

mixes pattern variables (shown in bold caps) with actual words (shown in plain text). **PERP** is less general than **NOUN**, since it will only match a restricted class of nouns identified in the lexicon as possible matches. Similarly other pattern variables, such as **LOCATION** and **DEVICE**.

This rule will match a sentence such as

> 'Terrorists attacked the Mayor's home in Bogota on Tuesday with grenades.'

but not the similar

> 'Bush charged the Democrats in the House on Tuesday with obstruction.'

thanks to the use of specific words and restricted pattern variables.

Nevertheless, many such patterns have to be written to catch all the different ways that things can be said, e.g.,

> 'The Mayor's home in Bogota was attacked on Tuesday by terrorists using grenades.'

> 'On Tuesday, the Bogota home of the Mayor was attacked by terrorists armed with grenades.'

and so on.[22] Although one is unlikely to catch all such wordings, a good number of them can be accounted for in this way.[23] Also problematical are unknown words that would fit the pattern variables if they had been anticipated, but which are not in the system's lexicon, e.g., Colombian towns that occur in the news but which are not recognized as place names by the program.

To make this clearer, let us look at a later version of FASTUS[24] that competed in MUC-5, where the task was to extract information about joint ventures from business news. Items to be extracted from this data included the partners in the joint venture, the name of the resulting company, its ownership and capitalization, and the intended activity, such as the goods or service to be provided. A typical text was the following:

> 'Bridgestone Sports Co. said Friday it has set up a joint venture in Taiwan with a local concern and a Japanese trading house to produce golf clubs to be shipped to Japan.'

> 'The joint venture, Bridgestone Sports Taiwan Co., capitalized at 20 million new Taiwan dollars, will start production in January 1990 with production of 20,000 iron and "metal wood" clubs a month.'

Table 3.5 Templates for the joint venture document set

Field	Filler
Name	TIE-UP-1
Relationship	TIE-UP
Entities	"Bridgestone Sports Co."
	"a local concern"
	"a Japanese trading house"
Joint Venture Company	"Bridgestone Sports Taiwan Co."
Activity	ACTIVITY-1
Amount	NT$20000000
Name	ACTIVITY-1
Activity	PRODUCTION
Company	"Bridgestone Sports Taiwan Co."
Product	"iron and "metal wood" clubs"
Start Date	DURING: January 1990

The information to be extracted from this short text is shown in the templates of Table 3.5.

Note that the first template, TIE-UP-1, contains a link to the second template ACTIVITY-1. Thus templates can be embedded in each other to allow fairly complex attributes and relationships to be expressed. Such templates are usually represented as data objects linked by pointers.

The MUC-5 version of FASTUS employed the following levels of processing to address this task.

Complex words
This stage includes the chunking together of 'multiwords', such as 'set up' and 'break down', which often consist of a verb and a particle. Locations, dates, times, and other basic entities are also identified at this level. Some proper names of people and companies in the lexicon may also be recognized here, although unknown names may require an analysis of context at a subsequent level, e.g., by inferring that capitalized words followed by 'Co.' are probably company names.

Basic phrases
Sentences are segmented into noun groups, verb groups, and particles. Noun groups consist of the head noun of a noun phrase, together with its determiners and left modifiers. Right modifiers, such as prepositional phrase attachments,[25] are ignored. Thus, in a noun phrase like

"The profitable West Coast manufacturer of gadgets for the food industry"

only the core noun phrase "The profitable West Coast manufacturer" would be
recognized.

Verb groups consist of the main verb, together with its auxiliaries and
any intervening adverbs. This stage also identifies other word classes, including prepositions ('at', 'in', etc.), conjunctions ('and', 'but', etc.), and relative
pronouns ('who', 'which', etc.).

For example, the first sentence in the joint venture text is segmented by this
stage into the following phrases:

Company Name:	Bridgestone Sports Co.
Verb Group:	said
Noun Group:	Friday
Noun Group:	it
Verb Group:	had set up
Noun Group:	a joint venture
Preposition:	in
Location:	Taiwan
Preposition:	with
Noun Group:	a local concern
Conjunction:	and
Noun Group:	a Japanese trading house
Verb Group:	to produce
Noun Group:	golf clubs
Verb Group:	to be shipped
Preposition:	to
Location:	Japan

Noun groups are recognized by a finite-state machine, which analyzes number, numerical modifiers such as 'approximately', other quantifiers ('all', 'some',
'many', 'most', etc.) and determiners ('the', 'a', 'this', etc.), participles in adjectival position, and adjectives of various kinds. It also recognizes orderings and
conjunctions of prenominal nouns and noun-like adjectives, e.g., "the home
insurance industry."

Verb groups are recognized by a finite-state grammar that tags them as Active, Passive, Gerund,[26] and Infinitive. Verbs can be locally ambiguous between
active and passive senses, as the verb 'kidnapped' in the two sentences,

'Several men kidnapped the mayor today.'

'Several men kidnapped yesterday were released today.'

These are tagged as both Active and Passive, and a later stage attempts to resolve the ambiguity.

As mentioned earlier, unknown or otherwise unanalyzed words will be ignored in subsequent processing, unless they occur in a context that indicates they could be names, such as a name prefix, like 'Mr.' or 'Dr.', or a company suffix, such as 'Co.' or 'Inc.'

Complex phrases

Complex noun groups and complex verb groups are identified on the basis of domain-independent, syntactic information. This includes the attachment of appositives[27] to their head noun group, e.g.,

'The joint venture, Bridgestone Sports Taiwan Co., ... '

the construction of measure phrases,

'20,000 iron and "metal wood" clubs a month'

and the attachment of 'of' and 'for' prepositional phrases to their head noun groups, as in

'production of 20,000 iron and "metal wood" clubs a month'.

Noun group conjunction, as in

'a local concern and a Japanese trading house'

is also performed at this level.

Domain events

Having recognized basic and complex phrases, we can identify entities and events, and build structures for them. Thus entity structures would be built for the companies referred to by the phrases 'Bridgestone Sports Co.', 'a local concern', 'a Japanese trading house', and 'Bridgestone Sports Taiwan Co.' in the 'joint venture' text shown above.

Similarly, complex verb groups, such as the following,

'GM *signed an agreement* forming a joint venture with Toyota.'

indicate events of interest, for which event structures need to be formed.

Patterns for interesting events are encoded as finite-state machines, where state transitions are driven by the head words[28] in the phrases identified earlier. Thus relevant head words and phrase types, such as 'company-NounGroup', and 'setup-ActiveVerbGroup', are paired and associated with a set of state transitions. So a domain-specific event pattern, such as

COMPANY SET-UP JOINT-VENTURE with COMPANY

could be instantiated with "Bridgestone Sports Co." matching the first **COMPANY** variable, "set up" matching **SET-UP**, "a joint venture" matching **JOINT-VENTURE**, and "a Japanese trading house" matching the final **COMPANY** variable. Extraneous material, such as "said Friday" in the original sentence, must either be discarded or anticipated in the patterns.

Merging structures
The previous levels of processing all operate within the bounds of single sentences, but this level operates over the whole text. Its task is to see that all the information collected about a single entity or relationship is collated into a unified whole. Thus structures arising from different parts of the text are merged, as long as they provide information about the same entity or event.

Three criteria can be taken into account in determining whether two structures can be merged:

- the internal structure of the noun groups
- nearness along some metric, and
- the compatibility of the two structures.

The rules for determining whether or not two noun groups refer to the same entity, and should therefore have their structures merged, are typically domain-dependent. For example, in the business world, a name, like 'General Motors' can be compatible with a description, like 'the company', provided the properties of the description are consistent with the properties associated with the name. Event structures, on the other hand, are typically merged only if there is a match among the names participating in the event in the corresponding subject and object roles.

Sidebar 3.4 Nondeterminism in FASTUS*

The finite-state mechanism used by FASTUS is *nondeterministic*. A nondeterministic FSM allows there to be more than one next state for any given pairing of state and input symbol.

Figure 3.4 shows an example that recognizes noun phrases that begin with a determiner (such as 'the'), and allow any number of modifiers, which can be nouns or adjectives, before ending in a noun. This FSM would accept or generate phrases such as:

'the red fire engine'
'a solid body electric guitar'
'the car window control button,'

as well as some anomalous phrases,[29] such as:

'the fire red engine.'

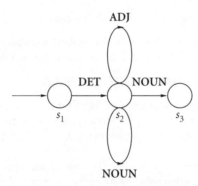

Figure 3.4 Machine diagram for a nondeterministic finite automaton

s_1 is the start state and s_3 is the end state. Thus state s_2 has two arcs labeled 'NOUN' exiting from it, one which terminates the phrase, and one which loops, allowing the phrase to be extended indefinitely. Nondeterminism arises because, at any given point when the FSM encounters a noun, it has a choice as to which transition to take.

In FASTUS, nondeterminism means that more than one extraction per sentence can be considered. With a few exceptions,[30] all of the events that are discovered are retained. Thus, the full content can be extracted from the sentence

'The mayor, who *was kidnapped yesterday, was found dead today.*'

As one branch discovers the incident encoded in the relative clause, while another branch marks time through the relative clause and then discovers the incident in the main clause. These incidents are then merged.

A similar device is used for conjoined verb phrases. Thus, in the sentence,

'Salvadoran President-elect Alfredo Cristiani *condemned the terrorist killing of Attorney General Roberto Garcia Alvarado* and *accused the Farabundo Marti National Liberation Front (FMLN) of the crime.*'

patterns such as

SUBJ Verb NG
SUBJ {VG | Other}* CONJ VG

allow the machine to find the information in the first conjunct, and then skip over the verb group and any intervening material in the first conjunct to associate the subject with the verb in the second conjunct.

In general, this kind of branching behavior permits the program to follow more than one thread, or interpretation, of a phrase.[31] In some instances, different branches will identify separate but complementary threads in a sentence, as in the last two examples. However, multiple branches can sometimes afford mutually exclusive interpretations of a sentence, in which case the sentence can be said to be ambiguous, e.g.,

'The terrorists attacked the soldiers with grenades.'

Do the grenades belong to the terrorists or the soldiers? Sometimes the preferred meaning is obvious, and will be found because only one regular expression exists, e.g.,

PERP attacked **HUMANTARGET** with **DEVICE**,

with the implicit interpretation (at template filling time) that the **DEVICE** belongs to the **PERP**. But, as a system's patterns become more numerous and complex, there may be occasions where more than one pattern will fit the same part of the data, allowing more than one interpretation of it.

Apparently, more recent versions of FASTUS use a lattice approach to represent ambiguities in the phrase recognition phase, enabling the program to defer ambiguity resolution to a later stage of processing.[32]

We can see from these examples that FASTUS has been applied to more than one domain.[33] As we noted above, the early stages of processing can be relatively domain-free, and the basic architecture of cascading FSMs is reusable. However, later stages of processing are more likely to be more domain-dependent, e.g., the lexicon of key nouns and verbs, and the semantic relationships that hold between them. Other domain-specific data includes the list of interesting proper names (and their variants) that one would like to be able to recognize, as well as cues for recognizing unknown words.[34] Thus there is an unavoidable amount of engineering involved in crafting domain rules that will govern how entities and events are identified and merged.[35]

In summary, FSMs have shown themselves to be extremely useful in many extraction tasks. Regular expressions as recognition rules have a familiar syntax and are relatively easy to specify. As we have seen, an FSM can also be used as a *transducer*, i.e., it can be programmed to output its analysis as it goes, emitting symbols as well as reading them. FSMs can be organized into layers, so that the output of one layer can be cascaded into the input of the next layer. This provides a nice architecture for managing complexity.[36]

FSMs are also relatively easy to implement. The most efficient method is to write a program that will simply compile a set of regexs into an FSM. The corresponding automaton can be coded as a table that says, for each pairing of internal state and input symbol, what its output and state change should be, as shown earlier in Figure 3.2.

3.4 Pushdown automata and context-free grammars

Despite the proven utility of FSMs as a means of extracting events from news, many texts contain complicating factors that may require additional or stronger methods. Using a stronger parser does not solve all the problems that we identified in the last section, such as the anticipation of all the different ways of saying things. However, it does provide more powerful tools for analyzing complex phrases and weighing alternative interpretations of ambiguous sentences.

3.4.1 Analyzing case reports

For concreteness, let us consider a particular kind of document, namely a U.S. court report, or case opinion. A case consists of a title, e.g., **John Smith v. Anne Jones**, some court information, such as a court name and a docket number, and the opinion of the court, which is the main body of the text.[37] The opinion usually culminates in one or more rulings, such as

> "We reverse the decision of the trial court, and remand the case for a new trial."

Such a text typically contains many different contexts that can serve as pitfalls for the unwary information extractor, whether human or mechanical.

1. *Facts* associated with the background to the case, concerning who did what to whom according to the plaintiff(s), may be intermingled with the *procedural history* of the case, concerning what previous courts have ruled on this matter, and how the case came to be before the current court. These two perspectives on the case, telling their rather different stories, are frequently mixed in the same sentence, e.g.,

   > 'Passengers brought action against airline to recover for intentional misrepresentation.'

2. The reporting of *precedents* (previous rulings) differs little from the way in which the ruling of the instant court is reported, and so tense is important, as is the correct attribution of subject, verb and object roles, e.g.,

    'The federal district court refused to allow any discovery or an evidentiary hearing and granted summary judgment denying the writ.'

3. Opinions frequently contain *quotations* from other proceedings, sometimes of an extensive nature, which could be confused with the ruling of the current court, if taken out of context, e.g.,

    'See *Dobson v. Kung*, ... "As plaintiff has failed to establish fraudulent intent, there is no genuine issue of material fact concerning common law and statutory fraud." '

4. The opinion may contain extended *discussion* of a hypothetical or counterfactual nature, or statements modified by qualifying phrases, e.g.,

    'We are not sure a new post-trial review and action will make appellant whole.'

5. An opinion usually addresses and pronounces upon many different *points of law*.

    'On December 1 1995, the defendants filed a motion to strike the plaintiffs' claims for bystander emotional distress in counts three, four, ten, and eleven, the claims for loss of consortium in counts five, six, twelve, and thirteen, the claim for relief seeking attorney's fees, the claim for relief seeking double or treble damages pursuant to General Statutes 14-295 in counts ten through fourteen, and the claim for relief seeking punitive damages.'

When faced with these difficulties, a deeper syntactic analysis may help a program identify matters of import, such as the judges' ruling in a case, or the name of the prior court whose previous judgment they are ruling upon. An alternative to a shallow parsing technique such as an FSM is to use a 'deeper' parser but still be prepared to cope with the challenges that will inevitably result.

Attempts to parse a sentence often fail simply because the lexicon and grammar that the parser is using are incomplete. Nonetheless, useful information can still be extracted from the parsed parts of a document. The phrase 'partial parsing' refers to a strategy in which a program attempts to perform a full parse of a sentence, but will settle for an incomplete syntactic analysis. It then does what it can to extract meaning from the structures it has identified. The 'partial' strategy can be applied to any parsing algorithm, e.g., it has been applied to cascaded finite automata.[38] However, using a more powerful parser may help an extraction program avoid certain errors to which FSM-based solutions are prone. For example, a deeper syntactic analysis will typically avoid some false assignments to subject and object roles, while an examination of broader sentential features will detect some opaque contexts.[39]

A good example of such an approach is provided by a program called History Assistant,[40] which integrates information extraction with information retrieval. The system extracts judicial language from electronically imported court opinions, and then uses this information to retrieve related cases from a database of citations, called a *citator*. The point of a citator is to link new decisions to earlier ones that they impact, so that a lawyer can tell whether or not a given case is still 'good law' and can be used as a precedent. The architecture has two principal components, a set of natural language modules and a prior case retrieval module, which perform the extraction and retrieval tasks respectively. We shall concentrate on the former here.

US appellate courts hand down approximately 500 new cases per day, so automated assistance to citator staff has the potential to reduce a significant workload, so long as results are reliable. This translates into a requirement for high recall (90% plus) and moderate precision (50% plus), so that human review of program output is not too onerous. The role of the information extraction program is to help an editor identify the relevant meta data to enter into the database, since links between cases are annotated by the nature of the decision, e.g., whether or not the old decision was affirmed, reversed, etc.

3.4.2 Context free grammars

We noted before that MUC-style information extraction programs typically use rather simple parsers, such as finite automata, to perform a very rudimentary syntactic analysis of the text. The CYK algorithm[41] is a somewhat stronger parsing method that has the computational power of a *push-down automaton* (PDA). A PDA is really an FSM with an additional tape that it can use as a stack.[42]

The stack functions as an external memory, which we can regard as being infinite.[43] The machine can both read from and write to the top of the stack. The basic 'push' operation adds another symbol to the top of the stack, while the basic 'pop' operation removes the top symbol. This arrangement means that such a device can use *context-free grammars* (CFGs) to recognize or generate deeply embedded and recursive structures, involving subordinate clauses and arbitrarily complex phrases. The stack can be used to save the context of the outer expression while the parser dives into the inner expression, and then reinstate the outer context when the inner analysis is done.

Thus, while parsing a sentence like:

> 'I reverse the ruling of the Federal District Court for the Northern District of New York and remand for a new trial.'

a PDA can save the parse of 'I reverse' on its stack while it analyzes the complex noun phrase 'the ruling of the Federal District Court for the Northern District of New York', and then recover its place to complete the parse of the whole conjunctive sentence. An FSM cannot do this reliably unless the regular language it recognizes can anticipate exactly how embedded the complex noun phrase is going to be.

CFGs are grammars consisting entirely of rewrite rules with a single symbol on the left-hand side.[44] In what follows, we use some notational conventions similar to those introduced in the last section. Upper case items in rules denote grammatical categories, while lower case items denote actual words from the English lexicon.

Context free grammar rules differ from regular expressions in that they contain recursion as well as repetition, so that

$$NG = DET + NOUN$$
$$NG = DET + MOD + NOUN$$
$$NG = NG + PREP + NG$$

allows us to define a noun group, NG, in terms of itself. Recursion is a convenient way of specifying complex noun groups, such as

> 'The rejection of the appeal from the ruling of the district court.'

CFGs allow nondeterminism as a matter of course, so that a noun group can be defined in multiple ways, as shown above.

The rules of such a grammar are sometimes called 'rewrite rules', because parsing proceeds by substituting one side of the rule for the other. Thus a pattern such as

DET MOD NOUN

in a larger pattern

DET MOD NOUN VERB ADVERB

can be recognized as an NG, and 'rewritten' as such to generate

NG VERB ADVERB.

Application of another rewrite rule,

VG = VERB + ADVERB,

might then result in the pattern

NG VG

which can be recognized as a sentence by the rule

S = NG + VG.

Such grammars are called 'context free' because they do not take the context of the left-hand symbol into account when specifying or applying a rule. When using the rule

NG = DET + MOD + NOUN

in the above example, we didn't care that the noun group was followed by a verb. We simply recognized the DET MOD NOUN pattern and applied the rule.[45]

3.4.3 Parsing with a pushdown automaton

The CYK algorithm is a parser for CFGs that uses a well-formed substring table (wfsst) to cache the results of constructing all alternative parses of a sentence. The use of the table avoids the duplication of effort commonly found in less sophisticated algorithms and aids efficiency. CYK is actually a kind of *dynamic programming* algorithm, in that it solves the overall problem by solving sub-problems, and then reusing those subsolutions appropriately while engaged in the search for an overall solution.

Figure 3.5 gives the algorithm, as described in a Pascal-like notation, taken from a well-known text on automata theory.[46]

Let S be a string of words, and V an (initially empty) substring table of size n. The table is accessed by subscripts in the range $[1, n]$, and $V_{i,j}$ denotes the cell in the ith column and the jth row of the table.

```
begin
    for i := 1 to n do
        V_{i,1} := {A|A = a is a rule and the ith word of S is a};
    for j := 2 to n do
        for i := 1 to n − j + 1 do
            begin
                V_{i,j} := {};
                for k := 1 to j − 1 do
                    V_{i,j} := V_{i,j} + {A|A = B + C is a rule and B is in V_{i,k} and C is in V_{i+k,j−k} };
            end
end
```

Figure 3.5 The CYK algorithm

The first loop essentially fills in the lexical categories associated with words in the string. $A = a$ is a rule that associates words with lexical categories, e.g.,

  TVERB = denies

where 'TVERB' denotes 'transitive verb,' i.e., a verb that takes an object.

The second, triple-nested loop fills in the non-lexical categories, by combining lower level categories in the table. This step uses rules such as

  NG = DET + NOUN.

Consider the example in Table 3.6. The wfsst corresponds to all but the top line of the table shown above. The Row 1 of the table consists of the lexical items in the sentence to be parsed – in this case "The court denies the motion." (We will omit row and column numbers from subsequent figures.)

The next row of the table contains the grammatical categories of these lexemes, which forms the first row of the wfsst. The subsequent rows then correspond to higher level syntactic structures constructed bottom-up from the lex-

Table 3.6 A well-formed substring table for a complete parse

	the	court	denies	the	motion
	1	2	3	4	5
1	DET	NOUN	TVERB	DET	NOUN
2	NG			NG	
3			VG		
4					
5	S				

ical categories. The ultimate category of the whole string resides in the bottom left-hand corner of the table.

Thus the entry VG in row 3, column 3 of the table – i.e., wfsst[3, 3] – indicates that "denies the motion" has been identified as a verb group, formed by combining a transitive verb, "denies," with a noun phrase "the motion." This formation is allowed by a grammar rule, such as

VG = TVERB + NG,

which says that a verb group consists of a transitive verb followed by a noun group.

The entry S in wfsst[5, 1] indicates that the whole string has been identified as a sentence. The sentence has been formed by combining a noun group, "the court," with the verb group "denies the motion" found earlier. The corresponding grammar rule would be

S = NG + VG.

The CYK algorithm tolerates both lexical and structural ambiguity.

– *Lexical ambiguity* means that a word may belong to more than one lexical category, in which case cells in the first row of the table may contain more than one entry.
– *Structural ambiguity* is where a group of words can be parsed in more than one way, resulting in overlapping, competitive substructures.

Structural hypotheses incorporating a substructure can use that substructure in any way sanctioned by the entry and the rules. In other words, a supposed phrase that has been discovered in the sentence can be combined with other material according to the rules, even if that hypothesis is false. However, such hypotheses will often fall by the wayside, because they will not fit into a structure that accounts for all the words in the sentence.

An example will make this clear. Consider the sentence

'The court that denied the motion is overruled.'

Most parsers would entertain the hypothesis that 'the motion is overruled' is a subsentence of the whole sentence, assuming a rule for forming passive verb groups, such as

VG = BVERB3 + TVERB,

where **BVERB3** stands for the third person singular of the verb 'to be', e.g., 'is' or 'was.'

Table 3.7 A wfsst with competing substructure hypotheses

	the	court	that	denied	the	motion	is	overruled
	1	2	3	4	5	6	7	8
1	DET	NOUN	RELPRO	TVERB	DET	NOUN	BVERB3	TVERB
2	NG				NG		VG	
3				VG				
4			RCLAUSE		S			
5	NG							
6								
7	S							

But this hypothesis is doomed to failure, if we want to parse the whole sentence. The correct bracketing[47] of the sentence is

  (S: (NG: The court that denied the motion) (VG: is overruled))

and not

  (?: The court that denied) (S: the motion is overruled).

'Denied' is a transitive verb, and must therefore take an object. So there is no grammar rule that will allow us to form a structural hypothesis for

  'The court that denied'.

The power of the pushdown automaton is that we can recognize this situation and avoid the error, whereas an FSM would be more likely to take the sub-sentence hypothesis at face value. A thorough parsing of the sentence using a CFG detects the presence of a relative clause, thereby uncovering embedded structure (see Table 3.7). Although

  'the motion is overruled.'

would still be parsed as a sentence, the structural hypothesis it represents crosses a clause boundary of the larger sentence in which it is embedded.

The parser's final output would ignore this embedded sentence hypothesis, since there is a better hypothesis that spans more of the data. The final parse is therefore

  (S:
    (NG:
      (NG: (DET: the) (NOUN: court))
      (RELPRO: that)
      (VG: (TVERB: denied) (NG: (DET: the) (NOUN: motion)))))

(**VG**: (**BVERB3**: is) (**TVERB**: overruled))
)

Structural ambiguity might seem like a rare occurrence, but it really isn't. Even noun groups can exhibit ambiguity. Look at our previous example:

'The reversal of the ruling by the Federal District Court for the Northern District of New York.'

The correct parse of this phrase is

(**NG**: (**NG**: The reversal of the ruling) (**PREP**: by) (**NG**: (**NG**: the Federal District Court) (**PREP**: for) (**NG**: the Northern District of New York)))

which indicates that the Federal District Court serves the Northern District of New York, and not, for instance

(**NG**: (**NG**: The reversal of the ruling) (**PREP**: by) (**NG**: the Federal District Court) (**PREP**: for) (**NG**: the Northern District of New York))

which suggests that the reversal was enacted expressly for the Northern District of New York by some Federal District Court (not necessarily serving New York).

The CYK algorithm is 'complete,' in the sense that it is guaranteed to find all parses sanctioned by the rules. Thus it will enumerate every structural hypothesis that the rules support, both for the sentence as a whole and for parts of it. It does not tell you how to decide between competing hypotheses, although certain heuristics can be devised to help make these decisions (see next section). We have already seen that it makes sense to prefer a 'spanning' hypothesis that explains the whole sentence to a competing subhypothesis that only explains part of it. In the absence of a spanning hypothesis, one might also prefer incomplete hypotheses that account for more of the data, i.e., which use more of the words.

The price you pay for completeness is polynomial complexity.[48] CYK's triple-nested loop dictates that the time taken to parse a sentence be a cubic function of its length.[49] But this is usually acceptable for an information extraction application, where you are not parsing every sentence.

3.4.4 Coping with incompleteness and ambiguity

For a parser to be usable for information extraction, it needs to be very robust. In other words, it must be tolerant of sentences that contain words that it does

Table 3.8 A well-formed substring table for an incomplete parse

the	court	of	appeals	denies	the	motion
DET	NOUN	GEN	?	TVERB	DET	NOUN
NG					NG	
				VG		

?

not have in its lexicon, and also syntactic structures that are not found in its grammar. Its main task is to identify and return key phrases from a sentence, while avoiding the problems caused by embedded contexts and ambiguity.

For example, suppose the lexicon does not contain an entry for "appeals". We would still expect the parser to be able to recognize some key phrases in a sentence such as:

"The court of appeals denies the motion."

This is because we could still form the wfsst in Table 3.8.

We cannot afford to extract nothing from a sentence that is incompletely parsed. So we proceed to make some assumptions about the structure of the half-analyzed sentence. We assume that, if there are no contrary indications, the noun and verb phrases that we have identified belong together. A little search will then allow us to use the rule,

S = NG + VG,

to form a sentence from the fragments, "the court" and "denies the motion." So we can discard "of appeals", and form a new wfsst from the joined substructures, which are already parsed. Then we reapply the CYK algorithm to fill out the superstructure of the new table.

In the context of the History Assistant program, this operation was called "splicing", and the program that performed splicing was invoked once the initial parse was complete. The Splicer also performed various checks, such as determining if the noun and the verb were semantically compatible. Confidence scores were also provided for retrieved fragments, based on how risky the splice appeared to be, e.g., in terms of how much material had been discarded (see Sidebar 3.5).

Sidebar 3.5 Heuristics for coping with ambiguity

Jackson et al. decided that they needed a measure of confidence that a string, S^*, extracted from a larger sentence, S, is a genuine phrase or subsentence of S, and not a random selection or splicing together of words from S.

Terminology & Notation

Let a *subsequence*, S^*, of S be any sequence of consecutive words in S. An *embedding* of S is obtained by extracting a subsequence of S that qualifies as a sentence according to the grammar rules. We assume that the embedding is shorter than S, i.e., it is not S itself. A *splice* of S is obtained by concatenating two non-adjacent subsequences of S that form a sentence according to the grammar rules. These must be concatenated in the order in which they appear in the sentence. For any string, S, let its length be s.

Desiderata

1. The measure, Q, should be a function only of the properties of S^* and S. Reason: We want the computation to involve only information local to the parse.
2. $0 \leq Q \leq 1$. Reason: The measures should behave like probabilities, e.g., with respect to the multiplication rule for evidence combination.
3. Q should monotonically increase as a function of s^*/s. Reason: The larger S^* is, the less chance that other significant material in S was missed.
4. Q should monotonically decrease with more 'dangerous' use of splicing, i.e., when we splice proportionally smaller and smaller units of S together. Reason: Smaller elements are informed by less of S's grammatical structure and may therefore combine things that do not belong together.
5. Q should monotonically decrease with the distance between spliced elements. Reason: The larger the 'gap', the more likely that interpolated material may be the true 'mate' of one of the elements.
6. The presence of other history phrases in S should increase our confidence in S^* as an *embedded* sentence. Reason: We are more likely to believe that "vacated" is a history phrase in the sentence "Vacated, summary judgment granted, case remanded to the district court" than in a sentence without other indications of history, e.g., "The tenant vacated the apartment."
7. The presence of other history words or phrases in S should *not* increase our confidence in S^* as a *spliced* sentence. Reason: The presence of other material introduces the possibility that we may have spliced the wrong pieces together.

The Measures

1. We define a simple base measure, $Q'(S^*, S)$, which we shall use to induce the full confidence measure, $Q(S^*, S)$.

$$Q'(S^*, S) = s^* / s.$$

Clearly, the more of S that is used by S^*, the more confident we are. Q' can be computed as soon as the string S^* is extracted.

2. *For embedded sentences only.* Let $S_1, ..., S_k$ be the totality of embeddings extracted from S. Then we allow the presence of the other embeddings to increase our confidence in a subsentence S^* as follows.

$$Q(S^*, S) = \frac{Q'(S^*, S) \cdot s}{s - \left(\sum s_i - s^* \right)} \qquad \text{for } 1 \leq i \leq k, \text{ where } S_i \neq S^*.$$

The score of a fragment increases monotonically as a function of both its length and the amount of other embedded material. Thus, the longer the fragment and the more of the full sentence that is used up by other embeddings, the more weight we accord to a given fragment. This reasoning does *not* apply to splices, and we do not use splices to increase our confidence in S^*, since these are more speculative than embeddings.

3. *For spliced sentences only.* Let S^* be a spliced sentence consisting of two halves, S_1 and S_2, separated by a gap of n unparsed words. Then

$$Q(S^*, S) = \frac{Q'(S^*, S)}{\sqrt{n} \cdot 2^m}$$

where m is 0, 1 or 2, depending on whether none, one or both of the halves are one-word strings. The idea is that we penalize moderately for the gap, since it is already counted as part of Q', but penalize more heavily for one-word fragments, since these are more likely to create spurious connections than multi-word fragments.

This parsing and splicing method has a number of advantages over more haphazard approaches to phrase extraction.

- In the interests of completeness, the parser examines all competing parses and splices. This gives History Assistant the option of returning more than one interpretation of a sentence to favor recall, or simply choosing the best scoring hypothesis, to favor precision.
- To aid correctness, History Assistant employs a number of other heuristics that forbid certain splices and embedded extractions. These checks are easy to incorporate into the splice algorithm as special cases, e.g., forbidding the discarding of negation.
- The scoring algorithm, though *ad hoc*, handles uncertainty by capturing the degree of danger associated with an extraction, a feature that allows History Assistant to present phrases to the user with an associated level of confidence.

In addition, History Assistant applied a few other filtering heuristics before passing the results of a parse on to the semantic level for interpretation. Thus extractions were discarded if their score was too low, e.g., one-word extractions whose score has not been boosted by the presence of other history language in a lengthy sentence. This threshold was arrived at by sensitivity analysis.

As in the FASTUS program, the output of the parser must be analyzed and used to fill event templates. The template format is meant to abstract away from the language actually used in order to represent the meaning of a phrase or sentence. Thus, variations on the same theme, such as

'The defendant's motion to strike is denied.'
'We deny the motion of the defendant to strike.'
'The court denies the motion to strike by the defendant.'

should all map to the same data object, along the lines of Table 3.9.

Table 3.9 Filled template for a 'Procedure' event

Procedure	
Type	petition
Purpose	strike
Party	defendant
Outcome	denied

These data objects are built by searching the well-formed substring table after the parse is complete, and mapping the structures identified by the parser into the fields of the record.

In the course of processing a document, the program may extract additional (possibly redundant) information about events that it has already encountered, and so such templates may need to be updated or merged. Thus, given two sentences describing a petition, such as:

'The defendant filed a petition for post-conviction relief.'

with a template as in Table 3.10, and

'The petition for postconviction relief is denied.'

with a template as in Table 3.11, the program needs to perform a limited kind of inference, in which it decides that the defendant's petition is the one that is denied.

Table 3.10 Incomplete template for a 'Procedure' event

Procedure	
Type	petition
Purpose	pcr
Party	defendant
Outcome	

Merging the two data objects collates these two sources of information to give a new template, as in Table 3.12.

Table 3.11 Template for a denied 'Procedure' event

Procedure	
Type	petition
Purpose	pcr
Party	
Outcome	denied

Table 3.12 Merged template for a 'Procedure' event

Procedure	
Type	petition
Purpose	pcr
Party	defendant
Outcome	denied

History Assistant draws such inferences incrementally as sentences are read. First, it checks that there are no conflicts among the fields of two candidates to be merged, and then it looks to see if the new record is capable of merging with more than one extant object. For example, if there are two petitions, P and Q, each of which could merge with a new petition, R, but could not merge amongst themselves, then neither is merged with R, since the identity of the new petition is ambiguous. Despite these precautions, data objects are sometimes merged in error.

In the next section, we discuss some of the shortcomings of FASTUS, History Assistant and extraction programs generally, as well as examining how such systems are usually evaluated.

3.5 Limitations of current technology and future research

Extraction programs are evaluated using the standard measures of recall and precision.[50] When calculating recall, programs are usually accorded partial credit for templates that have been filled out with some but not all of the desired information. Redundant extractions, such as failed merges of identical content, result in depressed precision, while incorrect merges depress recall.

Any knowledge that can be brought to bear concerning the domain of application, or the documents themselves, is likely to help performance, regardless of the parsing approach used. For example, in some court reports, the prior court that is being appealed from is listed soon after the title, before the opinion begins. In other reports, this information has to be extracted from the first paragraph of the opinion. However, many courts may be mentioned in the text. An early version of History Assistant used a data structure that encoded information about which courts can stand in an appellate relation to which other courts.[51]

Nevertheless, as we noted in the first section, extraction programs understand little or nothing about the events they are looking for. The rules, be they regular expressions or context-free, are purely syntactic, and have little or no semantic content (although see Sidebar 3.6). This fact can manifest itself in various ways, to the detriment of the system's performance.

Sidebar 3.6 Semantic grammar

A primitive semantics can be injected into grammar rules by organizing the lexicon into domain-specific categories, and then using these categories in the rules, instead of the content-free **NOUN**, **NG**, etc. Both FASTUS and History Assistant availed themselves of this technique.

For example, given that 'motion' is designated as a **PROCEDURE_NOUN**, and 'denied' as a **PROCEDURE_VERB**, you can write a rule like:

PROCEDURE_SENTENCE = PROCEDURE_NOUN + PROCEDURE_VERB

that will recognize such meaningful sentences as

'Motion denied.'

but not anomalous sentences, such as 'Court denied.' or 'Ruling denied.', because 'court' and 'ruling' are not **PROCEDURE_NOUN**s.

Such rule sets are called *semantic grammars*, because they enforce semantic constraints by making certain combinations of words ungrammatical.[52] Returning to our famous example from Chapter 1,

'Colorless green ideas sleep furiously'

one could insist that the modifier 'green' only be applied to nouns describing concrete objects, and not to abstract entities such as ideas.

However, semantic grammars do not solve all the problems of semantics, e.g., they cannot easily be used to detect the contradiction between 'colorless' and 'green' when applied to the same object.

3.5.1 Explicit versus implicit statements

For current extraction technology to work, the information sought must be explicitly stated in the text. It cannot be merely implied by the text. This lack of inferential capability can pose significant problems when extracting from documents that expect the reader to draw simple conclusions.

For example, bankruptcy cases posed special problems for History Assistant. The strategy of looking for dispositive language, such as "conversion denied" did not work reliably. In a typical scenario, a debtor might move to convert from Chapter 7 to Chapter 13. A creditor files a complaint to oppose this. The judge decides the case by "finding for the plaintiff."

The program would have to perform a number of steps of reasoning to identify the outcome correctly as "conversion denied". It would have to realize that:

1. the plaintiff is the creditor,
2. the creditor is asking for a denial of what the defendant (debtor) is asking for, namely a conversion, and
3. the Judge grants the denial.

This kind of reasoning is beyond the capabilities of History Assistant, and all other information extraction programs of which we are aware.

Even if the information is explicitly stated, there may be purely linguistic problems that need to be solved in order to extract it. The phenomenon of coreference is a common stumbling block to extraction programs. Coreference is where two or more linguistic expressions refer to the same entity, e.g., "IBM" and "the company", or "Bill Gates" and "he." Phrases like "the company" and "he" are called *anaphors*, and they typically corefer with a preceding expression, called the *antecedent*.[53]

In cases where the crucial sentence to be extracted contains anaphors, extraction must resolve reference if it is to be successful. The version of FASTUS used in the MUC-6 conference[54] had a coreference module that used specialized algorithms[55] to resolve pronouns ('she'), reflexives ('herself'), and definite descriptions ('the company'). The system achieved recall of 59% and precision of 72% on the MUC-6 coreference task.

A later version of History Assistant[56] developed an algorithm called TIARA for resolving references to court decisions associated with case citations. Although limited in scope, the program handles forward and backward references, intra- and inter-sentential references, as well as making a distinction between explicit and implicit coreference. Explicit coreference involves reference terms and expressions, as in 'it', 'that decision', 'the legislature', 'the district court', etc. Implicit coreference, on the other hand, lacks such terms and expressions but the language nonetheless implies the existence of 'co-specifiers.'

For example, a sentence such as

'There is a conflict in the circuit.'

implies the existence of at least two decisions that are in disagreement with each other. Subsequent sentences, such as

'The court in Jones held that ...'

and

'On the other hand, the district court held that ...'

provide the co-specifiers later.

We examine the whole problem of name recognition and coreference in Chapter 5, under the rubric of 'text mining.'

3.5.2 Machine learning for information extraction

In addition to systems that use hand-written patterns and rules, there are an increasing number of research vehicles which attempt to learn extraction patterns.[57] These machine learning approaches require a text corpus such as that provided for MUC in which the significant fragments are delineated with detailed annotations. Such markup needs to identify the roles played by different text features in providing the relevant information, e.g.,

'The parliament was bombed by Carlos.'

might be tagged as:

'The <TARGET>parliament</TARGET> was
<ACTION>bombed</ACTION> by <PERP>Carlos</PERP>.'

A program then needs to learn that a pattern like

NOUN was **PASSIVE-VERB** by **NOUNGROUP**

will cover examples of this type, if certain constraints are met, e.g., the passive verb needs to express the concept of attack.

The problem, of course, is that there may be many syntactic variations on this simple theme, and we want the learning program to generate rules that have reasonably broad coverage, rather than building a different rule for each variant. Managing the space of possible rules creates both conceptual and computational problems.

At the moment, rule-based learning programs are typically being applied to somewhat simpler domains than that of terrorist incidents and court reports. For example, there are programs that extract information from advertisements for jobs and real estate[58] and others that find company names in news stories.[59] But it seems likely that such programs may eventually reduce the amount of effort that is required to build an industrial strength information extraction application.

We examine machine learning approaches to text categorization in the next chapter.

3.5.3 Statistical language models for information extraction

An alternate approach to machine learning for information extraction is to train a statistical language model[60] on annotated data. Thus the sentence analysis system fielded by BBN Technologies at MUC-7, called SIFT,[61] employed a statistical process to map strings of words into more meaningful structures. The details of how this was done are somewhat beyond the scope of this text, but we can give the reader the flavor of this approach, and how it worked on a pair of extraction tasks.

The tasks SIFT was asked to perform were called 'Template Element' and 'Template Relationship.'

- The Template Element task required that information pertaining to organizations, persons, and artifacts mentioned in a text be captured in the form of templates consisting of a predefined set of attributes, as in previous MUCs.
- The Template Relationship task was new in MUC-7, and required that relationships among template elements, such as time and place, be captured in the form of relations between template elements.

SIFT was trained on both general knowledge of English sentence structure, using the Penn Treebank corpus[62] mentioned in Chapter 1, and specific knowledge of how domain entities and relationships are typically expressed, using half a million words of New York Times news stories on air disasters and space technology. The NYT text was annotated semantically with significant properties and relationships, rather than with a detailed parse of the sentence structure. Figure 3.6 gives an example of semantic annotation.

These two knowledge sources are combined in the following way.

- A sentence-level model is derived from the Penn Treebank, and then used to parse sentences from the NYT document collection. However, the parses are constrained to be consistent with the semantic annotation.

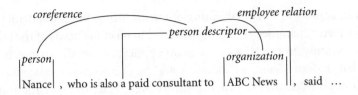

Figure 3.6 A semantically annotated sentence

– The resulting parse tree is then augmented with the semantic information, and the sentence-level model is then retrained on this combination
   of syntactic and semantic information.

Once SIFT has been trained, it can be given unseen sentences to analyze. The
program works by computing the most likely syntactic and semantic interpretation, which reduces to finding the most likely augmented parse tree for the
sentence. This search is conducted using the CYK algorithm we encountered
earlier, with the addition that there are now probabilities associated with parse
tree elements, which can be combined to compute the probability of the whole
tree.

   SIFT performed well at MUC-7 on both the Template Element and the
Template Relationship tasks, as shown in Table 3.13.

Table 3.13 SIFT's performance at MUC-7

Task	% Recall	% Precision	% F-Measure
Named Entity	89	92	90.44
Template Element	83	84	83.49
Template Relationship	64	81	71.23

   The 'Named Entity' extraction task involved recognizing names of organizations, people, and locations, along with expression for dates, times, monetary
amounts and percentages. We shall encounter the SIFT name recognizer, called
IdentiFinder, in Chapter 5.

3.6 Summary of information extraction

It can be seen that event extraction is a fairly complex process, and that no
program is going to perform at 100% precision and recall by identifying all
and only the items of interest. However, such systems are typically meant to be

used as an adjunct to a manual editing or intelligence-gathering system. In this scenario, system parameters need to be tuned to meet the needs of the task.

For example, in the History Assistant application, recall was much more important than precision, so editors would be prepared to tolerate a certain number of false positives in order to ensure high recall. In other applications, such as scanning the news for events of interest, precision might be more important than recall. Given the redundancy among stories in many news collections or feeds, one might assume that really important events will receive high coverage, and therefore have a good chance of being found in one story or another. By the same token, the high volume of most news feeds means that high precision is important if intelligence-gathering staff are not to be swamped by irrelevant information.

Writing event extraction rules is a fairly laborious activity, and such rule sets will need to be maintained over time. As we noted earlier, it is hard to write rules that anticipate all the possible ways that events or objects of interest can be described, and rule sets will often need to be extended to accommodate new patterns observed in text data. Although modifying declarative representations, such as patterns or grammar rules, will be easier than making changes to program code, it is nevertheless an ongoing task that requires skilled personnel. Systems that learn extraction rules from examples can theoretically be retrained from time to time on new data, but there have been few studies done on the effectiveness of this kind of automatic maintenance.

In spite of these caveats, the MUC systems show that it is possible to obtain recall and precision results that would be acceptable for many applications. Whether one employs FSMs or a chart parser such as CYK, these algorithms are efficient enough to process large document feeds, so long as one is only analyzing selected sentences in a document, e.g., sentences that contain certain target words. Information extraction programs now power a number of online applications in the business information arena,[63] so this technology can be said to have come of age.

Pointers

The proceedings of MUC-3 through MUC-6 were published by Morgan Kaufmann Publishers, although some of these may now be out of print. The proceedings of MUC-7 are published on the National Institute of Standards (NIST) website.[64]

An information extraction tutorial[65] and useful pointers to other resources are currently available at the Stanford Research Institute's web site.

For a summary of early work in information extraction and related areas, see Lehnert;[66] for early work on automating the creation of extraction rules, see Lehnert et al.[67]

For a thorough treatment of regular expressions, see Friedl.[68] For more about finite state approaches to language processing, see Roche and Schabes,[69] and also Kornai.[70]

Notes

1. The mandate is simply the ruling of the judge, or the panel of judges.

2. The initial MUC evaluations were carried out by Beth Sundheim of the Naval Ocean Systems Center (NOSC) and continued with DARPA funding under the TIPSTER Program by Nancy Chinchor of Science Applications International Corporation (SAIC).

3. Giving equal weight to recall and precision, we have

$$F_1 = \frac{2PR}{P + R}$$

where P stands for precision and R for recall.

4. We chose MUC-3's event extraction task as an exemplar, rather than taking a task from a later MUC, because it is a 'classic' application of information extraction from English texts that raises most of the technical issues we wish to discuss. We deal with some of the more specialized tasks from later MUCs (such as named entity extraction) in Chapter 5.

5. Sundheim, B. M. (1991). Overview of the Third Message Understanding Conference. *Proceedings of the 3rd Message Understanding Conference*, 3–16.

6. Actual texts were all upper case, as a result of the download process used.

7. See Levine, J. R., Mason, T. & Brown, D. (1992). *lex and yacc*. Sebastopol, California: O'Reilly & Associates.

8. It can't be done, because wherever you set your bound, β, we can provide you with a string that is so long that you have to remember more than β positions to predict the next symbol. This means that your 'regular expression' for characterizing the string can't be finite. Hence, the machine for recognizing it can't have a finite number of states. Furthermore, there is nothing in the regular expression notation that will allow you to make the number of b's depend on the number of a's. a*b* simply generates any number of a's followed by any number of b's.

9. See Chapter 1, Section 3.2.

10. So long as the actual language remains the same. Different languages, such as French and English, have different tokenization rules.

11. The Perl language was released as freeware by Larry Wall at the end of 1987. It is currently in its sixth incarnation. See http://www.perl.org and http://www.perl.com.

12. Appelt, D. E., Hobbs, J. E., Bear, J., Israel, D., & Tyson, M. (1993). FASTUS: A Finite-State Processor for Information Extraction from Real-World Text. In *Proceedings of the International Joint Conference on Artificial Intelligence* (pp. 1172–1178).

13. The acronym is flawed in more ways than one. The term 'finite state automaton' is redundant, given that an automaton was originally defined as a finite or infinite machine that moves from state to state in discrete steps. However, the term and its acronym (FSA) are now common usage in the literature, so it's a bit late to worry about that now.

14. Named entity recognition is simply the identification of proper names representing people, companies, organizations, places, and so forth. The relevant technologies are examined in detail in Chapter 5.

15. A *formal language* is a (usually infinite) set of strings defined over a finite alphabet of symbols by a finite set of concatenation rules. In other words, the language consists of all the strings that can be built out of a given character set according to the rules.

16. Kleene, S. C. (1956). Representation of events in nerve nets and finite automata. In *Automata Studies*, C. E. Shannon, & J. McCarthy (Eds.), *Annals of Mathematics Studies, 34*. Princeton, NJ: Princeton University Press.

17. Chomsky, N. (1959). On certain formal properties of grammars. *Information and Control, 2*, 137–167.

18. No finite automaton can accept a language containing arbitrarily nested, balanced parentheses, such as algebraic expressions like $(x + (yz)) - (wz)$. This applies to other recursive structures, such as deeply embedded clauses in a language, e.g., sentences like 'The cat that ate the bird that ate the worm is black.' As an example of crossed constraints, consider a sentence such as 'John and Mary are six and seven years old respectively,' in which the usual nesting and adjacency conventions are violated.

19. Church, K. W. (1980). *On Memory Limitations in Natural Language Processing.* MIT Laboratory of Computer Science Technical Report MIT/LCS/TR-245.

20. 'Heuristically' means 'using rules of thumb.' A heuristic is simply a rule that you try, hoping it will work. It isn't based on a law or a theorem, so it isn't guaranteed to work.

21. Now that we are no longer dealing with single letters as pattern variables, we will render patterns with spaces between variables, e.g., writing 'a b c' in place of 'abc.'

22. As an exercise, you might like to try writing rules to catch these variants.

23. These variations account for much of the lost recall in MUC systems. The problem is that, after the first 50% recall has been achieved, a law of diminishing returns sets in. A repeat of the initial investment of effort in the pattern writing process normally yields much less improvement in terms of recall points. In our experience, doubling, tripling and quadrupling the original investment typically results in taking recall from 50% to 75%, to 83%, and (if you are lucky) to 90% respectively. This additional effort is not usually cost effective, and it is not guaranteed to produce these 'best case' results.

24. Hobbs, J. E., Appelt, D. E., Bear, J., Israel, D., Kameyama, M., Stickel, M. & Tyson, M. (1996). FASTUS: A Cascaded Finite-State Transducer for Extracting Information from Natural-Language Text. In Roche and Schabes (Eds.), *Finite State Devices for Natural Lan-*

guage Processing. Cambridge MA: MIT Press. The current section draws heavily upon examples from this paper.

25. As we saw in Chapter 1, prepositional phrase attachments can be highly ambiguous.

26. A gerund is a noun-like use of a verb participle, e.g., "The CEO proposed *acquiring* the Acme Company," or "*Acquiring* a company is easier than *running* it profitably."

27. Appositives are simply modifying phrases that occur adjacent to a noun phrase, e.g., "Bill Gates, CEO of Microsoft" or "Secretary of State, Colin Powell."

28. The head word in a noun phrase is the single noun that other words are typically modifying, while the head verb in a verb phrase is the main verb, as opposed to one of the auxiliary verbs.

29. When using FSMs for recognition, designers tend not to worry about such anomalies, working on the assumption that they will never occur in text. In other words, having patterns that would over-generate, if so employed, is deemed less of a problem than having patterns that will under-recognize.

30. The exceptions involve clauses that are subsumed by other larger clauses, and therefore discarded as being redundant.

31. However, it can be shown that nondeterministic finite automata are actually no more powerful than deterministic ones. Any language accepted by the former can be accepted by the latter, even though the more expressive formalism may ease the programming process.

32. The details of how this is done have not been published, as far as we are aware.

33. Some aspects of FASTUS have apparently been incorporated into a Message Handler System that is being used for analyzing military messages in field operations. See http://www.ai.sri.com/~appelt/arpatu.html.

34. Unknown words are simply words that are not in the lexicon the FSM is using. In addition to contextual cues, such as 'Mr.' and 'Co.', we also hinted earlier (see Section 3.2) that morphology can help a program guess a word's class. Thus any uncapitalized English word ending in '-ness' is almost certainly a noun, while a word ending in '-ed' or '-ing' is probably a verb, although there are obvious known exceptions.

35. Interestingly, this technology has also been ported to another natural language. In MUC-5, FASTUS was entered into the Japanese task as well as the English one. The system read and extracted information from both romanji and kanji input, and contained rules for recognizing joint ventures in both English and Japanese business news with similar recall and precision results.

36. Although allowing nondeterminism complicates the design to some extent.

37. The main opinion may be followed by a dissenting opinion, authored by a minority of judges.

38. See e.g., Abney, S. (1997). Partial Parsing via Finite-State Cascades. *Journal of Natural Language Engineering, 2* (4), 337–344.

39. An 'opaque context' is a context where the declarative force of a statement is qualified or nullified by adjacent expressions, e.g., '*If* I grant the motion, *this will create a bad precedent*,' or '*The defendant contends that* the ruling should be reversed.'

40. Jackson, P., Al-Kofahi, K., Kreilick, C. & Grom, B. (1998). Information extraction from case law and retrieval of prior cases by partial parsing and query generation. *CIKM-98, 60–67.* New York: ACM Press.

41. This is also called the CKY algorithm. The letters stand for the names of the inventors: Cocke, Young, and Kasami. The twist is that each of them developed it quite independently of the others in the 1960s.

42. A 'stack' is a data structure to which items can only be added (and from which items can only be taken) at the 'top' or 'front.' It therefore differs from a queue, in which items are added at one end and taken from the other. Adding to a stack is called 'pushing' and taking from a stack is called 'popping.'

43. Of course, no stack medium is infinite. But we just assume that whenever our machine gets short of memory, a friendly neighborhood systems engineer instantly adds more. If only life were like that.

44. Regular grammars are also context free, with the further restriction that the right-hand side of the rule contain at most one nonterminal, always situated to the right. Thus a(b|c)* could be written as

$$S = a + T$$
$$T = b + T$$
$$T = c + T$$
$$T = b$$
$$T = c$$

45. But suppose we wanted to express the constraint that noun groups with a modifier (MOD) only occur in certain contexts, say where the NG is the grammatical subject of the sentence. Then we might insist that the NG be followed by a verb, along the lines of:

NG *VERB* = DET + MOD + NOUN

where *VERB* supplies the right context of NG, but is not part of the rewrite. Grammars which permit the specification of left and right contexts of this kind are called 'context sensitive' grammars (CSGs). Their properties are beyond the scope of this book, and they are not typically used in information extraction.

46. Hopcroft, J. E. & Ullman, J. D. (1969). *Formal Languages and their Relation to Automata.* Reading, MA: Addison-Wesley.

47. See Chapter 1.

48. 'Polynomial complexity' means that the time taken by the algorithm is a polynomial function of the size of the problem, i.e., it is given by a function of the form $an^m + bn + c$, where n is the key size variable.

49. This is a worst case analysis that is not always encountered in practice, especially when attempting to parse long sentences using a relatively small lexicon of targeted words. If we are processing row i of the table, and j is the last row where we assigned a non-lexical category, then it is only worth proceeding if $i > 2j$, where i is even, and $i > 2j + 1$ otherwise.

50. See Chapter 2, Section 2.4.2.

51. Later versions of History Assistant switched to using a statistical model, based on many years of accumulated data, to estimate the probability that a case from court C will go to court D on appeal.

52. See Allen, J. (1995). *Natural Language Understanding* (2nd edition). Redwood City, CA: Benjamin/Cummings, Chapter 11 for more about semantic grammars.

53. See Chapter 5, Section 5.2.2, for more precise definitions and further examples.

54. Appelt, D. E., Hobbs, J. R., Bear, J., Israel, D., Kameyama, M., Kehler, A., Martin, D., Myers, K., & Tyson, M. (1995). SRI International FASTUS system MUC-6 test results and analysis. In *Proceedings of the Sixth Message Understanding Conference (MUC-6)*. Columbia, MD.

55. Kameyama, M. (1997). Recognizing referential links: An information extraction perspective. In *Proceedings of the ACL'97/EACL'97 workshop on Operational factors in practical, robust anaphora resolution* (pp. 46–53). Madrid, Spain.

56. Al-Kofahi, K., Grom, B. & Jackson, P. (1999). Anaphora resolution in the extraction of treatment history language from court opinions by partial parsing. In *Proceedings of the Seventh International Conference on Artificial Intelligence and Law* (pp. 138–146).

57. Muslea, I. (1999). Extraction patterns for information extraction tasks: A survey. In Papers from the AAAI Workshop on *Machine Learning for Information Extraction*, Tech. Report WS-99-11 (pp. 1–6). Menlo Park, CA: AAAI Press.

58. Soderland, S. (1999). Learning information extraction rules for semi-structured and free text. *Machine Learning*, pp. 34, 233–272.

59. Freitag, D. (1998). Information extraction from html: Application of a general learning approach. *Proceedings of the 15th National Conference on Artificial Intelligence* (pp. 517–523).

60. Of the kind we encountered in Chapter 2, Section 2.3.4.

61. Scott Miller, Michael Crystal, Heidi Fox, Lance Ramshaw, Richard Schwartz, Rebecca Stone, Ralph Weischedel, and the Annotation Group. (1998). Algorithms that learn to extract information – BBN: Description of the SIFT system as used for MUC-7. In *Proceedings of the Seventh Message Understanding Conference*.

62. This corpus consists of about a million words of Wall Street Journal text that has been heavily annotated with part of speech information and parse trees indicating sentence structure.

63. For example, EDGAR Online People (http://www.edgar-online.com/people/) is indexed by NetOwl[TM] Extractor (www.netowl.com), which also processes real-time news feeds supplied by NewsEdge (www.newsedge.com). Extraction technology from WhizBang! Labs (www.whizbang.com) assembles job descriptions from corporate Web sites for online recruiters FlipDog.com.

64. http://www.itl.nist.gov/iad/894.02/related_projects/muc/proceedings/muc_7_toc.html

65. http://www.ai.sri.com/~ appelt/ie-tutorial/

66. Lehnert, W. (1991). A Performance Evaluation of Text Analysis Technologies. *AI Magazine*, pp. 81–94, Fall issue.

67. Lehnert, W., Cardie, C., Fisher, D., Riloff, E., & Williams, R. (1991). Description of the CIRCUS System as Used in MUC-3. In *Proceedings of the 3rd Message Understanding Conference* (pp. 223–233).

68. Friedl, J. E. F. (1997). *Mastering Regular Expressions*. Sebastopol, California: O'Reilly & Associates.

69. Roche, E. & Schabes, Y. (Eds.). (1997). *Finite-State Language Processing*. Cambridge, Massachusetts: MIT Press.

70. Kornai, A. (1999). *Extended Finite State Models of Language*. Cambridge, England: Cambridge University Press.

CHAPTER 4

Text categorization

With the Internet and e-mail becoming part of many people's daily routine, who is not familiar with the Yahoo! directory, or with Microsoft Outlook's highlighting of junk messages? These are but two applications of text classification. Web pages in the Yahoo directory have been assigned one or more categories by human editors, so we say that the classification was performed 'manually'. On the other hand, users of Outlook can write simple rules to sort incoming e-mails into folders, or use predefined rules to delete junk e-mails. This is an example of automated text classification, albeit a rather trivial one.

First, let us dispose of a few terminological issues. Some researchers[1] make a distinction between text classification and text categorization. 'Text categorization' is sometimes taken to mean sorting documents by content, while 'text classification' is used as a broader term to include any kind of assignment of documents to classes, not necessarily based on content, e.g., sorting by author, by publisher, or by language (English, French, German, etc.). However, these terms will be used interchangeably in the present context, as will the terms 'class' and 'category', with the assumption that we are always talking about the assignment of labels or index terms to documents based on their content.

The term 'classifier' will be used rather loosely to denote any process (human or mechanical, or a mixture of the two) which sorts documents with respect to categories or subject matter labels, or assigns one or more index terms or keywords to them. As a notational device, individual classes of documents, such as BUSINESS NEWS, will appear in small capital letters.

While text retrieval may be considered as a text classification task (the task of sorting documents into the relevant and the irrelevant), it is worth maintaining a distinction between the two activities. Text retrieval is typically concerned with specific, momentary information needs, while text categorization is more concerned with classifications of long-term interest.[2] Unlike queries, categorization schemes often have archival significance, e.g., the Dewey Decimal Classification system and the West Key Number system.

There is no question concerning the commercial value of being able to classify documents automatically by content. There are myriad potential applications of such a capability for corporate Intranets, government departments, and Internet publishers. Integration of search and categorization technology is coming to be seen as essential, if corporations are to leverage their information assets.[3]

Such uncertainty as surrounds this topic relates to the relative immaturity of the field, as well as a lack of clarity concerning the task itself. People frequently speak of categorization when they are really interested in the indexing, abstracting, or extracting of information. In this chapter, we both review the technology and try to identify the different kinds of categorization task to which current methods can be applied.

4.1 Overview of categorization tasks and methods

A number of distinguishable activities fall under the general heading of classification, but here is a list of the main types, with sample applications attached for illustrative purposes. The aim here is not to say how such problems should be solved, but to identify the main issues.

- *Routing.* An online information provider sends one or more articles from an incoming news feed to a subscriber. This is typically done by having the user write a standing query that is stored run against the feed at regular intervals, e.g., once a day. This can be viewed as a categorization task, to the extent that documents are being classified into those relevant to the query and those which are not relevant. But a more interesting router would be one that split a news feed into multiple topics for further dissemination.
- *Indexing.* A digital library associates one or more index terms from a controlled vocabulary with each electronic document in its collection. Wholly manual methods of classification are too onerous for most online collections, and information providers are faced with a large number of difficult decisions to make regarding how to deploy technology to help. Even if an extant library classification scheme is adopted, such as MARC[4] or the Library of Congress Online Catalog, there remains the issue of how to provide human classifiers with automatic assistance.
- *Sorting.* A knowledge management system clusters an undifferentiated collection of memos or email messages into a set of mutually exclusive categories. Since these materials are not going to be indexed or published, a certain level of error can be tolerated. It is obvious that some of these documents will be easier to cluster than others. For example, some may be

extremely short, yielding few clues to their content; some may be on one topic, while others cover multiple topics. In any event, there will be outliers, which will need to be dealt with by manual cleanup, if a high degree of classification accuracy is really necessary.

- *Supplementation.* A scientific publisher associates incoming journal articles with one or more sections of a digest publication where new results should be cited. Even if authors have been asked to supply keywords, matching those keywords to the digest classification may be nontrivial. However, there may be many clues to where an article goes, over and above the actual scientific content of the paper. For example, the authors may each have previously published work that has already been classified. Also, their paper may cite works that have already been classified. Leveraging this metadata will be key to any degree of automation applied to this process.

- *Annotation.* A legal publisher identifies the points of law in a new court opinion, writes a summary for each point, and classifies the summaries according to a preexisting scheme. Given the volume of case law, these tasks are most likely performed by teams of people. The written summaries will not be very long, and so any automatic means of classification will not have much text to work with. However, each summary comes from a larger text, which may yield clues as to how the summaries should be classified. It is possible that simply having a program route new summaries to the right classification expert would improve the workflow.

Such tasks can be analyzed along a number of non-orthogonal dimensions, which are mostly about the data. Understanding the data is one of the keys to successful categorization, yet this is an area in which most categorization tool vendors are extremely weak. Many of the 'one size fits all' tools on the market have not been tested on a wide range of content types.

Moreover, some of the currently available off-the-shelf tools work only with the text of a document. But documents often have useful data or metadata associated with them, such as the source of the document, its title, any keywords associated with it by the author, and so forth. Such tools are often difficult to customize in order to take advantage of this valuable information.

The points below attempt to cover some of the gross features of documents and category spaces, and to examine some of their implications for classification, whether by person or machine. The degree of complexity associated with the documents and the target categories under consideration is an important indicator of both how much human expertise is needed to perform reliable classification, and how sophisticated a classification program has to be in order to be effective. It is easy to underestimate the difficulty of classification tasks from both points of view.

The human factor is also important when attempting to evaluate text categorization software. If humans find the classification task difficult, then agreement among editorial staff may be low with respect to an irreducible number of categorization decisions. Evaluating program output will be extremely difficult, if limitations of human performance set an upper bound on the perceived accuracy of the program's decisions.

Here are some important issues with respect to the data.

- *Granularity*. How many categories are we assigning to, and how finely do they divide the document space? Routing to subscribers is typically coarse-grain, in the sense that recipients are working with a small number of categories. Even in the case of a narrowly-specified information need, the categorization task is typically a binary decision, namely does this document meet the need or not?

- *Dimensionality*. How many features are we using for classification purposes? In the case where every content word in the document collection is a feature, we are trying to perform classification in a high-dimensionality space that is sparsely populated with documents. If, on the other hand, we are classifying over a controlled vocabulary of keywords, or other linguistic metadata, the dimensionality will be greatly reduced.

- *Exclusivity*. Do documents belong to only one category, or a relatively small number of categories, or a much larger number? The indexing task typically involves assigning a relatively large number of terms to a document, and this can be a somewhat harder task than simply sorting documents into disjoint classes. In between, there are hierarchical classification schemes where it may be useful to have documents appear under more than one node in the tree.

- *Topicality*. Are documents typically about one thing, or can they contain multiple topics? Multiple topics require multiple document classifications and can complicate the task considerably. In particular, it may first be necessary to segment the document by topic, a task that is just as hard as classification itself.

It helps with the task analysis to think of approaches to text categorization as lying on a continuum. At one end are totally manual procedures in which various end-users, editors, or information science professionals assign documents to some classification scheme. At the other end are fully automatic procedures, in which computer programs cluster documents, name the clusters, and arrange those clusters in some way to create a tailor-made system of categories.

These extremes are rarely met with in practice. For example, very few editorial processes now have no computer involvement, especially where electronic documents are concerned. At the same time, generating sensible categories and error-free categorizations in a wholly automatic manner is somewhere beyond the current state of the art.

In between these two poles, there are various gradations of human versus computer involvement. A good person-machine system is one that encourages people to do what they are good at (usually creating frameworks, exercising judgment and critiquing solutions) and allows machines to do what they are good at (usually enumerating alternatives, performing iterations, and generating solutions). Getting the right balance is critical to both system performance and system cost, as we shall see in Section 4.6.

There are a number of other practical considerations to do with the context in which classification tasks are performed.

–   *Document management.* Classification is only one activity typically associated with a document feed. Other activities might include data conversion (e.g., XML tagging), duplicate document detection (particularly in syndicated news feeds), and the application of domain knowledge to add further value (e.g., by writing summaries). The question then arises as to where in the process classification belongs.

–   *Concept management.* In a real-time news feed, it may be necessary to detect new topics, as well as classifying documents to existing topics. In addition, existing topics may exhibit 'drift', e.g., as a minor scandal becomes a major public issue, or a major issue loses its importance. Both problems currently necessitate an editorial effort of some kind.

–   *Taxonomy management.* Consumers of information are often interested in having materials organized in a tree-like structure for reference through searching and browsing. Creating and maintaining these topics and their organization can be a major part of the publishing process. Classification tools that also support these ancillary tasks can add significant value.

Document management vendors have typically not done a very good job of integrating text categorization software or taxonomy management tools into their offerings. It seems that it is up to the next generation of enterprise portal vendors to address this problem. Such an effort would be greatly helped by the further development and publication of industry standard taxonomies for different vertical market segments, such as insurance, human resources, medicine, and the like.

Meanwhile, text categorization research has tended to focus on news materials, rather than scientific, business or legal text.[5] A favorite data set is a publicly available Reuters collection of over 22,000 news wires, each of which has been classified by hand to one or more of 135 categories, such as GRAIN and TRADE.[6] But attempts have also been made to classify emails[7] and cluster Web pages.[8]

Researchers in text retrieval and information extraction have concentrated on a relatively small number of well-understood methods, albeit with several variations on any given theme. Text categorization, by contrast, has been attacked by a bewildering variety of techniques that are both individually complex and hard to compare. It has been pointed out that there is little consensus in the literature concerning either the absolute or relative efficacy of some of these methods. [9]

There are a number of factors that need to be considered when evaluating a text categorization system. Some of these factors concern the underlying algorithm employed, while others relate more to the process as a whole. Here are the issues that we shall raise as we proceed to examine some proposed solutions to the text categorization problem.

– *Data requirements.* Many algorithms need to be trained on data that has already been classified, as we shall see in Section 4.3. Availability of such data can be a limiting factor in attempts to automate text categorization. Both the quality and the quantity of such data can be important.

– *Scale.* Many algorithms that perform well on up to 100 categories do not scale well to larger problems, involving 1,000 or more categories. Sometimes the problem is simply performance, in terms of the computational cost involved. Other times, it is a question of accuracy, as having more categories to choose from confuses the system.

– *Mode of operation.* Many algorithms run in batch mode, i.e., training and/or test examples must be presented all together, in a single session. Other algorithms can be run incrementally, with documents being encountered one at a time, without affecting either training or test performance.

It should be stressed that it would be presumptuous of us to assume that we have all the answers with respect to how existing text categorization algorithms and systems rate with respect to these factors. In many cases, neither the research literature nor trade publications provide enough data for the drawing of definitive conclusions. However, we share such information as we have gleaned from a variety of sources, including personal experience.

Classification problems and methods overlap to some extent with those of retrieval and extraction, as we shall see. As we noted earlier, information retrieval can be regarded as solving a binary classification problem, by distinguishing between documents that are relevant to the query and those that are not. Some methods, such as Bayesian statistics (see Chapter 2, Section 2.3.3 and Section 4.3 below) have been applied to both tasks. However, information retrieval has been researched for about 40 years, while text categorization has only received intense academic attention over the last 10 years.[10] These disciplines have developed along sufficiently different lines to merit separate treatment in a text of this kind.

4.2 Handcrafted rule based methods

One obvious approach to text categorization is to perform automatic full-text indexing of incoming documents and then manually write a query for each category of interest. The documents retrieved by a given query, via a search engine, are then classified to that category. With skillful query construction, this approach can work quite well for a relatively small number of disjoint categories.

Many document routing tasks, such as news clipping, are performed in just this way. Editors (or end users) construct standing queries, which are run against a document collection or feed to produce results. The precision and recall of such a process will depend upon how skillfully the queries were constructed and on which side of the trade-off an editor (or end user) wishes to err.

Experience tells us that professional query construction by editors takes up to two days per query, if we include significant testing. A query, once derived, must be run against a representative document feed, the results must be examined, and the query must be tuned in the light of these results. This is an iterative process, and the work must be done by a domain expert.

A more sophisticated approach is to construct an *expert system* that relies upon a body of hand-written pattern-matching rules[11] to recognize key concepts in documents and assign appropriate categories or index terms to them. One such rule-based system, called Construe-TIS, assigns zero or more labels to stories for a Reuters news database.[12] It was developed by the Carnegie

Group and went into production in 1989, applying 674 distinct categories[13] to a newswire feed, as well as recognizing over 17,000 company names.

The Construe pattern language can be thought of as an embellished query language. The core of the program is a set of *concept rules* crafted to identify key concepts in text and trigger the assignment of category labels. Thus, a pattern element, such as

(gold (&n (reserve ! medal ! jewelry))

is meant to detect the word 'gold', but pass on the phrases 'gold reserve', 'gold medal', and 'gold jewelry'. The exact syntax of the pattern language is not really important. What is important is the principle of using arbitrary query-like patterns[14] to identify not documents but concepts that will then drive *categorization rules*.

The categorization rules trigger not on individual words but on concepts derived from the actual text. Thus, the rule for the category AUSTRALIAN DOLLAR, looks something like this:

```
(if
test:
        (or [australian-dollar-concept]
    and   [dollar-concept]
          [australia-concept]
          (not [us-dollar-concept])
          (not [singapore-dollar-concept])))
action: (assign australian-dollar-category))
```

Without fretting too much about parentheses and other syntax, this rule states the following principle.

If the concept rules have already detected either
1. a clear reference to the Australian dollar, or
2. references to Australia and the dollar (with no confounding references to the US dollar or the Singapore dollar),
   then it's safe to assign the AUSTRALIAN DOLLAR category.

Other refinements are possible, such as searching for concepts having occurred in particular fields of the document. We might wish to impose the rule that an article is about gold either if it exhibits the gold-concept in the headline and once in the body, or if it contains four references to the gold-concept in the body. The following Construe-type rule achieves this:

```
(if
test:
    (or (and    [gold-concept :scope headline 1]
                [gold-concept :scope body 1])
        [gold-concept :scope body 4])
action: (assign gold-category))
```

Construe was tested on a set of 723 unseen news stories, with the task of assigning them to any of 674 categories. The system accomplished this with a recall of 94% and a precision of 84%. We shall see that this level of performance is somewhat better than the best of the current machine learning programs. This is not surprising, considering that the rules were handcrafted for this particular application.[15]

However, it can readily be appreciated that the handcrafting of such rule sets is a non-trivial undertaking for any significant number of categories. The Construe project ran for about 2 years, with 2.5 person-years going into rule development for the 674 categories. (Note that this figure is consistent with the "two days per query" rule of thumb we mentioned earlier.) The total effort on the project prior to delivery to Reuters was about 6.5 person-years.

Thus there is a powerful incentive to investigate automatic methods for text categorization. These run the gamut from fully automatic statistical methods that function as "black boxes" and require no human intervention, to programs that generate legible rules automatically, for subsequent editorial review. The remainder of this chapter provides an overview of these methods, and also attempts to evaluate their utility.

4.3 Inductive learning for text classification

The main alternative to handcrafting a rule base is to use machine learning techniques to generate classifiers. The most common approach is to employ an *inductive learning* program, i.e., a program that is not itself a classifier, but is capable of learning classification rules given a set of examples encoded with respect to a feature space.[16] Such techniques are called *supervised learning* methods, since the person supplying the examples is in effect teaching the program to make the right distinctions. Supervised learning can be contrasted with mere *rote learning*, where the classification rules are simply given to the program. It is also distinct from *unsupervised learning*, where a program somehow learns without human feedback, e.g., by clustering similar documents together.

For supervised machine learning to be applicable to a classification task, the following requirements should be met:

- The classes to which data will be assigned must be specified ahead of time
- In the simplest case, these classes should be disjoint.
- When classes are not disjoint, we can transform the problem of classifying documents to n categories into n corresponding sub-problems. Each subproblem classifies documents to one of two classes, those that belong to the corresponding category and those which do not. These binary decisions are now independent of each other, since categories are no longer 'competing' for documents.

Machine learning techniques are not restricted to building text classifiers, but can also be applied to a wider range of NLP tasks for online applications. For instance, some of the approaches introduced below have been applied to spelling correction, part-of-speech tagging, and parsing. In this section, however, we will focus on only those machine learning approaches which have been successfully used for building text classifiers.

Learning programs do not work with the texts themselves, but with some surrogate, e.g., a vector whose components are features, such as words or phrases, occurring in the text. In this and other respects, the representations used for text classification are similar to those used in document retrieval. Thus a text can be represented by a document vector of the kind we discussed in Chapter 2, with binary or numeric features recording occurrences of single words or phrases.

It can readily be appreciated that such vector spaces have extremely high dimensionality, since every term defines a dimension of the space. Depending upon the nature of the texts, even single word features can generate spaces with 10^5 dimensions. Such a feature space will be extremely sparse with respect to the distribution of documents, making it difficult to construct sets of documents for training and testing classifiers. Furthermore, words are noisy features (as we have seen), since they may have more than one meaning, while documents can obviously contain asides that are not germane to the principal subject matter.

Nevertheless, there are relatively simple methods available that are quite robust, if one is willing to tolerate a certain degree of error.

4.3.1 Naïve Bayes classifiers

Suppose that you have a feed of incoming documents. You have been manually assigning each such document to a single category for some time. Thus, for each category, you have a reasonable number[17] of past documents already assigned.

Bayes' Rule
One approach to automating (or semi-automating) this process is to build statistical models of the categories you are assigning to, leveraging the assignments that you have already made. This approach assumes that you can compute, or estimate, the distribution of terms (words, bigrams, phrases, etc.) within the documents assigned to these categories. The idea is to use this term distribution to predict the class of unseen documents, but this only works under certain conditions, which we shall present, in a somewhat simplified form.

Firstly, you need to be able to transform the probability of a term occurrence given a category (which you can estimate directly from your data) into the probability of a category given a term occurrence. Secondly, you need a method to combine the evidence derived from each of the terms associated with a document or category. In other words, you know

$$P(t|C_i),$$

for each term t and category C_i, but you are really interested in

$$P(C_i|t),$$

or better yet

$$P(C_i|T_D),$$

where T_D is the set of terms occurring in document D.[18] In the following, we make no more distinction between document D and its representation as a set of terms, T_D.

As we saw in Chapter 2, the term 'Naïve Bayes' refers to a statistical approach to language modeling that uses Bayes' Rule but assumes conditional independence between features (term occurrences).

We thus compute the probability that document D belongs to a given class C_i by:

$$P(C_i|D) = \frac{P(D|C_i)P(C_i)}{P(D)}.$$

In the most common form of Naïve Bayes, we assume that the probability that a document belongs to a given class is a function of the observed frequency with which terms occurring in that document also occur in other documents known to be members of that class.

In other words, 'old' documents known to be in the class suggest both:

1. terms to look for, and
2. the term frequencies one would expect to see in 'new' documents.

The 'old' documents function as training or conditioning data, providing probability estimates upon which a statistical argument for classification of unseen data can be built.

Ignoring conditional dependencies between terms, we can use the multiplication rule to combine such probabilities. More formally, given a document, D, represented by a term vector consisting of n components or terms,

$$D = (t_1, \ldots, t_n),$$

and a class, C_i, from the range of target classes, the formula

$$P(D|C_i) = \prod_{j=1}^{j=n} P(t_j|C_i)$$

captures the assumption[19] that the probability of a term vector being generated by a document of a given class can be decomposed into a simple combination of the distribution of the terms within that class.

Before we can apply Bayes' Rule, we also need to estimate the prior probability of a particular class being any document's destination.

Suppose we had no information regarding the terms in a document, and had to make a blind guess as to where it should be classified. Clearly, we would maximize our chances of success if we assigned it to the most popular class, according to our training data. The most direct way to estimate the prior for a given category is simply to count the number of training documents occurring in that category and divide by the total number of categories.

Given a value for $P(C_i|D)$, how do we decide whether the document belongs in the class or not? Given M classes, one approach is to compute

$$P(C_i|D)$$

for all i such that $1 \leq i \leq M$, and then assign the document to the class that scores best. We can express this tersely by the formula

$$C^* = \text{argmax}_{C_i} [P(C_i|D)]$$

where C^* is the favored class, and $\text{argmax}_y[f(y)]$ selects the value of subscript argument, y, that maximizes the function of y that follows in brackets. Thus we look for a category, C_i, that maximizes the value of $P(C_i|D)$. By Bayes' Rule,

$$\text{argmax}_{C_i}[P(C_i|D)] = \text{argmax}_{C_i}[P(D|C_i) \cdot P(C_i)],$$

enabling us to plug in the probability estimates discussed above. We can omit $P(D)$ from the right hand side of this equation, since it is an invariant across classes, and will therefore have no effect upon which category is selected.

There are at least two variations on Naïve Bayes to be found in the classification literature.[20] These variations, called the *Multinomial Model* and the *Multivariate Model*, differ on how the probabilities of terms given a class are computed. One counts frequencies of term occurrences, while the other simply records the presence or absence of terms.

The Multinomial Model

We start with the Multinomial Model, which represents documents by their word occurrences, sometimes called a 'bag of words.' By 'bag' we mean that the order of the words is discounted, but that the number of occurrences is recorded.[21]

Given enough training data, we can tabulate the frequencies with which terms occurring in new, unclassified documents occur in the documents associated with the various classes. From these counts, we can estimate simple probabilities, such as the probability that a document in the class NEWS will contain the term 'merger.' We write this as

$$P(\text{'merger'}|\text{NEWS}) = \frac{\text{frequency of 'merger' in known NEWS documents}}{\text{frequency of 'merger' in all classified documents}}$$

In practice, this simple estimate of $P(\text{'merger'} \mid \text{NEWS})$ is further refined (or smoothed) to avoid zero probabilities (see Sidebar 4.1).

Sidebar 4.1 Zero probabilities and smoothing

Even if we allow ourselves to assume that term occurrences in a document, D, are independent of each other, computing the probability of a term occurring in a class as a product will not work without some further tinkering. If we have

$$P(t_j|C_i) = 0$$

for the jth term, then

$$P(D|C_i) = 0$$

and so, by Bayes' Rule,

$$P(C_i|D) = P(C_i) \times \frac{P(D|C_i)}{P(D)} = 0$$

which is not what we want.

Hence the common practice of *Laplace smoothing*, in which one or more pseudo-counts are added to all frequencies, so that they do not zero out. The new counts are normalized by the size of the total number of counts (including pseudo-counts). Consequently, in very sparse data settings, this may result in too much probability mass being taken from observed events and assigned to unobserved events. Another method is to set a small epsilon value to be used in place of zero counts.

Sidebar 4.2   Assigning to more than one category

There remains the problem of what to do when we wish to assign documents to more than one class. One method is to set a threshold, θ, and then assign document D to all classes C_i where $P(C_i|D) \geq \theta$.

A related approach is to transform a multiple label assignment problem into multiple problems of assigning a single label. Indeed, if you wanted to decide whether to assign the categories BUSINESS NEWS and SPORTS NEWS to a document, you could first decide to assign BUSINESS NEWS, and then decide to assign SPORTS NEWS, independently of the knowledge that you have already assigned BUSINESS NEWS. This approach is often referred to as 'binarization' of text classification as, for each class, we need to make a binary decision: assign the label to documents, or not.

A final method that has been used is *proportional assignment*. Roughly speaking, we aim to route to each class the same proportion of test documents that it was assigned by the training phase. So if class C_i holds 20% of the training documents, it receives $(k \times 20)\%$ of its best scoring test documents, where k is a 'proportionality constant' that we tweak to balance false positives against false negatives.

However, this method assumes that you have a large set of test documents, and that this set is drawn from the same distribution as the training data. These conditions may not be met in many common situations. A real application may encounter unseen documents one at a time, or in small batches, and there may be no guarantee that such a batch is representative of the total document feed.

The Multivariate Model

An alternative way of modeling documents is the Multivariate Model, which uses a vector of binary components that encode, for each word in the vocabulary, whether or not it occurs in the document. We do not record the frequency with which terms occur in new documents, only their presence or absence. The probability of a given document is then obtained by multiplying together the probabilities of all the components, including the probability of an absent component not occurring.

The probability of a document vector D given a class C_i is then computed along the lines of

$$P(D|C_i) = \prod_{j=1}^{j=n} (B_j P(t_j|C_i) + (1 - B_j)(1 - P(t_j|C_i)))$$

where B_j is either zero or unity, depending upon whether the jth term is present or absent in the document.[22]

Assuming again that we have a training set of m documents, $\{D_1, \ldots, D_m\}$, we can derive the following estimate for the probability of a term, t, being associated with class, C_i:

$$P(t|C_i) = \frac{1 + \sum_{k=1}^{k=m} B_k P(C_i|D_k)}{2 + \sum_{k=1}^{k=m} P(C_i|D_k)}$$

where B_k is either zero or unity, depending upon whether term t occurs in the kth document or not, and $P(C_i|D_k)$ will be either zero or unity, depending upon whether D_k is in C_i or not. The class priors, $P(C_i)$, are estimated as before. Similarly, the decision to assign a class follows the same rule as before.

Experimental results[23] suggest that the multinomial method usually out-performs the multivariate at large vocabulary sizes, or when vocabulary size is manipulated so that it is optimal for each method. The multivariate method sometimes does better on small vocabularies.

One problem with the Naïve Bayes approach is that it needs a batch of pre-classified data in order to work well. Thus, if you have a backfile of manually categorized documents, you can leverage this to automate or semi-automate the process. But lacking a store of such documents, you must first invest a significant manual effort (although see Sidebar 4.3).

Given training data, classification using Naïve Bayes is an attractive approach, because it is easy to implement. Constructing classifiers is just a matter of keeping track of term counts. Classifying a new document only relies on retrieving probabilities (or counts) from the stored model.

Sidebar 4.3 Dealing with lack of training data or sparse training data

One solution to a lack of training data is to perform a rough and ready automatic labeling on some subset of the documents in your possession, e.g., using keywords, and then attempt to improve the model by other automatic means, such as Expectation-Maximization. This EM 'bootstrapping' approach iterates between two steps:

1. *The E-step.* Calculating training class labels $P(C_i|D)$ that are now continuous weights, instead of being unity or zero.
2. *The M-step.* Plugging these weights into the formulas to estimate new parameters for the classifier.

The E- and M-steps are repeated until the classifier converges. There is some evidence[24] that this technique results in a significant improvement in classification accuracy where labeled data is in limited supply, but there is a lot of unlabeled data to work with. However, it assumes that the unlabeled documents really do belong to one or other of the categories.

Another solution is to take advantage of additional information in order to smooth the data. When documents are organized into a large number of classes, these classes are often organized in a hierarchy, which presents us with an opportunity for smoothing. We saw earlier that we can use Laplace smoothing to avoid zero probabilities when there is no class data for a given feature. *Shrinkage* is another statistical technique for smoothing that takes advantage of a hierarchy of classes. In this instance, we are trying to compensate for the fact that a given class is sparsely populated with data, in the sense of having very few training examples.

If C_i is a sparse class, the probability $\Pr(t_j|C_i)$ for each term t_j can be smoothed with the probability of t_j in the ancestor[25] classes of C_i:

$$\Pr(t_j|C_i) = \lambda_i^1 \Pr(t_j|C_i) + \lambda_i^2 \Pr(t_j|P_i^2) + \cdots + \lambda_i^k \Pr(t_j|P_i^k),$$

where P_i^k is the kth ancestor of class C_i, and λ_i^k is the weight given to the kth ancestor. These weights can be estimated using a variant of the EM algorithm.[26] It has been shown that shrinkage using a hierarchy of classes noticeably improves the performance of Naïve Bayes when there is little data at the leaves of the hierarchy.

From a practical point of view, it remains an open question as to whether such methods are better than simply having someone label more training data, assuming that this is feasible.

4.3.2 Linear classifiers*

The Naïve Bayes methods described above attempt to model the distribution of textual features within a collection of classified documents, and then use that model to classify unseen documents. The conditional probability that a document belongs to a class, given its feature vector, is calculated from two other probabilities. One is the probability of observing vectors of feature values for documents of each class. The other is the prior probability that a document will be assigned to a given class.

A second approach is the use of *linear classifiers*, in which categorizers are modeled as separators in a metric space. It assumes that documents can be sorted into two mutually exclusive classes, so that a document either belongs to a category like BUSINESS NEWS, or it does not. The classifier corresponds to a hyperplane (or a line) separating the positive examples from the negative examples. If the document falls on one side of the line, it is deemed to belong to BUSINESS NEWS; if it falls on the other side of the line, it does not. Classification error occurs when a document ends up on the wrong side of the line.

These two approaches mirror the dichotomy between Bayesian information retrieval techniques and vector space techniques that we saw in Chapter 2. As in Chapter 2, these differences may be more apparent than real, in that linear separation can be cast in terms of probability theory. But it is fair to say that the Bayesian and vector space techniques provide rather different ways of looking at the same problem, namely how to derive decision rules for classification based only upon feature values.

Linear separation in the document space

A linear separator can be represented by a vector of weights in the same feature space as the documents. The weights in the vector are learned using training data. The general idea is to move the vector of weights towards the positive examples, and away from the negative examples.

As described in Chapter 2, documents are represented as feature vectors. Just like Naïve Bayes, features are typically words from the collection of documents. Some methods have used phrasal structures, or sequence of words as features, although this is less common. The components of a document vector can be 0 or 1, to indicate presence or absence, or they can be a numeric value reflecting both the frequency of the feature in the document and its frequency in the collection. The familiar *tf-idf* weight from Chapter 2 is often used.

When we classify a new document, we look to see how close this document is to the weight vector. If the document is 'close enough', it is classified to the category. The score of this new document is evaluated by computing the dot product between the vector of weights and the document.

More formally, if a document, D, is represented as the document vector

$$\vec{d} = (d_1, d_2, \ldots, d_n),$$

and the vector of weights

$$\vec{C} = (w_1, w_2, \ldots, w_n)$$

represents the classifier for class C, then the score of document D for class C is computed by:

$$f_C(D) = \vec{d} \cdot \vec{C} = \sum_{i=1}^{n} w_i \cdot d_i.$$

The computed score is a numeric value, rather than being a binary 'yes/no' indicator of membership. How do we decide whether document D belongs to class C given that score? The most commonly used method is to set a threshold, θ.[27] Then if

$$f_C(D) \geq \theta,$$

we decide that the document is 'close enough' and assign it to the class.

How do we compute these weights in the category vector? Just as we used training data to estimate probabilities in the Naïve Bayes framework, here too, we can use a set of labeled documents to compute the weights in the category vector. This training algorithm for linear classifiers is an adaptation[28,29] of Rocchio's formulation of relevance feedback for the vector space model (see Chapter 2, Section 2.5.2).

Sidebar 4.4 Linear functions in information retrieval

Linear functions have often been used in information retrieval. In the probabilistic model introduced in Chapter 2 documents were ranked using a linear function:

$$P(D|R_Q = 1) = \sum_{t \in Q} w_{t,d} = \sum_{t \in Q} 1 \cdot w_{t,d}.$$

$R_Q = 1$ denotes that the document D is relevant to the query, Q, considered as a set of terms. In the above formula, we explicitly introduced the weights associated with query terms as either 1, when the term is present in the query, or 0, when it is absent. Weights $w_{t,d}$ are the probabilistic estimates introduced in Chapter 2, Section 2.3.3.

Similarly, the classical vector space model[30] can be recast into a linear framework. It is not surprising that these models are intimately related, or that they can be couched in probabilistic terms. As noted earlier, they are all working from the same feature data.

Rocchio's algorithm

Rocchio's approach models each category using all the documents known to be in the category. The algorithm consists of applying the formula shown below to the current weight vector, W', to produces a new weight vector, W. Typically, the first weight vector will have all zero components, unless you have prior knowledge of the class, e.g., in terms of keywords that have already been assigned.

The jth component of the new weight vector, w_j, is:

$$w_j = \alpha w_j' + \beta \frac{\sum\limits_{D \in C} d_j}{n_c} - \gamma \frac{\sum\limits_{D \notin C} d_j}{n - n_c},$$

where n is the number of training examples, C is the set of positive examples (e.g., all training documents assigned to the class BUSINESS NEWS) and n_c is the number of examples in C. d_j is the weight of the jth feature in document D. α, β and γ control the relative impact of the original weight vector, the positive examples, and the negative examples respectively.

Rocchio's algorithm is often used as a baseline in categorization experiments.[31,32] One of its drawbacks is that it is not robust when the number of negative instances grows large. In its original context, relevance feedback, Rocchio's formula was used when there were only a few positive and a few negative documents.

In a classification context, there are typically more documents that do not belong to a given class than documents that do belong to that class. Many approaches have handled this problem by setting parameters β and γ to arbitrary values. For instance, negative examples can be entirely discarded by setting γ to 0.

However, experiments have shown that a refined version of Rocchio can be as effective as more complex learning techniques.[33] This approach distinguishes between negative instances that are similar to positive examples (these instances are called near-positives) and those that are not. Other approaches[34] take advantage of a hierarchy of classes and choose the near-positives from the set of positive instances in sibling categories.

To summarize, Rocchio's algorithm is both easy to implement and efficient. Its naïve implementation is often used as a baseline. It has shown good performance when only a few positive examples are available. Furthermore, its performance can be improved by reducing the number of negative examples, and other enhancements.

On-line learning of linear classifiers

Rocchio, as described above, is a *batch learning* method, in that the entire set of labeled documents is available to the algorithm all at once, and weights can be computed directly from the set. *On-line learning* algorithms, on the other hand, encounter examples singly and adapt weights incrementally, computing small changes every time a labeled document is presented. On-line learning is particularly attractive in dynamic categorization tasks like filtering and routing, so most linear classifiers are trained with on-line algorithms.[35]

In general terms, on-line algorithms run through the training examples one at a time, updating a weight vector at each step. The weight vector after processing the ith example is denoted by

$$\vec{w}_i = (w_{i,1}, w_{i,2}, \ldots, w_{i,n}).$$

At each step, the new vector, $\vec{w}_{i+1}$, is computed from the old weight vector, $\vec{w}_i$, using training example $\vec{x}_i$ with label y_i. For all methods, the updating rule aims at promoting good features and demoting bad ones.

Once the linear classifier has been trained, we can classify new documents using $\vec{w}_{n+1}$, the final weight vector.[36] Alternatively, if we keep all weight vectors, we can use the average of these weight vectors, which was reported to be a better choice:[37]

$$\vec{w} = \frac{1}{n+1} \sum_{i=1}^{n+1} \vec{w}_i.$$

When we want to train classifiers on-line, we need to choose how and when weights are updated.

It is common to use rather simple rules for updating weights. A rule can either be additive, i.e., we add some small value to the current weight vector, or multiplicative, i.e., we multiply each weight in the vector by a small value. In each case, that small value controls how quickly the weight vector is allowed to change, and how much effect each training example has on the weight vector. Examples of approaches that use an additive rule are the perceptron[38,39] and Widrow-Hoff,[40] while examples of training algorithms using an multiplicative update rule are Winnow[39] and Exponential Gradient (EG).[40]

The number of active features, or terms, that occur in a document is far smaller than the number of terms in the whole training corpus. Updating rules typically apply to only those weights that correspond to active features in training document $\vec{x}_i$.

After each training document, we can choose to update weights or not. Some approaches (Winnow and perceptron) are mistake-driven, that is to say they update weights only when example $\vec{x}_i$ is misclassified by weight vector $\vec{w}_i$. Others (Widrow-Hoff and EG) update weights after each training example, whether it has been correctly classified or not.

We discuss only Widrow-Hoff and Winnow here, for illustrative purposes.

Widrow-Hoff

The Widrow-Hoff algorithm, also called *Least Mean Squared*, updates weights by making a small move in the direction of the gradient of the square loss,

$$(\vec{w}_i \cdot \vec{x}_i - y_i)^2.$$

It typically starts with all weights initialized to 0, although other settings are possible. It then uses the following updating rule:

$$w_{i+1,j} = w_{i,j} - 2\eta(\vec{w}_i \cdot \vec{x}_i - y_i)x_{i,j}.$$

This rule is obtained by taking the derivative of the loss function introduced above. η is the learning rate, which controls how quickly the weight vector is allowed to change, and how much effect each training example has on the weight vector.

The weight-updating rule is applied to all features, and to every example, whether the example is misclassified by the current linear classifier or not.

Winnow

There are several instantiations of Winnow. Positive Winnow[41] is a multiplicative weight-updating counterpart of the perceptron algorithm. Initially, the weight vector is set to assign equal positive numbers to all features. Then, if example $\vec{x}_i$ is incorrectly classified, weights of the active features are updated using the following rule:

If the example $\vec{x}_i$ is a positive example, then

$$w_{i+1,j} = w_{i,j} \cdot \alpha.$$

If the example $\vec{x}_i$ is a negative example, then

$$w_{i+1,j} = w_{i,j} \cdot \beta.$$

The promotion rate is $\alpha > 1$ and the demotion parameter is $0 < \beta < 1$. These parameters have a role similar to the learning rate. The above rule is a simplified version of Winnow, which assumes that features reflect the presence or absence of terms. Positive Winnow furthermore constrains weights $w_{i,j}$ to be positive.

Balanced Winnow is a variant of Winnow that allows negative weights. This version of the algorithm keeps two weights for each feature, $w_{i,j}^+$ and $w_{i,j}^-$. The overall weight of a feature is the difference between these two weights $w_{i,j}^+ - w_{i,j}^-$.

Just like in Positive Winnow, weights are initialized to some small positive value.

The algorithm updates the weights of active features only when a mistake is made, as follows:

- If the example $\vec{x}_i$ is a positive example, the positive weight is promoted and the negative one is demoted:

$$w^+_{i+1,j} = w^+_{i,j} \cdot \alpha \quad \text{and} \quad w^-_{i+1,j} = w^-_{i,j} \cdot \beta.$$

- If the example $\vec{x}_i$ is a negative example, the positive weight is demoted and the negative one promoted:

$$w^+_{i+1,j} = w^+_{i,j} \cdot \beta \quad \text{and} \quad w^-_{i+1,j} = w^-_{i,j} \cdot \alpha.$$

The overall effect of the update rule is to increase $w^+_{i,j} - w^-_{i,j}$ after a promotion and decrease it after a demotion.

Effectiveness of linear classifiers

The effectiveness of these on-line algorithms has been proved in a number of experimental studies.[35–37] Some studies have compared additive and multiplicative update rules, e.g., Winnow versus perceptron, while others have compared these methods with earlier methods, such as Rocchio. Overall, effectiveness seems to depend upon the following parameters.

- *Document representation.* Experimental results have shown that the perceptron and Balanced Winnow performed better that Positive Winnow using a simple document representation (e.g. presence/absence of terms). On the other hand, a more complex document representation using term frequency, document length normalization and feature discarding improved the performance of all three methods, and especially Positive Winnow, which compared favorably to the Perceptron.
- *Target values.* Target values have been shown to impact performance. Target values are the values, y_i, representing the class membership of examples, $\vec{x}_i$. These values are typically set to 0 when $\vec{x}_i$ does not belong to the class, and to 1 when $\vec{x}_i$ is a member of the class. Experiments[42] have shown that this is not always the best setting.
- *Learning rate.* The learning rate is usually set by trial and error.

To summarize, on-line learning of linear classifiers produces adaptive classifiers, i.e., classifiers that can learn on the fly. These classifiers are very simple, but effective and easy to train. Update rules are also simple and efficient, although a complex document representation may use a lot of space.

4.3.3 Decision trees and decision lists

Naïve Bayes and linear classifiers model documents using a relatively large, fixed set of features, typically represented as vectors. Naïve Bayes looks at the distribution of terms, either with respect to their frequency or with respect to their presence or absence. Linear classifiers assume the existence of a multidimensional feature space, and membership in a class is determined by determining document's position in that space, based on feature weights.

Decision trees
A quite different approach is to construct a tree that incorporates just those feature tests needed to discriminate between objects of different classes. The unique root can be thought of as representing the universe of all objects to be categorized. A non-terminal node of the tree is a decision point that tests a feature and chooses a branch that corresponds to the value of the result.

A classification decision is then a sequence of such tests terminating in the assignment of a category corresponding to a leaf node of the tree. Leaf nodes represent the categories non-uniquely, i.e., there may be more than one leaf node with the same category label, with the path from the root to that leaf representing a distinct sequence of tests. It turns out that such trees can be formed by an inductive learning technique, based on a training set of preclassified documents and their features.

A simple example will help illustrate the general structure of decision trees, and their use in document categorization.

In Figure 4.1, we have a decision tree on the topic of whether or not a case law document is about bankruptcy, given the presence of a few words or phrases. The leaf nodes 'P' and 'N' stand for positive and negative judgments about this. The features and their possible values are given in Table 4.1. Note that feature values are intended to be both discrete[43] and mutually exclusive.

The decision tree in Figure 4.1 says that the document should contain the term 'bankruptcy', but also adds some further conditions. If 'bankruptcy' occurs only once, we insist that the term 'conversion' be present more than once. If 'bankruptcy' occurs more than once, we only require that the term 'assets' be present.

A decision tree therefore encodes an algorithm that states, for any conjunction of test outcomes along a valid path from the root, what the outcome

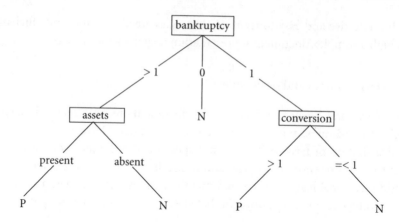

Figure 4.1 A decision tree for the 'bankruptcy' example

should be. Paths through the tree exhaust the space of alternatives, so that all objects find their way to a leaf node, and are so classified. As we shall see, it is also possible to decode such a tree into an ordered set of rules that encodes an equivalent decision procedure.

Note that the decision tree method characterizes a data object, such as a document, in terms of a logical combination of features, which is simply a statement about that object's attributes, and does not involve any numeric computation. In text categorization applications, these features are most likely to be stemmed words. This is quite different from representing a document as a vector of weighted features, and then performing a numeric computation to see if some combination of feature weights meets a threshold. Consequently, decision tree classifiers do not have to learn such thresholds, or other parameter values. What they learn is essentially a set of rules defined over a space of keywords.

A typical training algorithm for constructing decision trees (let's call it CDT) can be sketched as the following recursive function.

Table 4.1 Features and their values

Feature	Possible values
Bankruptcy	number of occurrences
Conversion	number of occurrences
Assets	present, absent

CDT(Node, Cases)

if Node contains no Cases, **then halt,**

else if the Cases at Node are all of the same class, **then** the decision tree for Node is a leaf identifying that class,

    else if Node contains Cases belonging to a mixture of classes,

    then choose a test and partition Cases into subsets based on the outcome, creating as many Subnodes below Node as there are subsets, and call CDT on each Subnode and its subset of Cases,

    else halt.

The main issue in the implementation of such an algorithm is how the program chooses the feature test that partitions the cases. Different systems have used different criteria, e.g., the ID3 decision tree program uses a measure of information gain, selecting the most 'informative' test.[44] The test that gains the most information is simply the test that most reduces the classification uncertainty associated with the current set of cases. Uncertainty is maximal when classes are evenly represented across the current set of cases, and minimal when the cases are all of the same class. We discuss this notion of 'information gain' in more detail in the next section.

We mentioned earlier that a decision tree can be considered as a set of rules, since each path between the root and a leaf node specifies a set of conjoined conditions upon the outcome at the leaf. Going down the left hand side of the tree in Figure 4.1, we find the positive outcome at the left-most leaf depends upon the term 'bankruptcy' occurring more than once, and the term 'assets' being present. We can write this rule as follows.

    if bankruptcy > 1 & assets = present

    then positive

Alternatively, we can consider all the different ways in which we can reach a positive leaf, and render these test conditions in *disjunctive normal form* (DNF) as a disjunction of conjunctions. There are two disjuncts in our Figure 4.1 example, because there are just two conditions under which a document is classified as being about bankruptcy.

    if bankruptcy > 1 & assets = present

    ∨

    bankruptcy = 1 & conversion > 1

    then positive

    else negative.

A complex rule like this can also be expressed as two simpler rules, each with a single conjoined condition. These rules are implicitly ordered, with the first rule whose conditions are satisfied making the decision. If no positive rule has its conditions satisfied, then the outcome is negative. Such rules are sometimes called *decision rules*.[45]

> **if** bankruptcy > 1 & assets = present
> **then** positive
>
> **if** bankruptcy = 1 & conversion > 1
> **then** positive
>
> **else** negative.

One of the most popular decision tree programs, C4.5, allows the user to compile the tree into a set of rules in this way.[46]

For an approach based on decision trees, or decision rules, to be applicable to a classification problem, the following requirements should be met.

- Decision-tree methods work best with large data sets. Training sets that are too small will lead to *overfitting*.[47]
- The data must be in a regular attribute-value format. Thus each datum must be capable of being characterized in terms of a fixed set of attributes and their values, whether symbolic, ordinal or continuous. Continuous values can be tested by thresholding.

Assuming that they are applicable, decision tree methods can have a number of advantages over more conventional statistical methods.

- They make no assumptions about the distribution of the attribute values (e.g., that they are normally distributed).
- They do not assume the conditional independence of attributes (as would be required by Naïve Bayes classifiers).

Studies[48] have shown that tree-based classifiers can perform on a par with most other text categorization methods for feature sets of moderate size. However, decision trees do not have to use all the available features, since not all features will make a contribution to the training phase. Nevertheless, it is worth removing stop words from the feature set, to prevent accidental distributions of such words attaining significance.

Decision lists
Decision lists are like the decision rules we encountered in the last subsection, except that they are strictly ordered and contain only Boolean conditions. Thus we can test for the presence or absence of word features, but not for features that have more than two values, unless they can be cascaded, or otherwise reduced, to a Boolean form. Various interesting results have been proved for bounded decision lists, including polynomial complexity.[49]

The best known application of decision lists to text categorization is a tool called RIPPER,[50] which classifies documents based solely on the presence or absence of words in the text. A decision list for a document, D, with respect to a category, C, is essentially a list of rules of the form,

if $w_1 \in D$ & ... & $w_n \in D$ then $D \in C$,

e.g.,

if 'bankruptcy' $\in$ Document & 'conversion' $\in$ Document & 'assets' $\in$ Document
then Document $\in$ BANKRUPTCY.

where BANKRUPTCY denotes the category of documents about bankruptcy. Since the role of the document can be understood, we shall write such a rule as:

if 'bankruptcy' & 'conversion' & 'assets' then BANKRUPTCY.

RIPPER is a 'non-linear' classifier, because the rules that it constructs test for combinations of terms, instead of weighing the contribution of individual terms without regard to their context of occurrence.[51]

Learning a category in RIPPER consists of first building a rule set (training phase) and then optimizing it (pruning phase). Given a set of positive and negative examples for the category, we use two-thirds of the data to build the rule set, and set aside the remaining one-third for the optimization process.

The training phase proceeds roughly as follows. Starting with a rule with no conditions, such as

if $\emptyset$ then BANKRUPTCY,

we grow the rule in stages, by adding conditions which identify positive instances of the concept. Thus

if 'bankruptcy' then BANKRUPTCY,

might identify some positive instances of the category, but also identify some negative instances, i.e., documents which are not primarily about bankruptcy, even though they contain the word.

Adding 'assets' to the rule might rule out some of those negative instances, yielding

> if 'bankruptcy' & 'assets' then BANKRUPTCY.

Two questions about this process may already have occurred to the reader:

- how does RIPPER decide which conditions to add, and
- how does it know when to stop?

At each stage, RIPPER seeks to maximize the *information gain*, given by

$$p' \cdot \left(-\log_2 \frac{p}{p+n} + \log_2 \frac{p'}{p'+n'} \right),$$

where p is the number of positive examples in the training set covered by the existing rule, and n is the number of negative examples so covered. p' (respectively n') represents the number of positive (respectively negative) examples covered by the new rule, formed by adding a condition.

The ratios represent the precision of each rule, and estimate its probability of success on unseen data. The log ratios represent the concept of information,[52] defined in terms of probabilities, so summing the logs is equivalent to multiplying the probabilities. The logarithms are base 2, because information is typically measured in terms of binary decisions, or bits.

Adding conditions to a rule continues until either

- no negative examples are covered by the rule, or
- no condition can be found which would result in information gain.

As soon as a rule has stopped growing, it is pruned. Thus the rule growing and rule pruning steps alternate as the rule set is built. Pruning involves deleting conditions from a rule to make it more general and avoid overfitting.

During pruning, the rule is considered in the context of the *pruning set*, not the training set. In choosing conditions to delete, we seek to maximize the expression

$$\frac{p'' - n''}{p'' + n''},$$

where p'' is the number of positive examples in the pruning set covered by the rule, and n'' is the number of negative examples so covered.

After pruning, all the positive examples covered by a rule are removed from the training set. Thus RIPPER requires that information gain be non-zero, and therefore stops adding rules when there are no positive examples left to classify.[53] The net result is a 'covering' or partitioning of the documents in the training set into mutually exclusive categories.

Another feature of RIPPER is that it allows the user to specify a 'loss ratio', which balances the cost of a false positive error against a false negative error.[54] In many applications, the cost of assigning a text to the wrong category might be greater than the cost of not assigning it to the correct category. For example, blatantly misclassified documents in a news feed might undermine a consumer's confidence in the feed. Numerical classifiers like Naïve Bayes or linear classifiers can make this trade-off by choosing similarity thresholds, i.e., high thresholds bias the system towards false negatives, while low thresholds bias the system towards false positives. RIPPER implements the loss ratio concept by manipulating the weights assigned to these different kinds of error during the pruning and optimization stages of the learning algorithm.

RIPPER has been shown to be an efficient learning program and an effective text classifier. Its performance scales almost linearly with the number of training examples, and its error rates compare favorably with other rule induction programs, such as C4.5,[55,56] and show modest improvements over approaches based on Rocchio's classifier.[57] Thus Thompson[55] found that RIPPER outperformed both C4.5 and a k-nearest-neighbor algorithm in assigning legal cases to 40 broad topical categories, such as BANKRUPTCY and TRANSPORTATION.

However, RIPPER is not available as a commercial system, and has not been used much outside of the research community. Although it scales well to large numbers of examples, one doubts that it would scale to a large number of categories. Most of the results in the research literature are derived from experiments in which documents are assigned across a few hundred categories. There are very few systems that have been applied to problems of a thousand or more categories, and those that have[58] rely upon editorial post-processing to tidy up the assignments.

Although decision trees and rules may not scale to a large number of categories, they remain attractive for some applications because they express classification rules explicitly, for instance:

If 'bankruptcy' and 'assets' then BANKRUPTCY.

With a limited number of categories, it is possible to learn classification rules automatically, but then refine these rules manually to better fit a given task.

Refining these rules, however, requires some understanding of how they are applied.

4.4 Nearest Neighbor algorithms

Naïve Bayes or linear classifiers learn through induction: they build an explicit model of the class by examining training data. The same can be said of decision tree and decision list classifiers, such as C4.5 and RIPPER. However, there is another kind of classifier that does not learn in this way.

'Nearest Neighbor' classifiers rely on rote learning. At training time, a Nearest Neighbor classifier 'memorizes' all the documents in the training set and their associated features. Later, when classifying a new document, D, the classifier first selects the k documents in the training set that are closest to D, then picks one or more categories to assign to D, based on the categories assigned to the selected k documents.

To define a k-NN (k-Nearest Neighbors) classifier, we first need to define the distance metric used to measure how close two documents are to each other. We could use the Euclidean distance between documents in the vector space, or we can use one of the measures defined in Chapter 2. Recall that search engines measure how relevant a document is to a given query by measuring how similar the query and the document are. Not surprisingly, we can use the same similarity metrics to measure the distance between pairs of documents, for instance the INQUERY[59] and the cosine similarity measures.[60]

Next, we need to define how to assign categories to a document, given the categories assigned to its k nearest neighbors. A simple approach to assigning a single class per document is to take the majority class among the k nearest neighbors. Multiple class assignment could be achieved by taking the top two or three best represented classes among the neighbors, but this may be overly simplistic.

A more sophisticated approach to both single and multiple class assignment is to use a distance-weighted version of k-NN, so that the further a neighbor is from the document D, the less it contributes in the decision to assign that neighbor's category, C_j. This preference can be expressed by computing scores for each potential class along the following lines of:

$$Sc(C_j, D) = \sum_{D_i \in Tr_k(D)} sim(D, D_i) \cdot a_{i,j}.$$

$Sc(C_j, D)$ is the score of class C_j for document D, $Tr_k(d)$ is the set of the k nearest neighbors of document D, $sim(D, D_i)$ is the similarity measure between documents, while $a_{i,j} = 1$ if document D_j is assigned to class C_j, and 0 otherwise.[61]

Applying this to binary classification, the best scoring class might differ from the majority class. In the multiple assignment case, we simply adopt a cut-off strategy[62] for assigning categories based on their scores, just as we did for assigning multiple classes with Naïve Bayes.

The last choice, the selection of k, remains mostly empirical.[59,60] It is usually computed on a validation set, i.e., a set of documents distinct from both training and test sets. In general, the value of k depends upon two things.

– How close the classes are in the feature space. The closer the classes, the smaller k should be.
– How typical the training documents are in a given class. If they are very heterogeneous, then a larger k is appropriate to ensure a representative sample.

Experimentally, k-NN classifiers have been shown to be very effective classifiers. Training k-NN classifiers is fast, because all one needs to do is store the documents represented as vectors of features. On the other hand, classification is not so fast, because a fair amount of computation is required to match documents against each other.

But they can still be reasonably efficient, and may be worth considering if the number of categories is large, since k-NN classifiers are document-centric, rather than category-centric. That is to say, a document is presented once, and multiple categories can be assigned, based solely on its neighbors. In this context, classifying a document requires N similarity computations, where N is the size of the training set. By contrast, Naïve Bayes and linear classifiers are category-centric, in that documents are matched against to each category. This requires M similarity computations, where M is the number of categories to assign.

Thus the attractiveness of k-NN depends upon the relative efficiency with which one can compare document vectors to category vectors, versus the cost of finding similar documents. If the documents to be categorized are quite short, e.g., abstracts or summaries, it may even be worthwhile to run them as queries against a collection of previously classified documents, using a ranked retrieval engine. The top k documents in the result list can then suggest classifications for the new document.

4.5 Combining classifiers

Individual text categorization programs often perform very unevenly across the target categories. Some categories will exhibit high recall, while others will have much lower recall scores, and similarly with precision. Some category pairs will be highly confusable, while others will be well separated in the space.

Consequently, it makes sense to try and combine different algorithms, in the hope that together they will provide better performance. Approaches that combine the judgments of multiple experts (classifiers, retrieval systems, etc.) have received a lot of attention in Artificial Intelligence,[63] Machine Learning[64] and Information Retrieval[65] over the last ten years.

4.5.1 Data fusion

The combination of classifiers in text categorization derives in part from concepts in Information Retrieval. The term 'data fusion' refers to the combining of search results retrieved from the same corpus by different mechanisms. These mechanisms may be known only through the list of documents they retrieve (i.e., they are typically used as "black boxes"). For instance, meta-search engines on the Web, such as MetaCrawler,[66] are faced with the data fusion problem of integrating search results from multiple search engines.

Experimental studies of data fusion have combined various representation schemes (terms and phrases for instance), various weighting instantiations of the same retrieval model (weighting schemes in the Vector Space Model), various (manual) formulations of the same information need,[67] and the outputs of different search engines.[68] A main issue is to decide how to combine multiple result sets. This requires choosing a combination model, and setting the parameters required by that model. In general, the model is selected manually, i.e., the systems designer decides to rely on simple averaging, or on a linear combination.

However, it is possible to set these model parameters (e.g., the weights in a linear combination) automatically using training data. For instance, Bartell et al.[69] rely on a linear combination, and derive the parameters using numerical optimization. They optimized the parameters using the squared error, and a measure derived from rank statistics and correlated to the retrieval performance measure used (average precision). This study emphasizes that the model parameters should be optimized using a function related to the performance measure used to evaluate the retrieval system.

Finally, recent studies have focused upon predicting when combined retrieval systems will work better than the individual systems. For instance, linearly combining two retrieval systems can improve overall performance, if the overlap of relevant documents is maximized, while the overlap of non-relevant documents is minimized.[70] Similar approaches have been taken to combine classifiers for binary text classification and text filtering tasks.[71]

In assigning medical codes to inpatient discharge summaries, one approach investigated linearly combining k-Nearest Neighbor, Naïve Bayes and Rocchio classifiers[72] using two different scoring methods. The first method relied on the (inverse) rank of a given category (categories were assumed to be ranked by the various classifiers). The other method normalized scores between 0 and 1. The score assigned by k-nearest neighbor was divided by k, while the score assigned by the Naïve Bayes classifier was divided by the maximal score for that category. The combination weights were tuned using a small validation set.

The conclusions drawn from this study were that using the normalized scores was superior to using the ranks, and that the combination of any two classifiers using normalized scores was always superior to the individual classifiers. Additionally, experimental results showed that a less effective classifier helped improve the effectiveness of the combination when its behavior (e.g., good precision at low recall) complemented the behavior of the other classifier (e.g., good precision at high recall).

4.5.2 Boosting

Boosting is a method that generates many simple "rules of thumb",[73] and then attempts to combine them into a single, more accurate rule for binary classification problems. A rule of thumb may be, for instance:

> If the word 'money' appears in the document, then predict that the document is relevant to the INVESTMENT class, otherwise predict that the document is not relevant.

A novel feature of boosting is that it associates weights with training documents. (The previous methods that we have examined treated each training document in the same way.) The training process is incremental, and proceeds as follows.

The boosting algorithm is an iterative one of R rounds, where a rule of thumb is derived from the training data at each round, using a weak learner. The method maintains a set of weights over training instances and labels so that, as boosting progresses, training examples and corresponding labels that are hard to predict get higher weights, while examples and their labels that are easy to predict get lower weights. New rules of thumb are generated as the weak learner takes into account that it is more important to classify documents with a higher weight. As a consequence, at any given round, the weak learner concentrates on hard documents, i.e., documents that were misclassified by the previously derived rules of thumb.

A rule of thumb is derived as follows. All words and bigrams (sequences of two words) are considered as potential terms. For each term, the weak learner computes the error generated by predicting that a document is relevant (should be assigned to the class) if and only if it contains that term. The term that minimizes the classification error is selected for that round, and the rule of thumb tests for the presence of that term.

The final combined rule classifies a new document by computing the value of each rule of thumb on this document and taking a weighted vote of these predictions of the form

$$ h_{final}(D_i) = \text{sign} \left(\sum_{r=1}^{R} \alpha_r h_r(D_i) \right), $$

where h_{final} is the combined hypothesis, h_s the rule-of-thumb at round r, and α_s its associated weight, while D_i is the new document.

Various suggestions have been made as to how rules of thumb, updating factors, and initial weights should be computed[74] in order to minimize classification error. For example, experimental studies have followed two different approaches to decide the number of rounds, R. The first simply fixes the number of rounds *a priori*, while the second relies on classification error on the training set to decide when to stop.

In a machine learning context, boosting has been successfully applied to more complex learners, such as decision trees. Using some dimensionality reduction techniques (described in Sidebar 4.5), boosting decision trees has been shown more effective than using stand-alone decision trees.[75] However, boosting even weak classifiers, like simple predictors based on the presence of a term or a sequence of terms, has been proven an effective technique for text classification and filtering.[76]

Boosting as we have presented it so far applies to binary classification tasks. The Boostexter system[77] has extended the approach to handle multi-class and multi-label problems. Multi-class refers to choosing a class among a set of classes, while multi-label refers to the assignment of multiple classes to the same document. The Boostexter system also expanded boosting to support ranking, i.e. labels are assigned in ranked order to documents. Boostexter has shown very good performance in a variety of text classification tasks, while boosting has also been applied successfully to the routing task.[78]

Sidebar 4.5 Dimensionality reduction

In any large collection of documents, there are tens of thousands of unique terms, and the number of phrases is even larger. However, not all terms are useful to distinguish between two classes. For instance, words like 'the' or 'and' will occur in every document. The word 'sport' may not help separating documents about FOOTBALL or BASEBALL. However, the term 'sport' is a pretty good indicator of the SPORT category, compared with other categories, such as STOCKS or TRAVEL. We can see that some words are more useful for a given classification task than others. Feature selection[79] focuses on finding these very words.

When feature selection is global, all classes are described using the same features. In that case, terms like 'the' and 'and' will be eliminated, but the term 'sport' may be kept. An alternative is local feature selection, which retains words that characterize a given category from the other categories in the classification task. As a result, the term 'sport' may be eliminated from the feature set used to describe FOOTBALL or BASEBALL, but kept to describe OLYMPIC GAMES. Terms are selected based on a numerical criterion that measures the association between categories and terms, usually statistical or information-theoretic measures.[80]

One very simple measure is document frequency. Only the most frequent terms are selected. Of course, before applying the criterion, we need to remove stopwords. Document frequency has mostly been used as a global selection criterion.

Another measure is the information gain, the same measure used to select a test when constructing decision trees or decision rules. Information gain is usually used as a local selection criterion, but can be adapted to be global.

Finally, χ^2 has been used as a local selection criterion. χ^2 is a common statistic that measures the lack of independence between variables. When we select features, the variables are terms and categories.

4.5.3 Using multiple classifiers

Boosting combines simple rules of thumb, but it is also possible to combine the results of multiple classifiers, by a more direct analogy with data fusion. A recent approach exploited distinct sets of features to address a hard categorization problem and successfully implemented a complex combination strategy.[81] The task was to assign headnotes (summaries of points of law) to sections of an analytical law publication. The multi-volume publication contains over 13,500 sections, each of which addresses a particular factual situation and is considered to be a category.

The program leveraged two different kinds of data associated to legal cases: the text of the headnotes themselves and key numbers[82] associated with these headnotes.

A headnote on the topic of ADMINISTRATIVE LAW AND PROCEDURE is shown below, together with its associated key number and hierarchical topic labels:

> In an action brought under Administrative Procedure Act (APA), inquiry is twofold: court first examines the organic statute to determine whether Congress intended that an aggrieved party follow a particular administrative route before judicial relief would become available; if that generative statute is silent, court then asks whether an agency's regulations require recourse to a superior agency authority.
> Key number: 15AK229 – ADMINISTRATIVE LAW AND PROCEDURE – SEPARATION OF ADMINISTRATIVE AND OTHER POWERS – JUDICIAL POWERS

The topical hierarchy is about seven layers deep and slanted towards legal concepts, such as negligence, whereas the publication to be supplemented consists of relatively flat sections that address specific fact patterns, such as leakage from underground storage tanks. Thus the match between the two is inexact, with respect to both structure and content. Furthermore, the section headings are rather fine-grained, representing quite narrow points of law that are easily confused, e.g.,

> ADEQUACY OF DEFENSE CONSEL'S REPRESENTATION OF CRIMINAL CLIENT REGARDING POST-PLEA REMEDIES.
>
> ADEQUACY OF DEFENSE CONSEL'S REPRESENTATION OF CRIMINAL CLIENT REGARDING GUILTY PLEAS.
>
> ADEQUACY OF DEFENSE CONSEL'S REPRESENTATION OF CRIMINAL CLIENT REGARDING PLEA BARGAINING.
>
> ADEQUACY OF DEFENSE CONSEL'S REPRESENTATION OF CRIMINAL CLIENT REGARDING SEARCH AND SEIZURE ISSUES.

The headnotes to be classified were represented by word features, as one might expect, but not just by individual words. One set of features consisted of all nouns, noun-noun, noun-verb and noun-adjective pairs present in headnotes. The second set consisted of key numbers associated with the headnotes.

Sections were modeled by similar features extracted from headnotes already assigned to them. This was found to be more effective than modeling the text of the sections themselves. These features were each used separately by two different classifiers, a Naïve Bayes classifier and a vector space classifier based on *tf-idf*, generating a total of four classifiers for each category.

For each section of the publication, the final score of a document was estimated by a linear combination of the scores of the individual classifiers. A headnote was then assigned to the section as a supplement, if that score exceeded a learned threshold. The weights and the threshold were parameters of the combination model, different for each classifier-class combination. Thus, for a problem involving m classes, the system would have $4m$ weights and m thresholds.

The combination of four classifiers on the headnote routing task outperformed each individual classifier, since both the different features and the different classification methods had different coverages of the data. The resulting program, called CARP for 'Classification And Routing Program', is now in production, performing regular semi-automatic supplementation of a legal encyclopedia. We discuss the evaluation of this system further in Section 4.6.4, where we attempt to decide how the utility of such programs should be assessed in practice.

4.6 Evaluation of text categorization systems

The methodology for evaluating a text classifier depends upon the task that the program is trying to perform, according to the analysis of tasks we provided in Section 4.1. Routing, filtering and categorization may each require different evaluation metrics that better reflect the task. For example, some routing tasks might place a premium on recall, if every document has to be sent somewhere. By contrast, a filtering task might want to emphasize precision, if the purpose of the filter is to alert a user to some event, or to prevent a user from seeing certain kinds of document.

4.6.1 Evaluation studies

When the Text REtrieval Conference[83] (TREC) started in 1992, its purpose was to provide the infrastructure necessary for large-scale evaluation of retrieval methodologies. However, there was an interest in evaluating a kind of categorization task, from the very beginning.

In the first year, TREC included two main tasks: "ad hoc" and routing.

- In the *ad hoc* task, unseen queries are being run against a static set of seen documents. This task is similar to how a researcher might use a search engine to find information.
- In the *routing* task, seen queries representing category profiles are run, but against a collection of unseen documents. This is more similar to the task performed by news clipping services.

While ad hoc and routing are distinct tasks, TREC followed the same evaluation protocol. For both tasks, relevance judgments were gathered using a pooling method,[84] and evaluation metrics included recall and precision.

Later on, the 4th TREC introduced *filtering* as a separate track. Routing was designed to be similar to ad hoc search, inasmuch as it was presented as a batch process, run on an entire collection of new documents, with routing results ordered by rank. Filtering, on the other hand, is more like an alert service, which selects incoming documents and forwards them to a user.

Filtering was therefore designed as a binary classification task for each topic, which required documents to be classified as they appeared. These requirements led to the introduction of new evaluation strategies that simulate immediate distribution of the filtered documents.[85] Given a topic, an incoming stream of documents, and possibly a small historical collection of relevant and non-relevant documents, systems were asked to construct a query profile and a filtering function that would make the binary decision to either accept or reject each new document as it is read from a feed.

Two years later, the 6th TREC introduced a sub-track, called *adaptive filtering*, which became the main filtering track in the subsequent conferences.[86] Adaptive filtering differs from filtering in that there is no historical collection of relevant and non-relevant documents for a given topic. However, a binary relevance judgment is provided for some of the filtered documents. This relevance information can be used adaptively to update both the filtering profile and the filtering function. So learning now occurs incrementally, as classifications are performed.

Other classification tasks from Section 4.1, e.g., indexing and sorting, have not been evaluated in such controlled evaluation studies. At first, classification approaches were mostly evaluated on proprietary data using common evaluation techniques, as they were centered on a given task.[87] Over the years, however, several collections of documents have become available to everyone, and classifiers can now be evaluated on the same set of documents and classes.

Among these collections, the most widely used is the Reuters collection,[88] a collection of news wire stories classifiers under categories related to economics.

Other frequently used collections include the OHSUMED collection,[89] the Associated Press (AP) news collection,[90] and the 20 Newsgroups collection.[91] The OHSUMED collection is composed of titles and abstracts of medical journal articles, where categories are posted terms of the MESH thesaurus. The AP collection consists of about 40 million words of newswires from 1989 and 1990, and was originally restricted to TREC[92] participants. The 20 Newsgroups collection was extracted from Usenet news groups; documents are messages posted to Usenet groups, and categories the news groups themselves.

For many academic studies, evaluations are equated to the comparison of a newly proposed method with previously published results, or more rarely, to the controlled comparison of several methods.[93] To conduct such evaluation studies, a common collection is necessary. However, a common collection does not ensure that results will be comparable. Indeed, previously published results may not use the same performance metrics, nor the same variant of the collection.

For instance, early results using the Reuters collection were reported using one metric, while later ones used another. More importantly, the set of documents and categories were not always kept constant across experiments. Indeed, there are at least 6 different variants of the Reuters collection. A comparative study by Yang[94] argues that results using Reuters-22173 ModLewis cannot be directly compared to any other results, but that results achieved using any of the other Reuters collections can be compared.[95]

4.6.2 Evaluation metrics

The performance metrics typically used in IR were the first metrics to be applied to the evaluation of text classifiers. Let us first address the problem of evaluating whether a given class is correctly assigned, i.e., the evaluation of a binary classifier.

Evaluating the performance of a binary classifier

The performance of classification systems is frequently evaluated in terms of effectiveness. Effectiveness metrics for a binary classifier rely on a 2×2 contingency table, similar to the one introduced in Chapter 2, Section 2.5.2, Table 2.4. TP_i denotes 'true positives', FP_i denotes 'false positives', FN_i denotes 'false negatives', and TN_i denotes 'true negatives.'

Table 4.2 Contingency table reflected the assignments performed by a binary classifier

Category c_i	Expert assigns YES	Expert assigns NO	Total
Classifier assigns YES	TP_i	FP_i	m_i
Classifier assigns NO	FN_i	TN_i	$N - m_i$
Total	n_i	$N - n_i$	N

Recall and precision have been adapted to text classification. Precision is the proportion of documents for which the classifier correctly assigned category c_i and is given by

$$P_i = \frac{TP_i}{m_i}.$$

Recall is the proportion of target document correctly classified and is given by:

$$R_i = \frac{TP_i}{n_i}.$$

Recall and precision are complements of one another, as we saw in Chapter 2. In fact, there is a trade-off between both measures: 100% recall can be achieved by always assigning every category to every document, in which case precision can be very low. As a result, it seems more appropriate to evaluate a classifier in terms of a combined measure that depends on both precision and recall.

Three main measures have been proposed: 11-point average precision, break-even point and the F_β measure.

– The *11-point average precision* metric is an IR metric and relies on ranking. Its value is the average of precision points taken at the fixed recall values:

  0.0, 0.1, 0.2, ..., 0.9, 1.0

  This measure has typically been used for the routing task. The use of the 11-point average precision is limited to systems that rank documents for a given category, or to systems that rank categories for a given document. In the latter case, classifiers may not be binary, i.e., the categories must not be mutually exclusive.

– The *break-even point* is the value at which recall equals precision. The break-even point is often interpolated from the closest recall and precision values. The break-even point was one of the first combined metric introduced. It has later been argued that the break-even point metric reflects more the properties of the recall-precision curve, rather than the performance of a given classifier.

- The F_β measure[96] is given by:

$$F_\beta = \frac{(\beta^2 + 1) \cdot P_i \cdot R_i}{\beta^2 \cdot P_i + R_i},$$

where $0 \leq \beta \leq \infty$ may be interpreted as the relative importance given to recall and precision. While a typical value for β is 1, other values may be used to bias the evaluation towards conservative or liberal assignments.

The TREC-9 filtering track has introduced a precision-oriented metric to evaluate adaptive filtering. This metric, called T9P, sets a *target number* of documents to be retrieved over the period of the simulation. This situation corresponds roughly with the cases where a user indicates what sort of volume he or she is prepared to see.

$$T9P_i = \frac{TP_i}{\max(T, m_i)},$$

where T is the target number, TP_i denotes 'true positives', as in Table 4.2.

Because text classifiers can be constructed using machine learning techniques, machine learning criteria such as the accuracy of the classifier, or the number of errors performed by the classifier, have sometimes been used to measure effectiveness. Accuracy is given by:

$$Acc_i = \frac{TP_i + TN_i}{N},$$

where TN_i denotes 'true negatives', as in Table 4.2.

However, such an accuracy measure has some limitations for the evaluation of text classifiers. A classifier that never makes a positive assignment to a class can have a higher accuracy than other non-trivial classifiers. As an alternative to accuracy, the number of errors ($FP_i + FN_i$) has sometimes been used.

Some evaluation measures are not strictly measuring effectiveness, but rather the utility of a classifier, by capturing the notion of gain and loss for a correct decision. Such measures have sometimes been put forward as an alternative to recall and precision in IR. A major change of emphasis came with the evaluation protocol for the TREC filtering track[85], in which utility measures were the evaluation measures of choice. Utility associates a gain (or a loss) to the cells in the contingency tables in Table 4.2.

Linear utility measures have been frequently used, and can be defined as follows:

$$U_i = \lambda_{TP} \cdot TP_i + \lambda_{FP} \cdot FP_i + \lambda_{TN} \cdot TN_i + \lambda_{FN} \cdot FN_i.$$

Examples of utility measures used for the TREC filtering track are

$$U_1 = TP_i - 3 \cdot FP_i,$$

and

$$U_3 = 3 \cdot TP_i - FP_i.$$

One can imagine a scenario where a user is willing to pay \$1 for each relevant document, but loses \$3 for each non-relevant document he reads. This corresponds to the utility U_1, which encourages high precision. In contrast U_3 encourages recall. While these two measures take into account only the documents accepted by the system, it is possible to take into account rejected documents. For instance, the following measure was used during TREC-6:

$$F_2 = 3 \cdot TP_i - FP_i - FN_i.$$

Utility measures may not be the best measures to evaluate the performance of filtering systems. First, utility measures are not normalized. It is therefore difficult to compare scores across topics (or categories). Second, all documents are considered equal, no matter how many documents have been seen by the system before, or how many documents are relevant to the topic. One way to address this second point is to use non-linear utility measures.

For instance, the following utility measure was used at TREC-8:

$$NF_1 = 6 \cdot TP_i^{0.5} - FP_i.$$

An interesting fact about linear utility functions is that they can translate into a threshold on the estimated probability of relevance.[97] If our text classifier computes accurate estimates of probability of relevance, we can derive the optimal thresholds for a given utility measure (for instance, U_1 corresponds to a conservative threshold of 0.75, while U_3 corresponds to liberal threshold of 0.25).

Evaluating the performance of a classification system
Until now, effectiveness and utility were measured for a single category. A classification system may handle hundreds of categories. How do we report the overall performance of such a system?

Two averaging methods have been adopted: micro- and macro-averaging.[98] *Micro-averaging* sums up all the individual decisions into a global contingency table (similar to Table 4.2) and computes recall and precision on the "global" contingency table:

$$P^{\mu} = \frac{\sum_{i=1}^{c} TP_i}{\sum_{i=1}^{c} m_i}, \qquad \text{and} \qquad R^{\mu} = \frac{\sum_{i=1}^{c} TP_i}{\sum_{i=1}^{c} n_i},$$

where c is the number of categories in the system.

Macro-averaging computes the recall and precision figures for each category, and averages these values globally:

$$P^{M} = \frac{\sum_{i=1}^{c} P_i}{c}, \qquad \text{and} \qquad R^{M} = \frac{\sum_{i=1}^{c} R_i}{c},$$

where c is the number of categories in the system.

Micro- and macro-averages can be computed for all of the effectiveness measures discussed above. These two methods may produce very different results, especially when some categories are more populated than others. Because micro-averaging adds individual cells into a global contingency table, it gives more importance to densely populated classes. Macro-averaging, on the other hand, does not favor any class.

No agreement has been reached in the literature on whether one should prefer micro- or macro-averages in reporting results. Macro-averaging may be preferred if a classification system is required to perform consistently across all classes regardless of how densely populated these are. One the other hand, micro-averaging may be preferred if the density of a class reflects its importance in the end-user system.

Simple averaging of utility measures gives an equal weight to every document. This means that average scores will be dominated by topics with large retrieved sets (as in micro-averaging). The filtering track at TREC has proposed two alternatives to averaging raw utility scores.

1. *Rank statistics.* Rank statistics expects several systems to be compared. For each topic, systems are ranked according to their utility score. Ranks are then averaged for each system over all topics. As a result, rank statistics provides a relative notion of the overall utility of a filtering system.
2. *Scaling.* For each topic, raw utility is scaled between 0 and 1. Systems can then be compared using the macro-average of the scaled utility scores.

To summarize, a large number of measures have been proposed and used to evaluate binary classifiers. We presented here only the most frequently used. We paid more attention to utility measures as they seem better suited to real filtering systems. However, the choice of utility function is an open question, i.e., there are no compelling theoretical reasons to prefer one function over another for a given task. Finally, we discussed alternative averaging approaches for reporting the overall performance of a classification system. Again, the choice of one method over another remains to some extent an open issue.

4.6.3 Relevance judgments

Our presentation of evaluation measures in the last section assumed that relevance judgments were available, i.e., we assumed that we knew the document labels. This is the case with collections such as Reuters and OHSUMED, where human experts have assigned classes to documents. We typically use most of the data to train the classification system, and the rest to test its performance on unseen data. Many collections of commercial value, like MEDLINE, have acquired retrospective classifications than can be used to evaluate system performance. Such evaluations, while they are informative of the quality of a system, are not predictive studies.

Performing predictive studies of classification systems indeed faces the same obstacles as introduced for IR systems in Chapter 2, Section 2.4. Recall how TREC adopted a pooling method for identifying documents in a collection that were relevant to a given query. Pooling selected the top 100 documents for each submitted run, and then experts judged the pool of these documents for relevance. Pooling based on the top 100 documents can not be used for the evaluation of filtering, because retrieved sets in that task are not ranked. Thus the pool of documents is created by taking random samples of some predetermined size, n, from the retrieved set of each system. If the retrieved set is smaller than n, all documents are selected.

This approach is less than ideal. For instance, documents in the pool will be of lesser quality using random sampling than pooled documents based on ranking. Moreover, topics with a large number of relevant documents will suffer the most from this approach. Fortunately, we know from sampling theory that the proportion of relevant documents in a simple random sample is an unbiased estimate of the proportion of relevant documents in the population, given a sufficiently large sample.

Relevance judgments or estimates can also help formulate utility measures. Because a utility function can be expressed using the proportion of relevant documents, we can convert an estimate of the proportion of relevant documents into the estimate of the utility score. Thus utility measure U_1 can be estimated by:

$$\widehat{U}_1 = \left(4 \cdot \frac{TP_i}{m_i} - 3 \right) \cdot m_i,$$

where TP_i is the number of relevant documents and m_i the total number of documents submitted.

4.6.4 System evaluation

Imagine a classification system built to support a manual classification process. Evaluating the performance of the automatic classification system, while informative, does not reflect the end goal of the manual process. Was consistency between human classifiers improved? Were costs cut, or was processing time reduced? Such questions go beyond mere classification effectiveness.

As an example, let us consider the CARP program outlined in Section 4.5 above. Evaluation of such a person-machine system consists primarily in comparing its performance with that of the previous, more manual, process. The process CARP replaced employed external contractors instead of in-house staff, and used a much less accurate pre-sorting program based on key numbers alone to suggest category assignments for vetting.

The old process used to result in about 700 new citations being posted from a typical weekly feed of 12,000 headnotes. In contrast, CARP makes about 1,600 suggestions per week, of which about 900 suggestions are accepted, 170 are rejected, and the remaining 530 are not used.[99] This is a net gain of 200 new suggestions per week, or a gain of 28%, at a precision rate of $(900 + 530)/1600 = 89\%$. In addition, supplementation now takes days instead of months, because CARP generates far fewer suggestions than the old pre-sorting program.[100] So the new system makes quality control easier, as well as making the online product more current.

The net gain is that contractor dollars are saved, the in-house editors regain control of the process, and overall performance is improved, measured in terms of both accuracy and timeliness. These are the real-world parameters of evaluation, as opposed to simple precision and recall statistics. Nevertheless, precision and recall are important, because a system that has poor coverage and is error-prone will never be accepted by the people part of the person-machine system.

As in any reengineering exercise, the final proof is an improved process. Automatic categorization has a role to play in many such back office applications, where attempts to streamline text and data processing work flows can leverage pre-existing stores of manually classified data. In many instances, the focus is not upon replacing human judgment, but facilitating human control and intervention in a system that is already automated to some extent. Allocating various data foraging and document ranking functions to a program can free up human experts to spend more time exercising their judgment and expertise. Such an approach can improve employee effectiveness, job satisfaction, and product quality all at the same time.

Pointers

Statistical classification algorithms, such as Naïve Bayes and maximum entropy, have been used in commercial applications by Whizbang![101] Whizbang![102] specializes in extracting targeted information from Web pages, such as job postings or company profiles. After crawling the Web to retrieve Web pages, the software determines and classifies whether or not these Web pages contain the target information, for instance whether the page contains a job posting or not.[103] Information extraction techniques are then applied to all pages classified as containing the targeted information.

Despite covering a lot of ground in this chapter, there are still some classification approaches that we did not describe. Some of them are complex, and require more mathematics than we wished to use in this text. For example, *support vector machines* have lately received a fair amount of attention, and experimental results suggest that they are effective for text classification.[104,105,106] Some of this work has been done at Microsoft Research, resulting in a Category Assistant tool for their SharePoint Portal Server.[107] *Neural networks* have also been applied to text classification.[108] For instance, RuleSpace uses neural networks[109] to create content filters for Web pages, and AOL uses RuleSpace products to support parental controls.[110]

The past few years have seen a growing interest in classification tools, and the number of vendors[111] has increased accordingly. At this point, it is hard to say whether or not a given product is able to provide a solution to a specific text classification task. The best one can do is to apply the task analysis provided in Section 4.1, and try to match the features of the tool with the task.

Notes

1. E.g., David Lewis has defined text categorization as 'the automated assignment of natural language texts to predefined categories based on their content', while using the term 'classification' to denote more general assignments of documents to classes defined in almost any fashion.

2. See Lewis, D. D. (1992). An evaluation of phrasal and clustered representations on a text categorization task. In *15th Annual International ACM SIGIR Conference on Research and Development in Information Retrieval* (pp. 37–50).

3. See Moore, C. (2001). Seeking far and wide for the right data. *InfoWorld*, August 27th/September 3rd.

4. MARC stands for MAchine-Readable Cataloging. There are five MARC formats available, covering Bibliographic Data, Authority Data, Holdings Data, Classification Data, and Community Information. See http://lcweb.loc.gov/marc/.

5. Although there has also been some work on medical document collections, see Section 4.4.1.

6. There are in fact two versions of this collection: Reuters-22173 and Reuters-21578. The latter is a tidied up version of the former.

7. See, e.g., Cohen, W. W. (1996). Learning rules that classify e-mail. In *Papers from the AAAI Spring Symposium on Machine Learning in Information Access* (pp. 18–25).

8. See, e.g., Pitkow, J. & Pirolli, P. (1997). Life, death, and lawfulness on the electronic frontier. In *Conference on Human Factors in Computing Systems*, CHI-97 (pp. 383–390). Atlanta, GA: Association for Computing Machinery.

9. See Yang, Y. & Lui, X. (1999). A re-examination of text categorization methods. *SIGIR-99*, 42–49, for both a critique and some interesting results.

10. See Maron, M. E. (1961). Automatic indexing: an experimental inquiry. *Journal of the ACM, 8*, 404–417, for an example of earlier work in text categorization for keyword indexing.

11. See Jackson, P. (1999). *Introduction to Expert Systems* (3rd edn.). Harlow, England: Addison-Wesley Longman, for a detailed discussion of rule-based systems, especially Chapter 5.

12. Hayes, P. J., & Weinstein, S. P. (1990). CONSTRUE/TIS: A system for content-based indexing of a database of news stories. In *2nd Annual Conference on Innovative Applications of Artificial Intelligence* (pp. 1–5).

13. Of these categories, 539 represent proper names (people, countries, organizations, etc.), while the rest are economic categories (mergers and acquisitions, commodities, etc.).

14. Such patterns can be distinguished from those formalized by regular expressions (see Chapter 3), since they are not limited to recognizing sequences of words or characters.

15. An expert system 'shell' called TCS was derived from Construe, but does not appear to have been widely used.

16. The learning of rules from examples is sometimes called 'inductive learning.'

17. Say 40, or more.

18. The fact that a term does *not* occur in the document may also be significant, as we shall see.

19. This is an independence assumption. Effectively, we are saying that the occurrence of the term 'company' in a document is rendered no more (or less) likely if we know that the term 'merger' also occurs in the document. This assumption is patently false, but the alternative is to specify a joint probability distribution for all $2^n - n - 1$ combinations of 2 or more terms, which is infeasible.

20. See McCallum, A. & Nigam, K. (1998). A comparison of event models for Naïve Bayes classification. In *Proceedings of AAAI-98 Workshop on Learning for Text Categorization* (pp. 41–48).

21. A *bag* is like a set in that elements are not ordered but, unlike a set, the same element can appear more than once.

22. As before, $P(t_j|C_i)$ may be zero, resulting in a zero value for the product $P(D|C_i)$, unless smoothing is employed.

23. See McCallum, A. & Nigam, K. (op cit).

24. Nigam, K., McCallum, A. K., Thrun, S., & Mitchell, T. (2000). Text classification from labeled and unlabeled documents using EM. *Machine Learning Journal, 39* (2–3), 103–134, May–June 2000.

25. The 'ancestor' classes of a given class are simply the classes higher up in the hierarchy that the given class belongs to. They can be systematically enumerated by traversing the hierarchy from the root node down to the given class, or traversing upward from the given class to the root node. In a strict hierarchy, each node has only one immediate ancestor, so this is a straightforward operation.

26. McCallum, A. K., Rosenfeld, R., Mitchell, T. M., & Ng, A. Y. (1998). Improving text classification by shrinkage of a hierarchy of classes. In *Proceedings of ICML-98, 15th International Conference on Machine Learning* (pp. 359–367). Madison, USA.

27. This is often done through trial and error, based on the training data.

28. Hull, D. (1994). Improving text retrieval for the routing problem using latent semantics indexing. In *Proceedings of SIGIR'94, 17th ACM International Conference on Research and Development in Information Retrieval* (pp. 282–291). Dublin, Ireland.

29. Ittner, D., Lewis, D., & Ahn, D. (1995) Text categorization of low quality images. In *Proceedings of SDAIR-95* (pp. 301–315). Las Vegas, NV.

30. See Chapter 2, Section 2.3.2.

31. Dumais, S., Platt, J., Heckerman, D., & Sahami, M. (1998). Inductive learning algorithms and representations for text categorization. In *Proceedings of CIKM'98* (pp. 148–155). Washington.

32. Lewis, D., Schapire, R., Callan, J., & Papka, R. (1996). Training algorithms for linear text classifiers. In *Proceeding of SIGIR'96* (pp. 298–306). Zürich.

33. Schapire, R., Singer, Y., & Singhal, A. (1998). Boosting and Rocchio applied to text filtering. In *Proceedings of SIGIR'98* (pp. 215–223).

34. See Ruiz, M., & Srinivasan, P. (1999). Hierarchical neural networks for text categorization. In *Proceedings of SIGIR-99* (pp. 281–282); and Ng, H., Goh, W., & Low, K. (1997). Feature selection, perceptron learning, and a usability case study for text categorization. In *Proceedings of SIGIR-97* (pp. 67–73).

35. In fact, Rocchio can be recast as an on-line algorithm.

36. For adaptive categorization tasks, time is a parameter and the final weight vector is a function of time. As the categorization system receives new information over time, the weight vector will be updated. However, documents that have already been classified at time t will usually not be reclassified at time $t + 1$.

37. Lewis, D., Schapire, R., Callan, J., & Papka, R. (1996). Training algorithms for linear text classifiers. In *Proceeding of SIGIR'96* (pp. 298–306). Zürich.

38. Ng, H., Goh, W., & Low, K. (1997). Feature selection, perceptron learning, and a Usability Case study for text categorization. In *Proceedings of SIGIR'97* (pp. 67–73).

39. Dagan, I., Karov, Y., & Roth, D. (1997). Mistake-driven learning in text categorization. In *Proceeding of the 2nd Conference on Empirical Methods for Natural Language Processing* (pp. 55–63).

40. Lewis, D., Schapire, R., Callan, J., & Papka, R. (1996). (op cit).

41. Dagan, I., Karov, Y., & Roth, D. (1997). Mistake-driven learning in text categorization. In *Proceeding of the 2nd Conference on Empirical Methods for Natural Language Processing* (pp. 55–63).

42. Callan, J. (1998). Learning while filtering documents. In *Proceedings of SIGIR'98* (pp. 224–231).

43. Continuous valued features can be split into ranges.

44. Quinlan, J. R. (1986). Induction of decision trees. *Machine Learning, 1,* 81–106.

45. Such decision rules should not be confused with *decision lists*, which we consider in the next subsection. Decision lists only perform Boolean (two-valued) tests in their conditions.

46. Quinlan, J. R. (1993). C4.5: *Programs for Machine Learning*. San Mateo, CA: Morgan Kaufmann.

47. In other words, the classification will be vulnerable to peculiarities among individual data items in the sample. The classifier will then perform badly on unseen data.

48. See e.g., Han, E. S., Karypis, G. & Kumar, V. (1999). *Text categorization using weight adjusted k-nearest neighbor classification.* Computer Science Technical Report TR99-019, Department of Computer Science, University of Minnesota, Minneapolis, Minnesota.

49. Rivest, R. L. (1987). Learning decision lists. *Machine Learning, 2,* 229–246.

50. Cohen, W. (1995). Fast effective rule induction. In *Proceedings of the 12th International Conference on Machine Learning (ML-95)* (pp. 115–123). San Mateo, CA: Morgan Kaufmann.

51. Unlike the 'naïve Bayes' classifiers we saw earlier, which assume that terms occur independently of each other.

52. The amount of information contained in a 'message', x, is defined in information theory as

$$I(x) = -log_2 P(x).$$

In other words, the amount of information in a message is inversely proportional to its probability. The concept of what constitutes a message can be interpreted fairly broadly, as in the example above.

53. In fact, Ripper uses an additional heuristic involving 'minimum description length' (MDL) to curtail rule generation in the face of noisy data sets, but that is beyond the scope of this text. See Quinlan, J. R. (1995). MDL and categorical theories (continued). In *Machine Learning: Proceedings of the Twelfth International Conference* (pp. 464–470). Lake Tahoe, CA; and also Cohen, W. W. & Singer, Y. (1996). Context-sensitive learning methods for text categorization. In *Proceedings of the 19th Annual International ACM Conference on Research and Development in Information Retrieval* (pp. 307–315). ACM Press.

54. For more about loss ratios, see Lewis, D. D., & Catlett, J. (1994). Heterogeneous uncertainty sampling for supervised learning. In Cohen, W. W. and Hirsh, H. (Eds.), *Machine Learning: Proceedings of the Eleventh International Conference on Machine Learning*, San Francisco, CA, 1994 (pp. 148–156). San Mateo, CA: Morgan Kaufmann.

55. Thompson, P. (2001). Automatic categorization of case law. In *Proceedings of the 8th International Conference on Artificial Intelligence & Law* (pp. 70–77).

56. Cohen, W. W. (1995). Fast effective rule induction. In *Machine Learning: Proceedings of the Twelfth International Conference* (pp. 115–123). Lake Tahoe, CA.

57. Cohen, W. W. (1996). Learning rules that classify e-mail. In *Papers from the AAAI Spring Symposium on Machine Learning in Information Access* (pp. 18–25).

58. See e.g., Al-Kofahi, K., Tyrrell, A., Vachher, A., Travers, T. & Jackson, P. (2001). Combining Multiple Classifiers for Text Categorization. *Proceedings of the Tenth International Conference on Information and Knowledge Management (CIKM-2001)* (pp. 97–104). New York: ACM Press.

59. Larkey, L., & Croft, W.B. (1996). Combining Classifiers in Text Categorization. In *Proceedings of SIGIR'96* (pp. 289–297). Zürich, Switzerland.

60. Yang, Y. (1994). Expert network: Effective and efficient learning from human decisions in text categorization and retrieval. In *Proceedings of SIGIR'94* (pp. 13–22). Dublin, Ireland; and Yang, Y. (1999). An evaluation of statistical approaches to text categorization. *Information Retrieval, 1* (1.2), 69–90.

61. Other aggregate scores have sometimes been proposed. See Cohen, W., & Hirsch, H. (1998). Joins that generalize: Text classification using WHIRL. In *Proceedings of KDD-98* (pp. 169–173). New York.

62. Only categories assigned to the k nearest neighbors are non-zero. Cut-off strategies normally apply to the score itself (e.g., assigning a category only if it scores over a threshold), or to the rank of the score (e.g., suggesting only the top 3 categories in the ranking).

63. Jordan, M., & Jacobs, R. (1994). Hierarchical mixtures of experts and the EM algorithm. *Neural Computation, 6,* 181–214.

64. Breiman, L. (1994). Bagging predictors. Technical Report 421. Department of Statictics, University of California at Berkeley.

65. Belkin, N., Kantor, P., Fox, E., & Shaw, J. (1995). Combination of evidence of multiple query representations for information retrieval. *Information Processing and Management, 31* (3), 431–448.

66. Selberg, E., & Etzioni, O. (1996). Multi-service search and comparison using the MetaCrawler. In *Proceedings of the 4th WWW Conference.*

67. Belkin, N., Cool, C., Croft, W. B., & Callan, J. (1993). Effect of multiple query representations on information retrieval system performance. In *Proceedings of SIGIR-93* (pp. 339–346).

68. Shaw, J., & Fox, E. (1995). Combination of multiple searches. In *Proceedings of the TREC-3 conference.*

69. Bartell, B., Cottrell, G., & Belew, R. (1994). Automatic combination of multiple ranked retrieval systems. In *Proceedings of SIGIR-94* (pp. 173–181). Dublin, Ireland.

70. Vogt, C., & Cottrell, G. (1998). Predicting the performance of linearly combined IR systems. In *Proceedings of SIGIR-98* (pp. 190–196); and Lee, J. H. (1997). Analyses of multiple evidence combination. In *Proceedings of SIGIR-97* (pp. 267–276).

71. Hull, D., Pedersen, J., & Schütze, H. (1996). Method combination for document filtering. In *Proceedings of SIGIR-96* (pp. 279–287).

72. Larkey, L., & Croft, W. B. (1996). Combining Classifiers in Text Categorization. In *Proceedings of SIGIR-96* (pp. 289–297).

73. In machine learning terminology, these are sometimes called 'weak classification rules,' or 'weak learners', since we do not expect them to work very well on their own.

74. See Schapire, R., & Singer, Y. (2000). Boostexter: a boosting-based system for text categorization. In *Machine Learning*, Vol. 39, No 2/3 (pp. 135–168).

75. Apte, C., Damerau, F., & Weiss, S. (1998). Text mining with decision trees and decision rules. In *Conference on Automated Learning and Discovery.* Carnegie-Mellon University, June 1998.

76. Schapire, R., Singer, Y., & Singhal, A. (1998). Boosting and Rocchio applied to text filtering. In *Proceedings of SIGIR'98* (pp. 215–223).

77. Schapire, R., & Singer, Y. (2000). (op cit).

78. Iyers, R., Lewis, D., Schapire, R., & Singer, Y. (2000). Boosting for document routing. In *Proceedings of CIKM-2000* (pp. 70–77).

79. See e.g., Lewis, D. (1992). Feature selection and feature extraction for text categorization. In *Proceedings of Speech and Natural Language Workshop* (pp. 212–217). San Mateo, CA: Morgan Kaufmann.

80. Yang, Y., & Pedersen, J. (1997). A comparative study on feature selection for text categorization. In *Proceedings of ICML'97* (pp. 412–420).

81. Al-Kofahi, K., Tyrrell, A., Vachher, A., Travers, T., & Jackson, P. (2001). Combining multiple classifiers for text categorization. In *Proceedings of CIKM-2001* (pp. 97–104).

82. Key numbers are manually assigned topics from a conceptual hierarchy of nearly 100,000 legal concepts.

83. See Chapter 2.

84. As described in Chapter 2, Section 2.4.3

85. Lewis, D. (1996). The TREC-4 filtering track. In *Proceedings of the Fourth Text Retrieval Conference*; and Lewis, D. (1997). The TREC-5 filtering track. In *Proceedings of the Fifth Text Retrieval Conference.*

86. Hull, D. (1999). The TREC-7 Filtering track: Description and Analysis. In *Proceedings of the Seventh Text Retrieval Conference.*

87. Fuhr, N., Hartmann, S. Knorz, G., Lustig, G., Schwantner, M., & Tzeras, K. (1991). AIR/X – a rule-based multistage indexing system for large subject fields. In *Proceedings of RIAO-91* (pp. 606–623).

88. The Reuters-21578 collection may be freely downloaded for experimentation purposes at http://www.research.att.com/~lewis/reuters21578.html

89. The OHSUMED collection may be freely downloaded for experimentation purposes at ftp://medir.ohsu.edu/pub/ohsumed

90. The AP newswire collections are now available for sale through the Linguistics Data Consortium at http://www.ldc.upenn.edu/ as part of its "Tipster" Volumes 1 and 2.

91. The 20 Newsgroups collection may be freely downloaded for experimentation purposes at http://www.cs.cmu.edu/

92. See Chapter 2, Section 2.4.1.

93. See Schütze, H., Hull, D., & Pedersen, J. (1995). A comparison of classifiers and document representations for the routing problem. In *Proceedings of SIGIR-95* (pp. 229–237), or see Yang, Y., & Liu, X. (1999). A re-examination of text categorization methods. In *Proceedings of SIGIR-99* (pp. 42–49).

94. Yang, Y. (1999). An evaluation of statistical approaches to text categorization. In *Information Retrieval*, Vol. 1, No 1/2 (pp. 69–90). Kluwer Academic Publishers.

95. Even this is debatable.

96. This measure (actually $E_\beta = 1 - F_\beta$) was introduced by van Rijsbergen, K. (1979). *Information Retrieval* (2nd edition). London: Butterworths, pp. 168–176. We have seen different versions of it before in Chapters 2 and 3.

97. Lewis, D. (1995). Evaluating and optimizing autonomous text classification systems. In *Proceedings of SIGIR-95* (pp. 246–254).

98. These averaging methods were introduced in IR by Tague, J. (1981). The pragmatics of information retrieval experimentation. In *Information Retrieval Experiment* (pp. 59–102). Butterworths, London.

99. The 'unused' suggestions are correct classifications, but they are rejected for editorial reasons, such as being redundant, too general, too numerous, etc.

100. The older program sometimes generated as many as 100,000 suggestions for a weekly feed.

101. See Aquino, S. (2001). Search engines ready to learn. *Technology Review*, April 24, Massachusetts Institute of Technology.

102. See http://www.whizbang.com/

103. See http://www.whizbang.com/solutions/wbwhite3.html

104. Joachims, T. (1998). Text categorization with support vector machines: Learning with many relevant features. In *Proceedings of ECML-98* (pp. 137–142). Chemnitz, Germany.

105. Dumais, S., Platt, J., Heckerman, D., & Sahami, Mehran. (1998). Inductive learning algorithms and representations for text categorization. In *Proceedings of CIKM-98* (pp. 148–155). Washington, USA.

106. Yang, Y., & Liu, X. (1999). A re-examination of text categorization methods. In *Proceedings of SIGIR-99* (pp. 42–49). Berkeley, USA.

107. See http://microsoft.com/sharepoint/techinfo/planning/SPSOverview.doc

108. See Schütze, H., Hull, D., & Pedersen, J. (1995). A comparison of classifiers and document representations for the document routing problem. In *Proceedings of SIGIR'95* (pp. 229–237); and Wiener, E., Pedersen, J., & Weigend, A. (1995). A neural network approach to topic spotting. In *Proceedings of SDAIR'95* (pp. 317–332).

109. See http://www.rulespace.com/contexion/technology

110. See http://www.rulespace.com/alliances/customers.html

111. http://www.searchtools.com/info/classifiers-tools.html gives a list of commercial vendors that offer classification tools.

CHAPTER 5

Towards text mining

In Chapters 2, 3 and 4, we looked individually at technologies for retrieving, extracting and classifying information from individual documents. As we have seen, these seemingly diverse text processing mechanisms share many common goals, are based on similar methodologies, and employ related statistical and linguistic techniques. It is therefore not a great leap to consider combining them into some grander vision, in which documents, and even whole *collections*, are 'mined' for information.

In this chapter, we look at the emerging area of *text mining*, envisioning what such applications might look like, and what the technical challenges will be. In particular, we emphasize applications to online publishing, digital libraries, and the World Wide Web. The focus will be upon processes that do more than simply finding or classifying documents, either by abstracting from documents and collections, or by building relationships between documents and collections based on the entities that they describe.

The link between text mining and natural language processing is that mining information out of text necessarily involves delineating at least some linguistic structures within the text. These structures could be as local as the occurrence of proper names and references to other documents, or as global as the division of a document into topical themes and segments. Having discovered such structures as part of the mining process, it often makes sense to mark them in the original document, e.g., with hypertext links or other tags, for subsequent use. These structures can then be related to records in other information sources at load or presentation time. Such sources could be directories of people and companies, encyclopedia and dictionary entries, or taxonomies and the like.

We shall concentrate here upon applications in two broad areas. One covers the automatic generation of metadata from documents in a collection, the most common forms of which are lists of proper names and document summaries. The other involves processing across single document boundaries, such as document clustering, cross-document summarization, and the detection of new topics.

But first let us look at the notion of text mining more closely.

5.1   What is text mining?

Talk of 'text mining' or 'text data mining' is in part inspired by the scarcely older field of data mining. 'Data mining' has been defined as the process of discovering patterns in data, sometimes distinguished from 'knowledge discovery', which can be seen as the higher order activity of judging which patterns are novel, valid or useful.[1] Thus the transformation from *data* to *knowledge* requires a critical evaluative step, which is distinct from the algorithms and procedures used to generate data patterns for consideration.[2]

Text mining is not information retrieval, or even information extraction, since these activities do not, strictly speaking, involve discovery.[3] Similarly, text categorization is not text mining, because categorizing a document does not generate new information. Presumably the author of the document knew what the document was about at the time of writing. However, the detection of novel topics, e.g., in a news feed, is deemed to be text mining, since it tells us something about the world, e.g., that a new incident or issue has arisen in the public consciousness. Mere categorization of a news feed to an existing hierarchy of concepts cannot detect such patterns, and would therefore run the risk of missing, or misclassifying, such stories.

Summarization is something of a borderline case. Sometimes, a document summary can succinctly capture the essence of a document in a way that adds something to the contents of the document itself. To the extent that a summary includes critical review, or links to related documents not referenced in the original text, we can consider it to add novel information. Many online publishers use document summaries as a convenient peg upon which to hang other metadata relating to their taxonomies, or point the reader at related documents.

Mostly, a summary is simply a cut-down version of the original document, composed largely of pieces of text extracted from it, as we shall see in Section 5.3.1. We shall nonetheless deal with cross-document summarization under the text mining rubric, since it involves the synthesis of information not present in any single document (see Section 5.3.3).

In summary, most authorities agree that text mining should involve something more than the mere analysis of a text. Programs that analyze document and sentence structure, assign keywords and index terms to documents, or route documents to various destinations are not doing text mining, according to this view. Ideally, text mining should uncover something interesting about the relationship between text and the world, e.g., what persons or companies

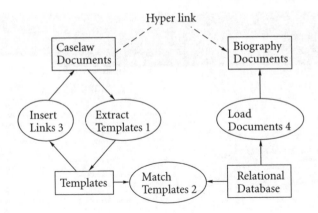

Figure 5.1 Overview of PeopleCite tagging system

an article is discussing, what trend or train of events a news story belongs to, and so forth.

Consequently, the concept of *reference* is crucial to the emerging notion of text mining. Proper names ("Bill Gates") and definite descriptions ("the Chairman of Microsoft") occurring in documents refer to real entities in the world, which have physical properties, such as age and location, abstract properties, such as being rich or powerful, and which are referred to by other documents. Current text mining efforts focus on elucidating such within- and cross-document relationships, typically building metadata repositories, such as directories of persons,[4] companies,[5] news threads,[6] and historical relationships between court decisions.[7]

Thus Dozier and Haschart describe an application that creates hypertext links from attorneys (and judges) featured in cases published on Westlaw to personal biographies of those persons in West Legal Directory. Their system, called PeopleCite, creates such links by extracting MUC-style templates[8] from text and linking them to biographical information in a relational database (see Figure 5.1). Their matching technique is based on a naïve Bayesian[9] inference network, and since its deployment in June 2000 the implementation has automatically created millions of reliable hypertext links in millions of documents. Their experiments show that this combination of information extraction and record linkage enables them to link attorney and judge names in caselaw to biographies with an accuracy rivaling that of a human expert.

The central problem addressed by the program is determining whether or not two names refer to the same person, given the rendition of the names, and any contextual information. For example, is the current biography of attorney

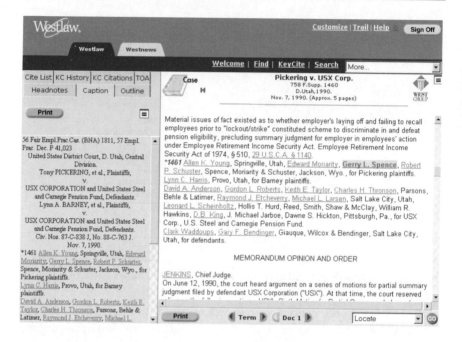

Figure 5.2 PeopleCite enhanced screen shot of a case law document on Westlaw

James Jackson of Palm Springs, California really the biography of a James P. Jackson practicing law in Sacramento, California in 1990? Probably. How PeopleCite goes about this computation is shown in Sidebar 5.1. Experiments have shown that PeopleCite can perform this task at 99% precision and 92% recall, which is as good as a human expert.

Figure 5.2 shows an actual screenshot from Westlaw with attorney names marked up by PeopleCite. Once an attorney has been matched against West Legal Directory, a number of other browsing options become possible. In addition to jumping from an attorney's name in a case to that person's biography, one can also bring up all the cases that a particular attorney has litigated, or all the law journal articles an attorney has written. This is obviously not possible unless a real connection has been established between a name string in the text and an actual person in the world.[10]

Given the central importance of reference, we shall begin our exploration of text mining by examining methods for extracting named entities from text and determining patterns of coreference among names and descriptions that refer to the same entity. We shall then proceed to survey techniques for docu-

ment summarization, some of which use named entity extraction and coreference as enabling technologies.

Sidebar 5.1   The matching module of PeopleCite

The job of the matching module is to find the biography record that most probably matches
each template record created by the extraction module. The process of matching one fielded
record (such as the template) to another fielded record (such as a biography record) is often
referred to as record linkage. The processing steps of the match module for attorneys are the
following.

1. For each template record, read the set of all biography records whose last names match
    or are compatible with the last name in the template. Call this set of biography records
    the 'candidate records'.
2. For each candidate record, determine how well the first name, middle name, last name,
    name suffix, firm, and city-state match the template fields.
3. Using the degree to which each piece of evidence matches, compute a match probability
    score for the linkage.
4. The candidate record with the highest match probability is the record used to build the
    hypertext link.[11]

Belief in the correctness of a match is computed using the following form of Bayes' rule:

$$P(M|E) = \frac{P(M) \prod_i P(E_i|M)}{P(M) \prod_i P(E_i|M) + P(\neg M) \prod_i P(E_i|\neg M)}.$$

$P(M|E)$ is the probability that a template matches a candidate record given a certain set of
evidence. $P(M)$ is the prior probability that a template and biography record refer to the
same person. $P(\neg M)$ is the prior probability that a template and biographical record do not
match. For attorneys, $P(M)$ is 0.000001 and $P(\neg M)$ is 0.999999, since there are approximately 1,000,000 attorney records in the biography database. For judges, $P(M)$ is 0.00005
and $P(\neg M)$ is 0.99995 since there are approximately 20,000 judge records in the biography
database.

   $P(E_i|M)$ is the conditional probability that E_i takes on a particular value given that a
template matches a biography record. $P(E_i|\neg M)$ is the conditional probability that E_i takes
on a particular value given that a template does not match a biography record. Conditional
probabilities for attorneys and judges were estimated using a manually tagged training set
of 7,186 attorney names and 5,323 judge names.

5.2 Reference and coreference

The concept of reference is one that exercised and entertained philosophers for a large part of the twentieth century, and will no doubt continue to do so. The fact that linguistic expressions (not to mention pictures and even musical phrases) can be understood to refer to real and imaginary entities is either totally transparent or completely mysterious, depending upon how sophisticated you want your analysis to be. In the present context, we are only concerned with inducing a mapping between occurrences of words and phrases in text and some external authority, such as the Yellow Pages, or a directory of companies and organizations.

The principal problem lies in determining whether the expression "Bill Gates", found in some random text, refers to the Chairman of Microsoft, or the relatively unknown schoolboy and dog owner, William Gates, of Milwaukee. Many contextual factors can help in making this decision, some external to the text (such as the source of the publication) and some internal (such as the occurrence of other expressions, like "Microsoft"). If the text is an article from Computer Weekly, it is more likely to be about Microsoft than if the text is from a school magazine.

However, even within the confines of a single article, a person or organization may be referred to in different ways, e.g., "Bill Gates", "Gates", "Chairman of Microsoft", "the Chairman", "he", etc. Suppose that we are interested in deciding whether an article is really about Bill Gates, or whether it merely mentions him in passing. Even if the former is in fact the case, the phrase "Bill Gates" may only occur once in the article, with other references to him using different words. How are we going to make this decision? Our best chance is to figure out that the various expressions listed above all refer to the same person, which brings us to the problem of coreference.

Coreference is the linguistic phenomenon whereby two or more linguistic expressions may represent or indicate the same entity. This is simple enough to state but, like many other linguistic phenomena, coreference admits of ambiguity. For example, in the sentence,

When *he* turned round, *John* saw *the man* with *his* jacket on.

it is *likely*, but by no means certain, that 'he' corefers with 'John', while 'the man' and 'his' corefer to another person distinct from John. But it *could* be the other man that turned round, and the other man could be wearing John's jacket. More perplexingly,

> *John* saw *the man* with *his* glasses on when *he* turned round.

admits of several interpretations, e.g., those in which John turns round and those in which the man turns round, cross-multiplied with those in which one or the other man is wearing the glasses.

Often context makes the meaning clear. But, the contextual rules that we use to make such judgments are not easy to articulate, and therefore not easy to represent in a computer program.

Coreference can be distinguished from the related phenomenon of *anaphora*, which is the linguistic act of pointing back to a previously mentioned item in speech or text.[12] It turns out that anaphors do not always corefer, as in

> The man who gave his *paycheck* to his wife was wiser than the man who gave *it* to his mistress.

Here 'it' points back to 'paycheck', but not the same paycheck, presumably.[13] In the parlance of linguistics, the first phrase is called the *antecedent*, and the second is called the *anaphor*. Sometimes the 'anaphor' points forward, in which instance it is, strictly speaking, a *cataphor*, as in:

> Sensing that *he* was being followed, *John* turned around.

Anaphora is not confined within sentences, e.g.,

> *John* turned around. *He* saw *the man* with *his* glasses on.

Inter-sentence cataphora is less common, and is most often used as a literary device that delays identifying a character, e.g., to create a suspenseful effect.

Linguists, both computational and otherwise, have worked hard to formulate the rules governing the assignment of coreference. Much of the early work focused upon the intrasentential case,[14] although later work has addressed intersentential and cross-document coreferences.[15] Although we still lack a general solution to all of these problems, some interesting progress has been made, and special purpose algorithms have also been devised for particular domains, such as legal citations.[16]

The conundrum of coreference would be of only passing interest here, if it were not for the fact that it is pervasive in documents of all kinds, and that even partial solutions can benefit online applications. Simply knowing that 'IBM' corefers with 'International Business Machines' in the same document will benefit indexing and retrieval, as well as knowing that the names 'James Prufrock', 'Jim Prufrock', and 'Alfred J. Prufrock' all refer to the same person in a collection of documents, such as public records. The ability to link proper names occurring in text to personal or company profiles depends crucially upon resolving cross-document coreferences of this kind.

Before examining coreference in more detail, it is worth understanding the technology behind named entity recognition, since this is a crucial preparatory step for resolving coreferences accurately.

5.2.1 Named entity recognition

The task of named entity recognition (NER) requires a program to process a text and identify expressions that refer to people, places, companies, organizations, products, and so forth. Thus the program should not merely identify the boundaries of a naming expression, but also classify the expression, e.g., so that one knows that "Los Angeles" refers to a city and not a person. This is not as easy as one might think.

Problems with NER
Many referring expressions are proper names and may therefore exhibit initial capital letters in English, e.g., "John Smith", "Thomson Corporation", and "Los Angeles." However, the mere presence of an initial capital does not guarantee that one is dealing with part of a name, since initial capitalization is also used at the start of sentences.[17] It might be supposed that this task could be simplified by using lists of people, places and companies, but this simply isn't so. New companies, products, etc. come into being on a daily basis, and using a directory or gazetteer doesn't necessarily help you decide whether "Philip Morris" refers to a person or a company.

Authority files of this kind might help with proper names, but not other referring expressions. Some are definite descriptions, e.g., "the famous inventor", while others are pronouns, such as "he", "she", or "it." Still other entities of interest might be dates, sums of money, percentages, temperatures, etc., depending upon the domain.

Most commercially available software packages[18] for NER concentrate upon identifying proper names that refer to people, places and companies. They may also try and find relationships between entities, e.g., "Bill Gates, President of Microsoft Corporation" will yield the person Bill Gates standing in a President relationship to the company Microsoft. A variety of methods are used to achieve such extractions, which we shall now summarize.

Heuristic approaches to NER
In Chapter 3, we encountered the Message Understanding Conferences (MUCs), which provided a stimulus for research and development in information extraction during the 1990s. In the seventh such conference, there was a track devoted to named entity recognition, with data collections and test conditions being set up along the lines of earlier conferences. The best MUC-7 system came from Edinburgh University,[19] and employed a variety of methods, combining lists, rules, and probabilistic techniques, applied in a particular order.

- First, the program applies a number of high-confidence heuristic rules to the text. These rules rely heavily upon syntactic cues in the surrounding context. For example, in *John Smith, director*, we know that *John Smith* refers to a person, because a string of capitalized words followed by a title or profession indicates the name of a person with high reliability. Similar rules can be written to recognize names of companies or organizations in expressions such as *president of Microsoft Corporation*.
- The system also uses lists of names, locations, etc., but at this stage it only checks to see if the context of a possible entity supports suggestions from the list. For example, a place name like *Washington* can just as easily be a surname or the name of an organization. Only in a suggestive context, like *in the Washington area*, would it be classified as a location.
- Next, all named entities already identified in the document are collected and partial orders of the composing words are created. Suppose the expression *Lockheed Martin Production* has already been tagged as an organization, because it occurred in the list of organization names and occurred in a context suggestive of organizations. At this stage, all instances of *Lockheed Martin Production, Lockheed Martin, Lockheed Production, Martin Production, Lockheed* and *Martin* will be marked as possible organizations. The annotated stream is then fed to a trained statistical model that tries to resolve some of the suggestions.
- Once this has been done, the system again applies its rules, but with much more relaxed contextual constraints. Organizations and locations from the lists available to the system are marked in the text, without checking the context in which they occur. If a string like 'Philip Morris' has not been tagged in the earlier stages as an organization, then at this stage the name grammar will tag it as a person without further checking of the context.
- The system then performs another partial match to label short forms of personal names, such as 'White' when 'James White' has already been rec-

ognized as a person, and to label company names, such as 'Hughes' when 'Hughes Communications' has already been identified as an organization.
-   Because titles of documents such as news wires are in capital letters, they provide little guidance for the recognition of names. In the final stage of processing, entities in the title are marked up, by matching or partially matching the entities found in the text, and checking against a statistical model trained on document titles. For example, in the headline MURDOCH SATELLITE EXPLODES ON TAKE-OFF, 'Murdoch' will be tagged as a person because it partially matches 'Rupert Murdoch' elsewhere in the text.

Let's look at this approach in a little more detail. As we mentioned earlier, disambiguating the first word of a sentence is typically problematical, because common words have initial capitalization in this context, but proper names also occur frequently in this position, e.g., as subject of the sentence. Other problematical positions occur after opening quotation marks, colons, and numbers of list entries.

Focusing specifically on this problem, Mikheev[20] studied a 64,000-word New York Times corpus, containing about 2,700 capitalized words in ambiguous positions, and found that about 2,000 of them were common words, listed in an English lexicon. About 170 of these were actually used as proper names, while 10 common words were not in the lexicon. Thus, using a lexicon as the sole guide for recognizing common words as non-names led to a decrease in accuracy of around 6.5%.

The question is how to improve on this level of performance. Using a part of speech tagger eliminated about 2% of the error, but various problems remained. In general, proper names that were also common nouns still tended to get assigned as non-names.

Real improvement came from the exploitation of coreference, namely in recognizing that ambiguous names are often introduced unambiguously earlier in the text. Thus the 'Bush' in

'Bush went to Los Angeles.'

is likely to have already been mentioned as 'Mr. Bush,' or 'George Bush,' thereby increasing the likelihood that the ambiguous occurrence of 'Bush' corefers with the earlier expression.

This insight led to an approach called the *Sequence Strategy*, in which the program looks for strings of two or more capitalized words in unambiguous positions before looking for similar or lesser strings in ambiguous positions. Thus, if the program finds the phrase 'Rocket Systems Development Co.' in the middle of a sentence on a first pass through a document, it can reliably identify this phrase as a proper name at the start of a sentence in a subsequent pass. Moreover, it can do the same for subphrases occurring elsewhere in the document, such as 'Rocket Systems', 'Rocket Co.', etc.

Proper names that are phrases can also contain lower case words, e.g., 'The Phantom of the Opera'. The heuristic rule is that the strategy allows proper name phrases to contain lower case words of length three or less. Subphrases must begin and end with a capitalized word, e.g., we allow 'The Phantom', but not 'Phantom of the'.

The Sequence Strategy has proved to be a high precision tool for finding names of companies and organizations. It is clear that the approach is not monolithic, but combines a number of different techniques and uses a variety of information sources. In the next subsection, we look at a more uniform approach based on statistical modeling.

Statistical approaches to NER

An alternate approach to NER is to write a program that *learns* how to recognize names. In this section, we explore the use of a powerful technology called Hidden Markov Models for extracting proper names from text. Some key work in this area derives from BBN, and resulted in the Nymble[21] system, which participated in MUC-6 and MUC-7, and has since morphed into the more highly developed Identifinder[22] system.

One way to think about NER is to suppose that the text once had all the names within it marked for our convenience, but then the text was passed through a noisy channel, and this information was somehow deleted. Our task is therefore to construct a program that models the original process that marked the names. In practical terms, this means learning how to decide, for each word in the text, whether or not it is part of a name. Typically, we are also interested in what kind of name we have found, so the word classification task reduces to deciding which name class a word belongs to. For convenience, we include NOT-A-NAME as a name class.

As with the heuristic approach, it is necessary to identify features of words that provide clues as to what kinds of words they are. The Nymble system used the features shown in Table 5.1. These mutually exclusive features sort all words and punctuation found in a text into one of fourteen categories.

These word features are not informative enough, in themselves, to identify names, or parts of names, reliably on a word-by-word basis. However, they can be leveraged, in conjunction with information about word position and adjacency, to provide better estimates of name class.

Table 5.1 Nymble's word feature set, based on Table 3.1 from Bikel et al.[14]

Word feature	Example text	Explanation
twoDigitNum	90	Two-digit year
fourDigitNum	1990	Four-digit year
containsDigitAndAlpha	A8-67	Product code
containsDigitAndDash	09-96	Date
containsDigitAndSlash	11/9/98	Date
containsDigitAndComma	1,000	Amount
containsDigitAndPeriod	1.00	Amount
otherNum	12345	Any other number
allCaps	BBN	Organization
capPeriod	P.	Personal name initial
firstWord	The	Capitalized word that is the first word in a sentence
initCap	Sally	Capitalized word in midsentence
lowercase	tree	Uncapitalized word
other	.net	Punctuation, or any other word not covered above

One important source of information is the name class assigned to the previous word in the sentence. (We assume that sentence boundaries have already been determined.) Another is the preceding word itself. Thus one component of assigning a name class, NC_0, to the current word, w_0, is given by the following probability:

$$P(NC_0|NC_{-1}, w_{-1}),$$

where NC_{-1} is the name class of the previous word, w_{-1}.

Another component looks at the probability of generating the current word and its associated feature, given the name class assigned to it and the name class of the previous word, i.e.,

$$P(\langle w_0, f_0 \rangle | NC_0, NC_{-1}),$$

where $\langle w_0, f_0 \rangle$ stands for the current word-feature pairing.

Nymble and Identifinder combine these probabilities into the following model for generating just the first word of a name class:

$$P(NC_0|NC_{-1}, w_{-1}) \cdot P(\langle w_0, f_0 \rangle | NC_0, NC_{-1}).$$

The model for generating all but the first word of a name class uses the word-feature pair of the previous word, and current name class:

$$P(\langle w_0, f_0 \rangle | \langle w_{-1}, f_{-1} \rangle, NC_0).$$

This approach is based on the commonly used bigram language model, in which a word's probability of occurrence is based on the previous word. The probability of a sequence of words $\langle w_1, \ldots, w_n \rangle$ is then computed by the product

$$\prod_{i=1}^{n} P(w_i|w_{i-1})$$

with a bogus START-OF-SENTENCE word being used to compute the probability of w_1. (See Sidebar 5.2 for a detailed breakdown of how this product is used in Nymble.)

Sidebar 5.2 Combining probabilities in the bigram model

For example, consider the sentence 'Mr. Smith sleeps', in which Smith is in the PERSON name class, and the other words are not names. To compute the probability of this sequence of words, we need to include the following probabilities.

$P(\text{"Mr."} \mid \text{NOT-A-NAME, START-OF-SENTENCE})$

is the probability of "Mr." starting the sentence, given that it is not a name.

$P(\text{PERSON} \mid \text{NOT-A-NAME, "Mr."})$,
$P(\text{"Smith"} \mid \text{PERSON, NOT-A-NAME})$

model with the occurrence of "Smith" as a person, given that it is preceded by a non-name, "Mr."

$P(\text{NOT-A-NAME} \mid \text{PERSON, "Smith"})$,
$P(\text{"sleeps"} \mid \text{NOT-A-NAME, PERSON})$

deal with the occurrence of "sleeps" as a non-name, given that it is preceded by a person name, "Smith".

The bigram model as used by Nymble requires other probabilities to represent the likelihood that any current word is the last word in its name class. E.g., given "Mr. John Smith sleeps", there is some value in explicitly representing the probability that "Smith" is the end of the person name. This is done by introducing a bogus +END+ word of the 'other' feature category after the current word, and computing its probability thus:

$P(\text{+END+, other}) \mid \langle w_0, f_0 \rangle, NC_0)$.

This usage introduces the following probabilities into our model for "Mr. Smith sleeps."

$P(\text{+END+} \mid \text{"Mr.", NOT-A-NAME})$,
$P(\text{+END+} \mid \text{"Smith", PERSON})$,
$P(\text{+END+} \mid \text{"sleeps", NOT-A-NAME})$.

Finally, we add other probabilities to cope with the start and end of the sentence, including the period at the end of the sentence:

$P(\text{NOT-A-NAME} \mid \text{START-OF-SENTENCE}, +\text{END}+)$,
$P(\text{“.”} \mid \text{“sleeps”, NOT-A-NAME})$,
$P(+\text{END}+ \mid \text{“.”, NOT-A-NAME})$,
$P(\text{END-OF-SENTENCE} \mid \text{NOT-A-NAME, “.”})$.

Multiplying all these probabilities together computes the probability of the sentence "Mr. Smith sleeps" being generated by the bigram model.

The needed probabilities are estimated from corpus counts, as usual. For example, we estimate

$$P(NC_0 | NC_{-1}, w_{-1})$$

by counting the number of times that a word of name class NC_0 follows word w_{-1} of name class NC_{-1}, and dividing by the total number of occurrences of word w_{-1} with name class NC_{-1}. Sparse and missing data are handled by back-off models and smoothing.[23]

Hidden Markov modeling generates a lattice of alternative labelings of the words in a sentence. Building this lattice is called 'encoding.' Thus, the subject of a sentence like

'Banks filed bankruptcy papers.'

could refer to an impecunious person called Banks, or to banking enterprises in a failing financial empire. A decision process is therefore required to find the most likely sequence of labels, i.e., to directly compare the probability of the assignment

<PERSON, NOT-A-NAME, NOT-A-NAME, NOT-A-NAME>

with that of

<NOT-A-NAME, NOT-A-NAME, NOT-A-NAME, NOT-A-NAME>.

Happily, there is an efficient algorithm[24] for performing this 'decoding' operation that is linear in the length of the sentence.

5.2.2 The coreference task

The 7th Message Understanding Conference defined a 'coreference layer' for the information extraction task, which links together multiple expressions that refer to a given entity.[25] In the context of information extraction, the role of coreference annotation is to ensure that information associated with multiple mentions of an entity can be collected together in a single data structure or template. MUC-7 confined itself to coreference in an identity relationship among nouns, noun phrases and pronouns – thereby leaving out verbs and clauses, as well as coreference relations such as part-whole.

The annotation used in MUC-7 was SGML,[26] so that

```
... <COREF ID="100">International Business Machines
</COREF>. <COREF ID="101" TYPE="IDENT" REF = "100">IBM
</COREF> ...
```

would indicate the phrase "International Business Machines" ending the first sentence corefers with the acronym "IBM" starting the second sentence in an identity relation.

Identity is the only coreference relation considered by MUC-7, although one can conceive of others, such as part-whole:

"The house was empty. He knocked on the door."

which could be rendered as:

```
<COREF ID="100">The house</COREF> was empty. He
knocked on <COREF ID="101" TYPE="PART" REF = "100">the
door</COREF>.
```

indicating that the door (with identifier '101') is part of the previously encountered house (with identifier '100').

Coreference relationships can therefore have different logical properties. Identity is a reflexive, symmetric, and transitive relation that divides entities into equivalence classes. The part-whole relation is anti-reflexive, anti-symmetric and transitive, and is therefore an ordering relation.

There are a number of common sentential contexts in which coreference occurs in English.

1. Predicate nominals, e.g., "*Bill Clinton* is the *President of the United States.*"
2. Apposition. "*Bill Clinton, President of the United States,* said ..."
3. Bound anaphors. "*The President* asked *his* advisor."

All three can occur across sentence boundaries, while (1) and (2) can also occur across document boundaries.

Existing products, such as NetOwl,[27] already use hand-written pattern matching rules, both to recognize and categorize names, and to recognize appositive and predicative relationships between them in contexts like (1) and (2) above. Meanwhile, university research has concentrated more upon the problem of anaphora resolution posed by (3). Early work by Hobbs[28] proposed the

Naïve Algorithm, which searches the sentence[29] in left-to-right order and concentrates upon finding antecedents that are close to a given pronoun, while preferring antecedents that occur in the subject position. Hobbs always acknowledged that this algorithm would never do as a stand-alone solution to the problem, but it is still used to gather candidate antecedents for more sophisticated approaches.

Heuristic approaches to coreference

Modern systems, such as CogNIAC, offer 90% or better precision on common pronoun usages that do not require either specialist knowledge or general knowledge for their resolution. CogNIAC works by performing a linguistic analysis and then applying a set of decision rules to the analyzed text.

The linguistic resources[30] that CogNIAC requires are well within the current state of the art as described in Chapter 1:

- Part of speech tagging.
- Simple noun phrase recognition.
- Basic semantic information[31] for nouns and noun phrases, such as gender and number.

Generating possible antecedents for a pronoun is not the hard part of this task. We have already seen that there exist efficient algorithms for identifying referring expressions, such as names. The hard part is picking the right antecedent when there is more than one candidate.

CogNIAC uses an ordered set of core rules to make such decisions. We reproduce them here, with an indication of their performance on a set of 198 pronouns taken from narrative text.[32] The rules assume that the candidates have already been identified, and have already been screened for restrictions like gender and number agreement.

1. *Unique in discourse.* If there is a single candidate in the text read in so far, then make it the antecedent. (8 correct, 0 incorrect.)
2. *Reflexive.* If pronoun is reflexive,[33] then pick the nearest candidate in the text read so far. (16 correct, 1 incorrect.)
3. *Unique in current + prior.* If there is a single candidate in the prior sentence and the read-in portion of the current sentence, then make it the antecedent. (114 correct, 2 incorrect.)
4. *Possessive pro.* If the anaphor contains a possessive pronoun,[34] and there is an exact string match of the anaphor in the prior sentence, then make the matching candidate the antecedent. (4 correct, 1 incorrect.)

5. *Unique in current sentence.* If there is a single candidate in the read-in portion of the current sentence, then make it the antecedent. (21 correct, 1 incorrect.)

6. *Unique subject/subject pronoun.* If the subject of the prior sentence contains a single candidate, and the anaphor is the subject of its sentence, then make the subject of the prior sentence the antecedent. (11 correct, 0 incorrect.)

Pronouns are considered in the order in which they occur in the text. For each pronoun, the rules are tried in the order in which they are listed above. If a rule succeeds, by having its conditions met, then its action is taken, and no further rules are considered for that pronoun. If a rule fails, because its conditions are not satisfied, then the next rule is tried. If no rules apply, then the pronoun is left unresolved.

The data show that these are high precision rules, when considered individually, and their recall when combined is 60%. As an example of a sentence where CogNIAC would fail to resolve a pronoun, Baldwin cites the following well-known example:[35]

> The city council refused to give the women a permit because they feared/advocated violence.

This example consists of two sentences: one in which violence is feared and one in which it is advocated. The preferred interpretation of 'they' is strongly influenced by the choice of verb. Resolving the coreferent of 'they' would require a fairly sophisticated analysis of verb meanings, as well as some real world knowledge to the effect that a city council is more like to be anti-violence than pro-violence.

Statistical approaches to coreference

An alternate approach to hand-written heuristic rules is to have a program learn preferences among antecedents from sample data. Researchers at Brown University[36] used a corpus of Wall Street Journal articles marked with coreference information to build a probabilistic model for this problem. This model then informs an algorithm for finding antecedents for pronouns in unseen documents.

The model considers the following factors when assigning probabilities to pronoun-antecedent pairings.

1. *Distance* between the pronoun and the proposed antecedent, with greater distance lowering the probability.

   Hobbs' Naïve Algorithm is used to gather candidate antecedents, which are then rank ordered by distance. The probability that the correct antecedent lies at distance rank d from the pronoun is then computed from corpus statistics as

$$\frac{\text{the number of correct antecedents at distance } d}{\text{medium the total number of correct antecedents}}.$$

2. *Mention count.* Noun phrases that are mentioned repeatedly are preferred as antecedents.

   As well as counting mentions of referents, the authors make an adjustment for position of the pronoun in the document. The later in the document a pronoun occurs, the more likely it is that its referent will have been mentioned multiple times.

3. *Syntactic analysis* of the context surrounding the pronoun, especially where reflexive pronouns are concerned.

   Preferences for antecedents in the subject position and special treatment of reflexive pronouns are supplied by the Hobbs algorithm.

4. *Semantic distinctions*, such as number, gender, and animate/inanimate, which make certain pairings unlikely or impossible.

   Given a training corpus of correct antecedents, counts can be obtained for such semantic features.

The probability that a pronoun corefers with a given antecedent is then computed as a function of these four factors, and the winning pair is the one that maximizes the probability of assignment.

The authors performed an experiment to test the accuracy of the model on the singular pronouns ('he', 'she', and 'it'), and their various possessive and reflexive forms ('his', 'hers', 'its', 'himself', 'herself', 'itself'). They implemented their model in an incremental fashion, enabling the contribution of the various factors to be analyzed. The results were quite interesting, and can be summarized as follows.

Ignoring Hobbs' algorithm, and simply choosing the closest noun phrase as the referent, had a success rate of only 43%. Using the syntactic analysis afforded by the Naïve Algorithm increased accuracy to 65%. Adding semantic information, such as gender, raised the success rate to 76%. Adding additional information, such as mention counts, obtained a final increment to 83%.

In restricting themselves to singular pronouns with concrete referents,[37] the authors set out to solve a simpler problem than that addressed by Cog-NIAC, but the results are still impressive. These are very common usages, and there is considerable utility for text mining in being able to analyze them accurately. In many documents, long chains of coreferences form a thread of meaning in which a single person or thing is mentioned, described and discussed. Such threads can form the basis of a document summary with respect to that entity, and such summaries could be provided in response to a query that contains a recognizable reference to the entity. Before exploring this topic further, we survey the general field of document summarization.

5.3 Automatic summarization

In Chapter 2, we echoed the common complaint that it is often hard to find documents relevant to our information needs, but actually the situation is much worse than that. Having found some relevant documents, the typical knowledge worker then has to find the time to read them, summarize them, and probably write some kind of survey or report that will serve as a basis for recommendations. The subsequent processing of retrieved documents is at least as arduous and time consuming as finding them in the first place.

High-quality browsing tools for scanning single large documents, or sets of documents, would be a boon to many people whose business is information. In Section 5.1, we saw how the named entities identified by PeopleCite can be used as a jumping off point for the browsing of documents. Similarly, document summaries are a useful adjunct in the sifting process, as well as providing report writers with material for their own abstracts.

Text summarization can be defined as a process that takes a document as input and outputs a shorter, surrogate document, which contains its most important content. 'Importance' can be determined with respect to a number of different reference points. The most common reflect user requirements, such as being relevant to a given topic, or helping the user perform a certain task. For example, intelligence agencies might wish to monitor message traffic for certain topics, or have long documents that feature associated key words or phrases summarized, but only with respect to the chosen topics.

One can think of a summary as being an extract or an abstract, with rather different implications. An *extract* is a summary that is constructed mostly by choosing the most relevant pieces of text, perhaps with some minor edits. An *abstract* is a gloss that describes the contents of a document without necessarily featuring any of that content.

In both cases, one can think of summarization as *compressing* or condensing a document. An extract performs compression by discarding less relevant material, whereas an abstract performs compression in more sophisti-

cated ways, e.g., by suppressing detail and replacing specific facts with gener-
alities. Obviously, one could mix these two modes of compression in a longer
summary, although doing this effectively raises many design issues.

Another distinction that one finds in the literature is between *generic* and
query-relevant summaries. Generic summaries give an overall sense of a document's content, while query-relevant summaries confine themselves to content
that is relevant to a background query.[38] The latter type of summary might be
extremely useful when dealing with documents that are either large, such as a
manual or textbook, or contain diverse subject matter, such as court opinions.

In this chapter, we begin with an examination of summarization tasks
and the results of some experiments before reviewing actual approaches to
automatic summarization. The chapter ends with an assessment of current
methodologies for both training and evaluating summarization programs.

5.3.1 Summarization tasks

Systematic attempts to build and evaluate automatic summarization software
received a boost in 1996 from a research programme called TIPSTER-III. This
was a DARPA[39] program involving government security agencies[40] intended to
support R&D in natural language processing.[41] It was sponsored by the MUC
and TREC organizations, under the auspices of the National Institute of Standards and Technology, which should be familiar to readers from the earlier
chapters of this book.[42]

The SUMMAC Summarization Conference[43] of TIPSTER-III performed
a large-scale evaluation of automatic text summarization technologies for relevance assessment tasks. We shall see that summaries produced at relatively
low compression rates[44] allowed for the assessment of news articles almost as
accurate as that achieved using the full-text of documents. Since relevance assessment is a primary use case for summarization of online documents, these
findings have significance beyond the intelligence community.

SUMMAC defined a number of summarization tasks, all of which were
based on activities carried out by information analysts in the U.S. Government.

–   The *ad hoc* task focused on generic summaries that were tailored to a
    particular topic.
–   The *categorization* task investigated whether a generic summary could con-
    tain enough information to allow an analyst to quickly and correctly cate-
    gorize a document with respect to a given set of topics.

- The *question-answering* task evaluated an 'informative' topic-related summary in terms of the degree to which it contained answers to a set of topic-related questions that could be found in the original document.

The ad hoc topics are shown in Table 5.2. The reader can see that these are fairly diverse, although certain pairs of topics might be confusable as a result of shared vocabulary, e.g., 'Nuclear power plants' and 'Solar power.' The 20 topics were chosen from a larger set of over 200 topics used by TREC.

For each topic, a 50-document test set was created from the top 200 most relevant documents retrieved by a standard search engine. Each document in each set came with relevance judgments for that topic provided by TREC. The 20 sets of documents were disjoint, and most of them were news stories from Associated Press and Wall Street Journal.

Two measures of performance were used to assess the usefulness of the summaries for relevance assessment tasks.

- Time. This is simply the time taken for a human subject to assess the relevance of a document by reading the summary.
- Accuracy. This was assessed using a contingency table, as in Table 5.3, where TP denotes 'true positive', FP denotes 'false positive', FN denotes

Table 5.2 20 TREC topics chosen for the ad hoc summarization task

Nuclear power plants	Cigarette consumption
Quebec independence	Computer security
Medical waste dumping	Professional scuba diving
DWI regulations	Cost of national defense
Infant mortality rates	Solar power
Japanese auto imports	Volcanic activity levels
Capital punishment	Electric automobiles
Lotteries	Violent juvenile crimes
Procedures for heart ailments	For-profit hospitals
Environmental protection	Right to die

Table 5.3 Contingency table for ad hoc summarization task

Ground truth	Subjects' judgment	
	Relevant	Irrelevant
Relevant is true	TP	FN
Irrelevant is true	FP	TN

'false negative' and TN denotes 'true negative.' Recall and precision metrics can be computed from this table in the usual way (see Chapter 2).

The design for the ad hoc experiment compared the performance of 21 professional information analysts on the relevance assessment task using full-text, fixed-length summaries,[45] variable-length summaries and baseline summaries.[46] See Sidebar 5.3 for a sample document and sample summaries.

Statistical analysis of the results showed that:

- Performance on variable-length summaries was not significantly different from that on full-text. Time taken to read the summaries was approximately half that of reading the full text (roughly, half a minute versus a minute).
- Performance on fixed-length summaries was not significantly faster than on baseline summaries, but produced significantly better accuracy.
- These performance gains are due to increased recall, not increased precision.
- The main weakness of the various kinds of summary versus full-text is false negatives, not false positives, i.e., summaries sometimes miss relevant information from the source. This is particularly true at high compression rates.

Concerning the effect of compression rate upon performance, the data showed that time increased more or less linearly with summary length, while accuracy increased only logarithmically.

These are encouraging results, since they demonstrate that automatic summarization can deliver real performance gains on a common class of information processing tasks, namely those involving the judgment of a document's relevance to a set of topics.

We now move on to the technology itself.

Sidebar 5.3 Sample document and sample summaries

Here is a sample full-text document from the 'Cigarette consumption' topic.

Cancer Map Shows Regional Contrasts
Striking regional variations are revealed by the first atlas of cancer incidence in England and Wales, published yesterday, Clive Cookson writes. The atlas, commissioned by the Cancer Research Campaign, shows that lung cancer, the most common form of the disease in men, is much more prevalent in the north than in the south. The reverse is true for breast cancer, the most common cancer in women.

Dr Isabel Silva and Dr Anthony Swerdlow of the London School of Hygiene and Tropical Medicine analysed information about 3m new cancer patients between 1968 and 1985 to give a county-by-county variation in cancer risks. They compared these with the geographical distributions of risk factors such as smoking and occupation. The figures in the map above are an index of the number of new cases in each county over the period.

In some cancers there is an obvious link with risk factors. The north-south gradient in lung cancer is caused mainly by the greater prevalence of smoking in the north. The authors say that greater industrial exposures to smoke, dust and toxic fumes in the north are not sufficient to account for the regional differences.

Malignant melanoma, the most virulent skin cancer, has a strong south/north gradient – someone living on the south coast is three times more likely to suffer than someone in northern England. There is a clear correlation with hours of sunshine.

The reason why breast and ovarian cancers are more common in the south is not obvious. The fact that southern women have fewer children on average may be a partial explanation, Drs Silver and Swerdlow say, because they have higher levels of the hormones related to these cancers.

(Atlas of Cancer Incidence in England & Wales. Oxford University Press)

Here is an automatically generated variable-length summary.

Striking regional variations are revealed by the first atlas of cancer incidence in England and Wales, published yesterday, Clive Cookson writes.

They compared these with the geographical distributions of risk factors such as smoking and occupation.

The north-south gradient in lung cancer is caused mainly by the greater prevalence of smoking in the north.

The fact that southern women have fewer children on average may be a partial explanation, Drs Silver and Swerdlow say, because they have higher levels of the hormones related to these cancers.

Here is an automatically generated fixed-length summary.

In some cancers there is an obvious link with risk factors. The north-south gradient in lung cancer is caused mainly by the greater prevalence of smoking . . .

Here is baseline summary, consisting of the first 10% of the document.

Striking regional variations are revealed by the first atlas of cancer incidence in England and Wales, published yesterday, Clive Cookson writes. The atlas, commissioned by the Cancer Research . . .

5.3.2 Constructing summaries from document fragments

The most popular way to construct a summary for a single document is to have a program select fragments from the document and then combine them into an extract.[47] Many different approaches along these lines have been tried and reported in the literature. However, it is not possible to compare these approaches systematically, since most of the studies were done on different corpora and under different experimental conditions. We can do little more than outline the most salient research and report the results here. But we shall see that a fairly consistent pattern of findings emerges with respect to the effectiveness of more sophisticated summarization techniques over simpler methods.

Summarization by sentence selection
A common way to tackle a hard research problem is to translate it into a simpler task that gets most of the job done. Selecting sentences for inclusion in the summary reduces summarization generation from a complex cognitive task to an exercise in sentence ranking. More precisely, one is interested in estimating, for each sentence, how likely it is that the sentence would or should appear in a summary. Having a ranking allows one to include or exclude sentences depending upon the desired summary length. This reduction leaves to one side the question of how the selected fragments should be combined to form a coherent whole.

The sentence is frequently (but not always) selected as the unit from which summaries are constructed, although there are obviously advantages (and disadvantages) to the use of larger units (such as paragraphs) and smaller units (such as phrases). Paragraph selection has its advantages if the required summary is relatively large, or if the material is such that the gist of a document is likely to be contained in a single paragraph. Most news articles are well summarized by their first paragraph, while most scientific papers contain a small number of paragraphs that motivate, report and interpret results. The problem with phrases is how to flesh them out into coherent sentences, possibly by combining them with other phrases. This can be done manually, of course, but the effort is greater than with the editing and arrangement of sentence units.

Rating sentences with respect to their suitability to appear in a summary is not a trivial task, but various heuristics have been put forward in the literature. These are based upon statistical studies of summary versus non-summary sentences for corpora containing documents that already have summaries. In the interests of brevity, we shall refer to sentences rated highly to appear in summaries as 'summary sentences' (SSs).

–   *Summary sentences should contain 'new' information.* SSs are more likely to contain proper names and are more likely to begin with the indefinite article 'A' than non-SSs. Clearly proper names, especially the full names of people, companies, etc., are often used to introduce new objects of interest that the document might be about. By the same token, the presence of pronouns is a good source of negative evidence, since these refer to previously mentioned entities. Similarly, indefinite descriptions, such as 'a major earth tremor,' often signal the introduction of a topic of interest, as opposed to a definite reference, such as 'the tremor.' The same is true of long noun phrases 'the most recent earth tremor' versus shorter references, such as 'the tremor.'

–   *Summary and non-summary sentences have distinctive word features.* SSs and non-SSs appear to be differentiated by a ragbag of other features at the phrase and word level. SSs often begin with words or phrases that suggest a conclusion being drawn, e.g., 'finally', 'in conclusion', etc. They also tend to contain words that have a high density of related words occurring in the text, such as synonyms, hyponyms, and antonyms. Non-SSs tend to contain miscellaneous indicators, such as negations ('no', 'never', etc.), integers ('1', '2', 'one', 'two', etc.), and informal or imprecise terms ('got', 'really', etc.). These results are in accordance with intuition, since SSs are usually positive, general, formal statements.

Most summarization systems employ a mixture of linguistic knowledge, such as the above, and more generic statistical methods, such as Bayes' Rule or the cosine distance metric, which we met in Chapter 2.

An example of such a hybrid approach is that of Kupiec's *Trainable Document Summarizer,*[48] which uses the following set of discrete features for selecting sentences:

–   *Sentence length feature.* Summaries rarely contain really short sentences, so we expect SSs to be longer than a threshold, such as 5 words.
–   *Fixed phrase feature.* Certain phrases suggest summary material, e.g., 'in conclusion.'
–   *Paragraph feature.* The first and last several paragraphs of a document are most likely to contain summary material.
–   *Thematic word feature.* The most frequent words in a document can be regarded as thematic, and summary sentences are likely to contain one or more of them.
–   *Uppercase word feature.* Proper names and acronyms (especially with parenthesized explanations) are often important for summaries.

Given k such features, $F_1, \ldots, F_k$, every sentence in a document can be scored according to its probability of being in the summary using Bayes' Rule,

$$P(s \in S | F_1, \ldots, F_k) = \frac{P(F_1, \ldots, F_k | s \in S) P(s \in S)}{P(F_1, \ldots, F_k)}$$

which can be written as

$$P(s \in S|F_1,\ldots,F_k) = \frac{\displaystyle\prod_{j=1}^{j=k} P(F_j|s \in S)P(s \in S)}{\displaystyle\prod_{j=1}^{j=k} P(F_j)}$$

if we assume independence among the features. The prior $P(s \in S)$ can be approximated by a constant factor, such as the reciprocal of the number of sentences in the document, and therefore ignored. $P(F_j|s \in S)$ and $P(F_j)$ can be estimated from counts over training data.

In order to derive such counts, it is necessary to create a training corpus by taking a document collection and matching sentences from known summaries with sentences in the corresponding original documents. As we shall see, there are many ways in which one might do this, but Kupiec et al. used the fairly simple approach of (1) looking for very close sentence matches, and (2) looking for summary sentences ('joins') composed of two or more sentence fragments from the original. 'Incomplete' single sentences and incomplete joins contain some fragments from the original, but also some material that appears to be wholly new. Other summary material is deemed to be unmatchable.

In their corpus (of engineering documents), 83% of summary sentences were either exact matches or joins, and therefore deemed to be correct in a manual process. The trained summarizer chose 35% of these summary sentences. When the summary sentences being searched included the 'incompletes', recognition rose to 42%, i.e., 42% of the summary sentences derived from the original documents by full or partial matching were identified.

Looking at the performance of individual features, it appeared that the 'paragraph' and 'fixed phrase' features were especially useful in picking out summary material from the original text, with 'sentence length' also performing well. Single word features, such as 'uppercase word' and 'thematic word', performed less well.

Summarization by paragraph selection

One problem with sentence selection as a strategy is that the resulting summaries are often disjointed and do not read well. Using larger building blocks can help with coherence. Thus an alternate approach to summarization is to assume that a text contains a small number of 'best' paragraphs, which can stand for the text as a whole. This is particularly effective for certain kinds of material, such as news stories and encyclopedia entries, where an early paragraph, typically the first, provides a coherent outline of what follows. Many news stories start with a succinct statement of who did what to whom, together with where and when. (The 'how' and 'why' usually comes later.)

Paragraph selection has been well studied, although it has not been as popular with researchers as sentence selection. One approach[49] is to begin by attempting an analysis of text structure, e.g., by linking similar paragraphs together. Similarity is estimated using the vector space techniques described in Chapter 2. Once the text has been segmented in this way, it is possible to identify the most heavily linked paragraphs. These have many links because they share terminology with many other paragraphs, and are therefore likely to contain overview or summary material.

Merely reproducing these paragraphs in the order that they occur in the text may cover the salient points of a document but fail to read well as a summary. Consequently, other strategies have been tried, such as starting with the most heavily linked paragraph and then visiting the next most similar paragraph, and so on. The chain of such paragraphs may improve on the previous approach, depending upon the material to be summarized.

Another approach by Strzalkowski et al.[50] also identifies paragraph structure, but then uses anaphors and other backward references to group passages together. Once passages have been connected in this way, they cannot be separated; either they all appear in the final summary, or none of them do. In addition to the document itself, the summarizer (called SDOCTOOL) takes a desired summary length and a topic description as inputs. Query terms extracted from the topic description are used to score combinations of passages. The passages with the best score appear in the final summary, the number of passages being determined by the length constraint.

Discourse based summarization

Moens[51] takes a quite different approach in which the first step is to model the structure of documents to be summarized. Thus, when attempting to abstract Belgian criminal cases, she began with an analysis of the 'typical form of discourse' of such materials. The result was a *text grammar*, in which prototypical segments of text are arranged in a network of nodes and links.

Different kinds of case have variations on this structure, and so a case can be categorized initially by recognizing the presence or absence of key segments. A given text is then tagged for further analysis by running a 'partial parser'[52] over it to identify commonly occurring word patterns that signal the start of a new segment. A knowledge engineering effort was required to construct these patterns by hand.

The system, called SALOMON, could then abstract selected parts of the case, such as the title, the parties, and the verdict, to provide a summary of the case. Clearly, such a system is predicated upon a particular type of document, being used in a particular context, such as legal research. Some general techniques were used to cluster paragraphs into segments (as in the preceding section on paragraph based summarization), but the resulting summaries were also informed by the overall structure of the case.

Marcu's approach[53] is both more general and more formal, in that it relies upon a methodology for text analysis called Rhetorical Structure Theory[54] (RST). A detailed discussion of RST is well beyond the scope of this book, but the basic idea is that texts can be decomposed into two kinds of elementary units: *nuclei* and *satellites*. These are non-overlapping spans of text that stand in various relations to each other. A nucleus expresses something essential to a writer's purpose, whereas a satellite expresses something less essential, e.g., it may provide the setting of a nucleus, or elaborate upon it. Nuclei may also stand in relationships to one another, such as contrast, in constructions such as 'on the one hand ... on the other hand.'

Applying RST to summarization, Marcu reduces the generation of a summary to a small number of (admittedly large) steps. First, take a text and decide what percentage of its length, $p\%$, you want the summary to be. Then, proceed as follows.

1. Identify the discourse structure of the text, using his 'rhetorical parsing algorithm.'
2. Determine a partial ordering on the units of the discourse structure.
3. Select the first $p\%$ of the units in this ordering.

The rhetorical parsing algorithm is cue-based, i.e., it identifies cue phrases and punctuation which mark important boundaries and transitions in the text, informed by corpus analysis. These 'discourse markers' suggest rhetorical relations between clauses, sentences and whole paragraphs, which are then rendered as tree structures. Where ambiguity exists, a weight function is used to prefer hypothetical text structures that are skewed towards introducing nuclei first and satellites later, since this is the most common way of expounding a topic.

Coreference based summarization
The two previous methods have been studied primarily in the context of 'generic' summaries, as defined earlier in this section. Coreference based methods are more focused upon the task of summarizing a document so that the

user of a retrieval system can determine whether or not a document is relevant to a query, and therefore worth reading. As we saw in Section 5.2, the basic concept behind coreference is that two linguistic expressions, such as 'Bill Gates' and 'the Chairman of Microsoft', corefer when they both refer to the same entity.[55]

If a query contains the name of an entity, such as a person or company, a reasonable summary of a document with respect to that query may be obtained by extracting sentences that contain references to that entity. This is simple to state, but hard to do, when references to Bill Gates might include such words and phrases as 'Gates', 'he', 'Microsoft Chairman', 'the billionaire', and so forth. Then think of the even more oblique relationships that hold between phrases such as 'the President', 'the White House', 'Washington', and 'the US', when used to refer to the government of the United States taking some action, e.g.,

'The President is expected to ratify the missile treaty.'
'The White House is expected to ratify the missile treaty.'
'Washington is expected to ratify the missile treaty.'
'The US is expected to ratify the missile treaty.'

More general meaning relationships also enter into coreference, especially among descriptions of events. Thus, a program may need to realize that

'the assassination of the President'

and

'the shooting of the President'

refer to the same incident.

Coreference determination for summarization is currently handled via a combination of string matching, acronym expansion, and dictionary lookup. At document retrieval time, names occurring in queries must be compared with referring expressions in documents. Such associations can be used to rank and then select sentences from the document for incorporation into a summary.

Using such methods, Baldwin and Morton[56] were able to generate summaries that were almost as effective as the full text in helping a user determine relevance.

5.3.3 Multi-document summarization (MDS)

If the summarization of single documents is difficult, summarization across multiple documents poses even more problems. Yet success in this endeavor would offer real utility to many researchers and 'knowledge workers', by enabling them to process whole document collections with far less effort than today. And, unlike single-document summarization, the multi-document case is more like real text mining, in that such summaries may well make it possible for users to make novel connections and undercover implicit relationships that cannot be gleaned from any single text.

Stein et al.[57] point out that single-document summarization is only one of the critical subtasks that need to be performed for successful MDS, e.g., the program must also

- identify important themes in the document collection;
- select representative single-document summaries for each of these themes; and
- organize these representative summaries for the final multi-document summary.

They use the paragraph-based, single-document summarizer SDOCTOOL, described in Section 5.3.2, to generate a summary for each document in the collection, then they group the summaries into clusters using Dice's coefficient (see Sidebar 5.4) as the similarity metric. Representative passages are selected from the clusters rather in the same manner as SDOCTOOL selects representative passages from a single document. The cross-document summarizer, XDOCTOOL, then presents selected passages with similar passages being grouped together. There is no other organizing principle used in constructing the final summary.

Sidebar 5.4 Another similarity measure

Dice's coefficient scales the overlap of sets of features A and B in terms of the size of these sets. Thus

$$DICE(A, B) = \frac{2N_{AB}}{N_A + N_B}$$

where N_A is the size of set A, N_B is the size of set B, and N_{AB} is the size of the overlap between them. Note that

$$0 \leq DICE(A, B) \leq 1$$

and

$$DICE(A, A) = 1.$$

Basing cross-document summarization on clustered paragraphs avoids some of the problems inherent in trying to bootstrap the sentence extraction model to the multi-document case. Simply extracting important sentences from single documents and pooling them for presentation to the user is bound to result in long, repetitive summaries.

Picking paragraphs from clusters helps reduce redundancy, but does nothing to integrate information from different documents at the paragraph level. Researchers at Columbia University[58] have taken a somewhat different approach to MDS, called 'reformulation.' As well as clustering similar paragraphs by theme, they also identify key phrases within paragraphs, reducing phrases to a logical form called 'predicate-argument structure' in order to effect the comparison (see Sidebar 5.5).

Phrases are matched using a machine learning algorithm, called RIPPER, described in Chapter 4. Important sentences and key phrases are then 'intersected' to form new, more informative sentences for inclusion in the summary. For example, the sentence,

"McVeigh was formally charged on Friday with the Oklahoma bombing."

might be merged with the phrase,

"Timothy James McVeigh, 27"

to produce the more informative sentence:

"Timothy James McVeigh, 27, was formally charged on Friday with the Oklahoma bombing."

This merge process is performed upon the logical form of the sentences and phrases, instead of trying to work with the raw text. Finally, summary sentences are *generated* from the underlying logical forms, so that the system can produce novel sentences that did not occur in any of the texts. This is done using a language generation program called FUF/SURGE.[59]

Sidebar 5.5 Predicate-argument structure

Predicate-argument analysis reduces a sentence to a logical form, using notation borrowed from the predicate calculus. Thus, "The Federal Court rebuked Microsoft" and "Microsoft is rebuked by the Federal Court" would both reduce to an expression like "rebuke(Federal

Court, Microsoft)". This mapping eliminates some of the syntactic variation of English and therefore allows sentences with similar meaning to be recognized in a pairwise comparison. A simple word match without regard to order would not be able to distinguish between "The Federal Court rebuked Microsoft" and "Microsoft rebuked the Federal Court".

More complex sentences can be represented by a more sophisticated notation, such as *dependency grammar*. This kind of analysis allows verbs to be annotated with tense and voice, nouns to be annotated with number and other features, and accommodated complex syntactic structures, such as prepositional phrases. For example, "The court rebuked the defendants" could be represented along the lines of:

<rebuke, past>(<court, definite, singular>, <defendant, definite, plural>).

More sophisticated still are analyses that attempt to account for synonymy, e.g., recognizing that verbs such as 'rebuke', 'criticize', 'reprimand', etc., have a common semantic core. This leads to further complexity, in which words are represented by bundles of features, which can then be matched.

The purpose of all such analyses is to uncover similarities in the 'deep structure' of words and sentences that are obscured by different 'surface structures' of the language, such as word order and lexical choice.

The multi-document summarization problem has received more attention in recent years, due to the Topic Detection and Tracking[60] (TDT) initiative. In 1996, a DARPA-sponsored initiative began investigating the problem of automatically finding and following new events in a media stream of broadcast news stories. This task requires that a system be able to accomplish the following subtasks.

1.   Segment the stream of speech data into distinct stories.
2.   Identify stories that describe new events[61] in the news stream.
3.   Identify stories that follow on from these new stories.

Here we shall neglect (1) in favor of (2) and (3), since speech recognition and the segmentation of audio data are out of scope for this book. We shall assume that news stories are already rendered as text, and that their boundaries are therefore known. (2) really boils down to detecting stories that are not similar to previous stories, while (3) looks for stories that *are* similar to stories identified as new.

Events can be detected 'retrospectively' in an accumulated collection, or 'on-line' in documents arriving in real time. These are somewhat different tasks. The input to a retrospective system is an entire corpus of documents, and the output will be sets of documents clustered by the events that they describe. The input to an on-line system is a stream of stories, read in chronological order, and the output is a YES/NO decision, indicating whether or not a given story describes a new event.

Given that new events are, by definition, events about which we have no knowledge, it is clear that we cannot identify them by running queries against either a document collection or a stream of documents. One is essentially mining the text for new patterns, which can be seen as a query-free form of document retrieval. There is also a text classification component to this problem, since we are interested in grouping documents into ad hoc categories.[62]

The Carnegie Mellon (CMU) group used a conventional vector space model[63] for their clustering system, based on the SMART retrieval system developed at Cornell University.[64] As usual, documents are preprocessed as follows: stop words are removed, the remaining words are stemmed, and term weights are calculated.[65] The weight of a term t in story d is defined as

$$w(t,d) = \frac{1 + \log_2 TF_{t,d} \times IDF_t}{\sqrt{\sum_{\vec{d}=\langle d_i \rangle} d_i^2}}$$

where TF and IDF are term frequency and inverse document frequency, as defined in Chapter 2, and the denominator is the 2-norm[66] of the document vector. The similarity between two stories is then defined as the cosine metric between their two vectors, as explained in Chapter 2.

A cluster of documents is represented by a *centroid vector*, which is just the normalized sum of the story vectors in that cluster. Similarity between clusters is likewise determined by the cosine measure, as is similarity between a story and a cluster. Thus, new stories can be added to a cluster if the cosine measure between them scores above a predetermined threshold, in which case the centroid is updated. If the story is insufficiently similar to any existing cluster, then it describes a new event, and a new cluster is created for it. This cluster will then attract follow-up stories to the new story, if they are sufficiently similar to it.

At the heart of CMU's method is an 'agglomerative algorithm' that it collects data into clusters. Called *Group Average Clustering*, it maximizes the average pairwise similarity between stories in a cluster. The algorithm[67] works in a bottom-up fashion as follows.

- Individual stories are leaf nodes in a binary tree of clusters, and are treated as singleton clusters.
- Any intermediate node is the centroid of its two children, which are more similar to each other than any other cluster.
- The root of the tree contains all clusters and therefore contains all stories.

The University of Massachusetts (UMass) group tried two methods for the retrospective task. One was an agglomerative algorithm similar to CMU's. Using the INQUERY[68] search engine, two documents are compared by running each against the other as if one were a query and the other a document to be retrieved. The similarity between the two documents is then computed as the average of the two belief scores. Documents are only clustered if the average so derived is more than two standard deviations above the mean comparison score. The mean comparison score is simply the average of all the two-way pairwise similarity scores for all the documents in the training collection.

The other method tried by UMass placed more emphasis on timing. Novel phrases occurring in the documents to be rated are examined to see if their occurrences are concentrated at a particular point in time, or reasonably narrow range thereof. If so, the term is allowed to trigger an event, and the documents containing the term are handed to a relevance feedback[69] algorithm, which generates a query for finding subsequent stories about that event.

Participants in the 1996 study touched upon the following open issues with respect to TDT in their 1998 report:

1. How do we give analysts monitoring news stories an overview of the whole information space, so they can navigate (i.e., search and browse) through it?
2. How do we choose the right level of granularity for clusters, so that users don't find them too big to browse or too small to consider?
3. How to summarize the clusters, the stories in them, and the themes in the stories?

As we have seen, researchers have begun to address (3), using 'ready to hand' techniques present in the literature. Thus vector space models, cosine similarity measures, and centroid clustering have all been pressed into the service of TDT. (2), on the other hand, requires a better understanding of how to parameterize clustering systems (see Sidebar 5.6). (1) is somewhat beyond the scope of this text, in that it assumes the availability of dynamic visualization software for graphically representing clusters of documents and relationships between them.

Columbia University was not involved in the TDT Pilot Study, but entered a system (called CIDR) for the subsequent TDT-2 evaluation. The system was put together in a short period of time as a testbed for exploring ideas about clustering and summarization. Like CMU and UMass, they used a form of the tried and true *tf-idf* weight function to generate clusters of documents. Their approach to multi-document summarization is called CBS, for 'Centroid Based

Summarization.' Centroids can be thought of as pseudo-documents that represent a whole cluster, and contain word lists, together with their corresponding counts and inverse document frequencies, or IDFs. To satisfy the 'on-line' task, they estimated IDFs from another collection of articles, rather than from the news feed they were incrementally reading.

Their actual summarization system, called MEAD, takes as input centroids from the clusters generated by CIDR (plus a compression rate). It then produces as output sentences that are topical for the documents in the clusters, constructing summaries in the form of sentence extracts. This work is, in some ways, less ambitious than the work on summarization by reformulation, described above, in which the logical contents of topical sentences are merged prior to language generation. However, it does contain the notion of *subsumption* between sentences, namely the idea that one sentence can contain the meaning of another, while sentences that have essentially the same meaning are arranged in equivalence classes. Subsumption is computed by word overlap, using the Dice coefficient (see Sidebar 5.4), rather than any kind of grammatical analysis. During summary construction, more informative sentences will be preferred over less informative ones, and more than one sentence will not be used from the same equivalence class.

Sidebar 5.6 Clustering parameters

Various system parameters were instituted in the interests of efficiency and then methodically varied to assess their effects upon CIDR's performance.

- DECAY_THRESHOLD. Processing ignores all but the first 50–200 words in a document to speed up the construction of *tf-idf* vectors. This works fine for news articles, since their salient points are usually contained in the first paragraph or two.
- IDF_THRESHOLD. Processing ignores any words with high document frequency, which reduces the size of the vectors.
- SIM_THRESHOLD. This parameter controls when a new cluster is created, and helps tune precision and recall when clustering.
- KEEP_WORDS. A centroid is typically represented by only the 10–20 highest scoring words on *tf-idf*.

Experiments have shown that a relatively small number of words is sufficient to capture the topic of a cluster, and that properties of these terms, such as inverse document frequency, remain reasonably stable as new documents are added to a cluster. Best clustering results, in terms of misses versus false alarms, were obtained with DECAY_THRESHOLD = 100 and KEEP_WORDS = 10.

5.4 Testing of automatic summarization programs

Machine-generated summaries are notoriously hard to evaluate. What makes a good summary? Intuitively, a summary should capture the important points in a document and be easy to read. Sentence selection algorithms can be good at gathering the main points, but a summary consisting of strung-together sentences plucked out of the text may not read well. Such methods may nonetheless be effective for discursive materials, such as legal opinions and magazine articles. Selected paragraphs will read well (to the extent that the original was well written), but may miss important points if material is distributed throughout the text. Such methods may work better on news articles than on magazine articles or legal cases.

5.4.1 Evaluation problems in summarization research

Researchers have typically used two methods in trying to quantify the performance of summarization programs. One is to compare the machine's output with an 'ideal' hand-written summary, produced by an editor or a domain expert. This has been called 'intrinsic' evaluation,[70] and it is the more widely used of the two. The other, 'extrinsic', approach is to evaluate the usefulness of a summary in helping someone perform an information processing task. Both methods are known to be very sensitive to basic parameters of the experimental context, such as summary length.[71]

First, let us consider intrinsic evaluations. When human subjects are asked to generate 10% summaries of news articles by sentence extraction, intersubject agreement can be as high as 95%, but declines somewhat when the compression ratio increases to 20%. When other materials, such as scientific articles, are used, agreement declines significantly to 70% or less. Not surprisingly, the perceived accuracy of automatically generated summaries also declines as length increases.

Other experiments have shown that a given pair of *hand-written* summaries may only exhibit about 40–50% overlap in terms of their content. As Mitra, Singhal and Buckley[72] point out:

> 'If humans are unable to agree on which paragraphs best represent an article, it is unreasonable to expect an automatic procedure to identify the best extract, whatever that might be.'

Interestingly, the authors found that their paragraph extraction program was able to generate summaries that had a similar 40–50% overlap profile with a given human-generated summary, indicating that the agreement between the program and a human was typically no worse that the agreement between two humans. They also found that extracting the initial paragraphs of an article formed summaries that were deemed as good as more sophisticated paragraph selection algorithms. (Another consistent finding is that taking the first 10 or 20 percent of a text, and treating that as a summary, can be as effective as sentence selection[73] on many kinds of material.)

Extrinsic evaluations typically treat a summarization system as a post-process to an information retrieval engine. The summary generated is meant to be tailored to the user's query, rather than reflecting the document as a whole. Human subjects then use the summaries to decide whether or not the document is relevant to the query. Their performance on this task is measured with respect to time taken, the accuracy of their decisions, and sometimes the degree of confidence they are prepared to place in their decisions. The assumption is that, given good summaries, users will be faster to judge the relevance of search results than if they had to delve into the documents themselves, and that accuracy and confidence will not suffer too much.[74]

For extrinsic evaluations, there appears to be no consistent relationship between summary length and system performance. Rather the data suggest that systems perform best when allowed to set their own summary lengths. Forcing task-based summaries to conform to a particular compression ratio neglects the user's information need, the genre of the document, and the specific content and structure of the documents themselves.

These results illustrate both the imperfect state of automatic summarization and the imperfect state of our evaluation methods. The evaluation of summarization technology may ultimately remain a subjective matter, since there is no unique right answer to the question 'What is a good summary?' for a given document or set of documents. Nevertheless, researchers are increasing our understanding of what makes for a good evaluation, and this is probably the best we can hope for.

5.4.2 Building a corpus for training and testing

Building a working summarizer based on Bayes, or some other statistical method, depends upon having a large amount of training data, i.e., a corpus of documents and their associated hand-written summaries. However, even if the number of examples to hand is small, there are automatic methods for mapping extant summary fragments to portions of original text that may help generate more training data over unseen texts and also help train a program to generate summaries for further unseen texts.

The rationale behind such a bootstrapping approach is that human summarizers frequently employ a cut-and-paste method for constructing summaries. Programs can therefore examine a given summary sentence and see (1) if it was derived from the text by cut-and-paste, and if so (2) what parts of it were taken from the text, and (3) where in the original text the used fragments come from. Researchers have used problem simplification to formulate a tractable answer these questions. Locating summary fragments in the original text can be posed as a mapping problem (see Sidebar 5.7), where the solution is to assign each word in a summary sentence to its most likely source in the text.[75] This is a more granular approach than that employed by Kupiec, and requires much less manual intervention.

In addition to building a corpus for summarization research, the ability to map summary fragments back onto the text can be used in an online environment to link from a summary sentence to that part of the text which deals with the topic of the sentence. This could be a valuable aid for browsing long documents. The mapping might also be useful for segmenting a document into subtopics, e.g., to support fielded search, as defined in Chapter 2.

Sidebar 5.7 Locating summary fragments in text

More precisely, given as input a sequence of words from the summary, $\langle I_1, \ldots, I_N \rangle$, we want to determine, for each word, its most likely source within the document. We can represent positions within a document by ordered pairs, $\langle S, W \rangle$, where S is the sentence number and W is a word position within that sentence. Thus, $\langle 2, 3 \rangle$ would represent the third word in the second sentence.

Any given word can therefore be represented by a set of such positions, namely those positions in where it occurs in the document. Finding the most likely source for a summary fragment can then be posed as the problem of finding the most likely position sequence that its words occupy in the original text. We will obviously prefer close and consecutive positions to positions that are widely dispersed and jumble the order of the words in the summary sequence.

Here we make another simplifying assumption: namely that the probability that a summary word derives from a particular position in the original text depends only upon the word that precedes it in the summary sequence. This assumption leads to a *bigram model* of the summarization process, in which the probability that a given word from the input sequence is derived from a particular position in the text is conditioned upon the position of the preceding word.

Thus, if I_i, and I_{i+1} are adjacent words from the input sequence, we write

$$P(I_{i+1} = \langle S_2, W_2 \rangle | I_i = \langle S_1, W_1 \rangle)$$

to denote the probability that I_{i+1} was derived from word W_2 of sentence S_2, given that I_i was derived from word W_1 of sentence S_1. We can abbreviate this as

$P(I_{i+1}|I_i)$.

To find the most likely sequence of assignments of positions to a sequence of N input words, we then need to maximize the joint probability, $P(I_1, \ldots, I_N)$, which can be approximated as follows, using the bigram model:

$$P(I_1, \ldots, I_N) = \prod_{i=0}^{i=N-1} P(I_{i+1}|I_i).$$

This can be done efficiently using the Viterbi algorithm[24] that we encountered in Section 5.2.1.

5.5 Prospects for text mining and NLP

Natural language processing, by its very nature, is difficult to automate. This is not primarily because grammar is complicated (although it is), or because word and sentence meanings are hard to analyze (although they are). It is largely because of the complexities of language usage, e.g., our habitual reference to previous linguistic or non-linguistic context, and our tendency to rely upon a reader or listener's common sense or shared experience. Computers are not becoming more like humans, and we should not rely upon software being able to bridge this gap any time soon.

While some progress has already been made on text mining, it is clear that we have a long way to go. Fully automatic methods for identifying proper names are both available commercially and being used in production at electronic publishing houses, but summarization software still leaves a lot to be desired, and is best used as an adjunct to a manual process. Indeed, many 'back office' applications can benefit from a semi-automatic approach in which human editors review the suggestions of programs, e.g., when constructing indexes, classifying documents, and choosing citations. We have seen a number of examples of successful applications along these lines in earlier chapters.

We have also seen that core technologies, such as information retrieval, information extraction and text categorization, are available in various forms, and can function as useful tools, so long as their limitations are understood. Exaggerated claims for these technologies, which suggest that computer programs can somehow 'understand' the meanings of words, or the intentions of users, are counterproductive in this regard. Even claims by software vendors that their programs can perform search or classification based on 'concepts' should be viewed with suspicion. Philosophers have yet to agree on what concepts are, but we can safely say that they are not words or word sequences that happen to occur frequently in documents.

Progress in text processing for online applications will benefit greatly from efforts to make information on the Web and elsewhere more machine-comprehensible. These efforts will involve data interchange standards such as XML,[76] and formats that are being defined over XML, such as RDF.[77] The 'Semantic Web'[78] initiative by the World Wide Web Consortium (W3C) can be seen as an attempt to annotate the Web with metadata to enable more complex transactions between software. Although such standards may be a few years away, researchers are already thinking about how they would exploited.[79]

One can view such endeavors as the other side of the NLP coin. NLP seeks to move machines into the arena of human language, while XML and related technologies seek to move human language into the realm of the machine. These approaches have the potential to be complementary, although at the time of writing they are largely being pursued by separate groups of technologists. W3C is one of the very few organizations attempting to promote synergy between the two areas.

These two different ways of approaching the problem of language processing have implications for systems design. We have seen that finding the right allocation of function between person and machine is often the key to a successful application. Programs can be good at tirelessly enumerating alternatives or generating possibilities, while humans can be good at critiquing and qualifying suggestions. In many instances, fully automatic solutions may be less desirable than semi-automatic ones, in which editors and end users retain control of the process.

The most promising way forward is typically to design a person-machine system in which sophisticated language processing serves as an adjunct to human intelligence. Such systems provide a domain expert with a 'smart clerk' capable of sifting through vast amounts of information and making suggestions concerning interesting documents or parts of documents that should be brought to the experts attention. The clerk may even be empowered to perform whole tasks on its own, in applications that are not mission-critical, or where 'good enough' performance is acceptable.[80] But a degree of editorial oversight will normally be required for 'top drawer' products and services that are a company's primary offerings.

Furthermore, we have seen that successful applications of natural language processing to online applications need not be intelligent in the traditional AI or science fiction sense. Knowledge workers in the 21st century need tools for finding relevant documents, extracting relevant information from them, and assimilating them into existing document classification systems. They also need aids (or aides) for navigating the World Wide Web, corporate Intranets, and digital libraries. But they do not need to conduct a conversation with an Eliza-like program of the kind we encountered in Chapter 1, or to be told what is significant or insignificant by a machine.

Future aides will pose as intelligent agents, and software vendors will no doubt give them names, faces, voice capabilities, and even personalities, using sophisticated 3-d modeling and animation coupled with state of the art speech synthesis. But our prediction is that these devices will be powered mostly by hand-written scripts, or statistical techniques that do not have a significant semantic component. They will perform important roles, such as reminding, suggesting, enumerating, and bookkeeping, but will not exercise judgment or make decisions. Most creative and analytical functions, such as the weighing of evidence and the crafting of recommendations, will remain firmly in the purview of human judgment, which is probably as it should be.

Pointers

The Named Entity Task Definition for MUC7 can be found at the National Institute of Standards and Technology (NIST) Web site.[81]
Another NIST site[82] contains further information about the TIPSTER Text Summarization Evaluation Conference (SUMMAC). The Association for Computational Linguistics,[83] ACL, held specialist workshops on anaphora (1999) called "Coreference and Its Applications", and "Intelligent Scaleable Text Summarization" (1997). The ACL journal, Computational Linguistics, is one of the main venues for publishing research on natural language processing.

For more about XML and RDF, see the World Wide Web Consortium[84] home page.

Notes

1. See Frawley, W. J., Piatetsky-Shapiro, G., & Matheus, C. J. (1991). Knowledge discovery in databases: An overview. In G. Piatetsky-Shapiro & B. Frawley (Eds.), *Knowledge Discovery in Databases* (pp. 1–27). Cambridge, MA: AAAI/MIT Press.

2. Much of this data is relational in nature, but not exclusively so.

3. See Hearst, M. A. (1999). Untangling text data mining. In *Proceedings of the 37th Annual Meeting of the Association for Computational Linguistics* (pp. 3–10). See also http://mappa.mundi.net/trip-m/hearst/

4. Dozier, C. & Haschart, R. (2000). Automatic extraction and linking of personal names in legal text. In *Proceedings of RIAO-2000 (Recherche d'Informations Assistée par Ordinateur)* (pp. 1305–1321).

5. Wasson, M. (2000). Large-scale controlled vocabulary indexing for named entities. *Proceedings of the Language Technology Joint Conference: ANLP-NAACL 2000.*

6. Dalamagas, T. (1998). NHS: A tool for the automatic construction of news hypertext. In *Proceedings of the 20th BCS Colloquium on Information Retrieval.* Grenoble, France.

7. Al-Kofahi, K., Tyrrell, A., Vachher, A., & Jackson, P. (2001). A machine learning approach to prior case retrieval. In *Proceedings of 8th International Conference on Artificial Intelligence and Law* (pp. 88–93). New York: ACM Press.

8. See Chapter 3.

9. See Chapter 2.

10. PeopleCite's statistical analysis uncovered a few anomalies in the West Legal Directory, such as an entry for an attorney named Luke Skywalker, probably submitted by a law student with a passion for Star Wars and a sense of humor.

11. Besides having the highest match probability, a candidate record must meet three additional criteria before we link it to the template. First, the date on the candidate record must be earlier than the template record date. Second, the highest scoring record must have a probability that exceeds a minimum threshold. Third, there must be only one candidate record with the highest probability. If two or more records share the highest score, no linkage is made.

12. The word 'anaphora' derives from Ancient Greek: 'ανα' meaning 'back' or 'upstream', and 'φορα' meaning 'the act of carrying.'

13. This example is taken from Mitkov, R., Evans, R., Orasan, C., Barbu, C., Jones, L., & Sotirova, V. (2000). Coreference and anaphora: Developing annotating tools, annotated resources and annotation strategies. In *Proceedings of the Discourse, Anaphora and Reference Resolution Conference (DAARRC-2000).* Lancaster University, 16–18 November, 2000.

14. E.g., Hobbs, J. E. (1986). Resolving Pronoun References. In Grosz, B. J., Jones, K. S., & Webber, B. L. (Eds.), *Readings in Natural Language Processing* (pp. 339–352). San Francisco: Morgan Kaufmann.

15. See Baldwin, B. (1997). CogNIAC: High precision coreference with limited knowledge and linguistic resources. *ACL-97/EACL-97, Workshop on Anaphora Resolution.* Madrid, Spain.

16. Al-Kofahi, K., Grom, B. & Jackson, P. (1999). Anaphora Resolution in the Extraction of Treatment History Language from Court Opinions by Partial Parsing. In *Proceedings of the Seventh International Conference on Artificial Intelligence and Law* (pp. 138–146).

17. Thanks to the tendency to slap a lowercase "e" on the front of any word to do with the Web, absence of an initial capital letter is less reliable than before as a negative indicator of namehood. Thus eBay is a company name, despite the lack of initial capitalization.

18. For example, NetOwl™ Extractor (http://www.netowl.com) classifies names into the following categories: PERSON, ENTITY (including ORGANIZATION, COMPANY, GOVERNMENT, etc.), PLACE (including COUNTRY, COUNTY, CITY, etc.), ADDRESS, TIME, and various NUMERIC expressions.

19. See Mikheev, A., Grover, C., & Moens, M. (1998). Description of the LTG system used for MUC-7. In *Proceedings of 7th Message Understanding Conference (MUC-7)*. The Language Technology Group (LTG) system scored 93.39 on the F-measure, with precision and recall weighted equally. The runners-up were IsoQuest, scoring $F = 91.60$, and BBN, scoring $F = 90.44$. Interestingly, two human annotators scored 96.95 and 97.60 on the same task under test conditions. So LTG's system scored close to the performance of an individual human editor. It's good to bear in mind when rating computer programs on various extraction and categorization tasks that human performance is never 100%.

20. Mikheev, A. (1999). A Knowledge-free Method for Capitalized Word Disambiguation. In *Proceedings of the 37th Conference of the Association for Computational Linguistics (ACL-99)* (pp. 159–168).

21. Bikel, D. M., Miller, S., Schwartz, R., and Weischedel, R. (1997). Nymble: A high-performance learning name-finder. In *Proceedings of the 5th Conference on Applied Natural Language Processing (ANLP-97)* (pp. 194–201).

22. Bikel, D. M., Schwartz, R., & Weischedel, R. (1999). An algorithm that learns what's in a name. *Machine Learning, 34*, 211–231.

23. See either of the Bikel et al. papers for details.

24. Viterbi, A. J. (1967). Error Bounds for Convolutional Codes and an Asymptotically Optimum Decoding Algorithm. *IEEE Transactions on Information Theory, 13* (2), 278–282.

25. There were only four participants in the Coreference Task and they were all academic institutions, namely Durham, Manitoba, Pennsylvania, and Sheffield Universities.

26. SGML is the document markup standard (ISO 8879) that inspired HTML, the markup language of the Web, and is now being superseded by XML, the World Wide Web Consortium's eXtensible Markup Language. See Goldfarb, C. F. (1990). *The SGML Handbook*. Oxford University Press.

27. See the footnote in Section 5.2.1.

28. Hobbs, J. R. (1977). Resolving Pronoun References. *Lingua, 44*, 311–338. See also Grosz, B. J., Jones, K. S., & Webber, B. L. (Eds.), *Readings in Natural Language Processing* (pp. 339–352). San Francisco: Morgan Kaufmann.

29. Actually, the algorithm searches the parse tree of the sentence in a breadth-first fashion.

30. One version of the system also uses full parse trees, i.e., a complete grammatical analysis of each sentence.

31. One can think of other, non-basic, semantic information that could help with this task. For example, the ability to categorize proper names with respect to their referents could help determine whether or not a pronoun should refer back to a person, place, or organization. But then one is going beyond mere linguistic analysis into real world knowledge.

32. Rules and data are taken from: Baldwin, B. (1995). CogNIAC: A high precision pronoun resolution engine. University of Pennsylvania Department of Computer and Information Sciences Ph.D. Thesis.

33. E.g., *myself, yourself, himself, herself, itself, ourselves, yourselves, themselves.*

34. E.g., *my, your, his, her, its, our, their.*

35. The example is from: Winograd, T. (1972). *Understanding Natural Language.* New York: Academic Press.

36. Ge, N., Hale, J., & Charniak, E. (1998). A statistical approach to anaphora resolution. In *Proceedings of the Sixth Workshop on Very Large Corpora.*

37. The authors did not address the special problems posed by plural pronouns, such as *they*, which are often used to refer to singular referents which have a 'collective' quality, as in the sentence: 'Now that Acme is losing money, they may lay off more employees.' They also do not address the vacuous use of 'it' in sentences such as 'It is raining' and 'It was not worthwhile to purchase the shares.'

38. See e.g. Goldstein, J., Kantrowitz, M., Mittal, V. & Carbonell, J. (1999). Summarizing text documents: Sentence selection and evaluation metrics. In *SIGIR-99* (pp. 121–128).

39. The Defense Advanced Research Projects Agency.

40. The Central Intelligence Agency and the National Security Agency partnered with DARPA in TIPSTER.

41. TIPSTER-I (1992–1994) focused on information retrieval and extraction, while TIPSTER-II (1994–1996) focused on natural language processing applications and prototypes.

42. See Chapters 2 and 3.

43. See http://www.itl.nist.gov/iaui/894.02/related_projects/tipster_summac/final_rpt.html

44. The degree to which a summary is smaller than the original document is often called the level of *compression*. Thus a 'lower' compression rate is taken to mean a smaller summary.

45. Fixed-length summaries were limited to 10% of the character length of the source.

46. Baseline summaries were produced by extracting the first 10% of the source document.

47. An alternative route to the same place is to *delete* unwanted material from the document and combine what is left into an extract. This approach has been used to identify places in the text from which existing summary sentences that have been derived, but it is less popular as a method of deriving new summaries.

48. Kupiec J., Pedersen, J. & Chen, F. (1995). A Trainable Document Summarizer. In *Proceedings of the Eighteenth Annual International ACM SIGIR Conference on Research and Development in Information Retrieval (SIGIR-95)* (pp. 68–73).

49. Mitra, M., Singhal, A., & Buckley, C. (1997). Automatic text summarization by paragraph extraction. In Mani & Maybury (Eds.), *Advances in Automatic Text Summarization* (pp. 31–36). MIT Press.

50. Strzalkowski, T., Stein, G. C., Wang, J. & Wise, G. B. (1999). A robust practical text summarizer. In Mani I., & Maybury, M. T. (Eds.), *Advances in Automated Text Summarization*. MIT Press

51. Moens, M.-F. (2000). *Automatic Indexing and Abstracting of Document Texts*, Chapter 7. Norwell, MA: Kluwer Academic.

52. See Chapter 3, Section 3.4.3.

53. Marcu, D. (2000). *The Theory and Practice of Discourse Parsing and Summarization*. Cambridge, MA: MIT Press.

54. Mann, W. C. & Thompson, S. A. (1988). Rhetorical Structure Theory: Toward a Functional Theory of Text Organization. *Text, 8* (3), 243–281.

55. Coreference is an aspect of language usage, and therefore dependent on contextual factors, such as time, since there may come a day when 'Bill Gates' and 'the Chairman of Microsoft' no longer corefer.

56. Baldwin, B., & Morton, T. (1998). Coreference-Based Summarization. In T. Firmin Hand & B. Sundheim (Eds.), *TIPSTER-SUMMAC Summarization Evaluation. Proceedings of the TIPSTER Text Phase III Workshop*. Washington, D.C.

57. Stein, G. C., Bagga, A. & Wise, G. B. (2000). Multi-document summarization: Methodologies and evaluations. In *Proceedings of TALN-2000*, 16–18 October, 2000.

58. McKeown, K. R., Klavans, J. L., Hatzivassiloglou, V., Barzilay, R. & Eskin, E. (1999). Towards multidocument summarization by reformulation: Progress and prospects. In *Proceedings of the National Conference on Artificial Intelligence (AAAI-99)*. Orlando, Florida.

59. See Elhadad, M. (1993). Using argumentation to control lexical choice: A functional unification based approach. Ph.D. thesis, Columbia University.

60. See Allan, J., Carbonell, J., Doddington, G., Yamron, J. & Yang, Y. (1998). Topic detection and tracking pilot study: Final report. In *Proceedings of the DARPA Broadcast News Transcription and Understanding Workshop*, February 1998.

61. The notion of an *event* is somewhat more restricted than that of a topic. Events are specific, and occur at a particular time and place, whereas topics are more general, and may encompass whole classes of events. Thus a plane crash is an event, whereas airline safety is a topic.

62. Yang, Y., Ault, T., Pierce, T., & Lattimer, C. W. (2000). Improving text categorization methods for event tracking. In *Proceedings of the 23rd ACM SIGIR Conference on Research and Development in Information Retrieval (SIGIR-2000)* (pp. 65–72).

63. See Chapter 2.

64. Salton, G. (1989). *Automatic Text Processing: The Transformation, Analysis, and Retrieval of Information by Computer*. Reading, MA: Addison-Wesley.

65. Terms can be words or phrases, as before.

66. To compute the 2-norm of a vector, square each element, sum the squares, and take the square root of the summation, as shown in the equation.

67. The GAC algorithm has quadratic complexity, i.e., computing time is of the order n^2, where n is the number of stories to be processed.

68. See Chapter 2, Section 2.3.3.

69. See Chapter 2, Section 2.5.2.

70. Sparck Jones, K. & Galliers, J. R. (1996). *Evaluating natural language processing systems: An analysis and review*. New York: Springer.

71. Jing, H., Barzilay, R., McKeown, K., & Elhadad, M. (1998). Summarization evaluation methods experiments and analysis. In *AAAI Intelligent Text Summarization Workshop* (Stanford, CA, Mar. 1998) (pp. 60–68).

72. Mitra, M., Singhal, A., & Buckley, C. (1997). Automatic text summarization by paragraph extraction. In Mani and Maybury (Eds.), *Advances in Automatic Text Summarization* (pp. 31–36). MIT Press.

73. Brandow, R., Mitze, K., & Rau, L. (1995). Automatic condensation of electronic publications by sentence selection. *Information Processing and Management, 31*, 675–685.

74. Performance on this task is typically averaged over different users, queries and documents, to minimize bias.

75. Hongyan, J. & McKeown, K. (1999). The decomposition of human-written summary sentences. In *SIGIR-99* (pp. 129–136).

76. eXtensible Markup Language. XML is a language for defining document structures.

77. Resource Description Framework. RDF is a language for describing information resources.

78. See Berners-Lee, T., Hendler, J. & Lassila, O. (2001). The Semantic Web. *Scientific American* [May issue].

79. See e.g., Grosof, B. N., Labrou, Y. & Chan, H. Y. (1999). A Declarative Approach to Business Rules in Contracts: Courteous Logic Programs in XML. In Wellman, M. P. (Ed.), *Proceedings of the 1st ACM Conference on Electronic Commerce (EC-99)*. New York, NY: ACM Press.

80. Fully automatic processing may also be useful for processing the 'back file' of a text archive when new editorial features are introduced prospectively.

81. http://www.itl.nist.gov/iaui/894.02/related_projects/muc/proceedings/ne_task.html.

82. http://www-nlpir.nist.gov/related_projects/tipster_summac/results_eval.html.

83. http://www.cs.columbia.edu/~ acl/home.html.

84. http://www.w3c.org.

Index

In the series NATURAL LANGUAGE PROCESSING (NLP) the following titles have been published thus far, or are scheduled for publication:

1. BUNT, Harry and William BLACK (eds.): *Abduction, Belief and Context in Dialogue. Studies in computational pragmatics.* 2000.
2. BOURIGAULT, Didier, Christian JACQUEMIN and Marie-Claude L'HOMME (eds.): *Recent Advances in Computational Terminology.* 2001.
3. MANI, Inderjeet: *Automatic Summarization.* 2001.
4. MERLO, Paola and Suzanne STEVENSON (eds.): *The Lexical Basis of Sentence Processing: Formal, computational and experimental issues.* N.Y.P.
5. JACKSON, Peter and Isabelle MOULINIER: *Natural Language Processing for Online Applications.* 2002.
6. ANDROUTSOPOULOS, Ioannis: *Exploring Time, Tense and Aspect in Natural Language Database Interfaces.* N.Y.P.